Sardar Patel and Partition of India

Sardar Patel and Partition of India

Edited by
Dr. (Mrs.) PRABHA CHOPRA

KONARK PUBLISHERS PVT LTD

KONARK PUBLISHERS PVT LTD
A-149, Main Vikas Marg, Delhi-110092 (India)
e-mail: konarkpublishers@hotmail.com

ISBN 81-220-0776-7

Typeset by The Laser Printers, New Delhi-110027 and printed at
Rashtra Rachna Printers, Delhi

Contents

Preface

Sardar Patel was a prominent member of the Congress Organisation and played an important role in the freedom movement with an ultimate goal of complete independence. India's greatness and unity were his guiding stars throughout his political life.

Sardar Patel was critical of the British policy of divide and rule by granting separate electorates and communal awards in order to create internal dissensions between the two major communities. Hindu-Muslim differences came as a handy pretext to the British for denying India Independence. The Linlithgow-Amery-Churchill axis fully exploited this pretext, thereby helping Jinnah's dream of Pakistan assuming concrete shape despite Sardar Patel's effort to maintain Hindu-Muslim unity. Sardar Patel's one criterion used to be whether any particular policy of British Government was in the interest of the country. He, however, felt that sooner the British left India, the better for the country. To Muslim League's constant demand for Pakistan, Sardar Patel exhorted both Hindus and Muslims to have Independence first by their joint efforts and then decide the fate of India after British left for "slaves have neither Pakistan or Hindustan".

To preserve India's unity was his primary concern and with this objective he accepted the Cabinet Mission plan despite its many undesirable features as it insisted on India's unity. "There should be a Union of India" and categorically turned down the claim of the Muslim League for a separate state of Pakistan. Sardar Patel rejoiced that the idea of Pakistan has been "buried for ever", as he wrote to his friend.

However, the Jinnah was livid when the issue of minorities was treated as a domestic problem by the Congress President, which vouchsafed no British interference. The Muslim League resorted to "non-constitutional methods" and Jinnah called upon Muslims to observe 16th August as "Direct Action Day", and this decision had a most tragic sequence in Bengal with riots and bloodbath which had its equally serious reprisals in Uttar Pradesh and Bihar. There were widespread disturbances in Assam, Punjab, Bengal and NWFP, also where riots broke out and there were murders on large scale. When the Congress asked the Britishers to leave early they said that they would leave "if you mutually agree".

Gandhiji wrote in *Harijan* on 20th July, 1947, "Britain was leaving India as a cockpit between two organised armies, in pursuance of the policy of one community against another".

Mountbatten who took over as Viceroy from Lord Wavell announced his plan on 3 June 1947. It accepted the principle of partition. The plan was accepted by the Congress and the Muslim League. Sardar Patel said that he agreed to partition because he felt convinced that "in order to keep India united it must be divided now". Defending partition Pt. Nehru also observed, "Partition was better than murder of innocent citizens."

Both Pt. Nehru and Sardar Patel bluntly told the Congress Committee that "it was either to accept partition or be faced with complete balkanisation and anarchy".

On another occasion Sardar Patel said that "we had to agree to partition ... after a great deal of heartsearching and sorrow. But I felt that if we did not accept partition, India would be split into many bits and completely ruined. Even after partition 75 per cent of the population is on this side, we have to uplift them," he added.

Even Gandhiji with whom the Sardar was in perfect agreement for several years felt that he could not agree with this conclusion, "but he told me that if my heart bore testimony to the rightness of my convictions I could go ahead".

This volumes is the sixth in the series of thematic volumes, the earlier five being Kashmir and Hyderabad, Muslims and Refugees, Nehru, Gandhi and Subhas Bose, Economic Policy and Foreign Affairs and Sardar Patel and Administrative Services.

I have tried to give a comprehensive Introduction for the benefit of the readers which is based on the Documents contained in the fifteen volumes of *Collected Works of Sardar Patel* edited by Dr. P.N. Chopra and Dr. Prabha Chopra; volumes of Sardar Patel's Correspondence edited by Durga Das; and two volumes of Selected Correspondence of Sardar Patel by V. Shankar. The relevant documents from the above-mentioned sources have been carefully selected and appended with the Introduction.

I am thankful to Shri M.P. Chawla, Accounts Officer, and Shri Rabindra Kumar Das, Research Officer, who took pains to type out the manuscript accurately and promptly.

My thanks are also due to M/s. Konark Publishers (P) Ltd., for undertaking the publication.

New Delhi PRABHA CHOPRA
January, 2010

Abstracts of Documents

Introduction

With the passing of the historic resolution at the Lahore Congress Session in December, 1929, which declared "*Purna Swaraj*" or "Complete Independence" as its ultimate goal, a new phase in India's freedom struggle started. Keeping this goal in view, the Congress Working Committee in its meeting of February, 1930, authorised Mahatma Gandhi to launch the Civil Disobedience Movement. Sardar Vallabhbhai Patel was a prominent member of the Congress Working Committee. Gandhiji decided to start this movement on 6th April, 1930, violating the law by preparing salt at "DANDI" on the seashore.

The Bombay Government in a secret telegram from the Viceroy on 17th January, 1930, informed that "a Civil Disobedience or no-tax campaign may at any time be launched in parts of Gujarat, (Doc.1). Sardar Patel, who was a born campaigner and leader since his schooldays and an important figure in the campaign, was arrested by Bombay Government on 7th March, 1930 in Borsad for inciting "villagers to manufacture salt" (Doc.2). His arrest and conviction of three months' imprisonment sent a signal that the fight had begun. As Nehru observed, "it means that we are in the thick of the fight" (Doc.3)."

Sardar Patel was secretly shifted from Sabarmati to Yervada Jail by a special train. In jail he was given a diet of "Jowari Gruel" in the morning and Jowari Roti and Dal or Roti and vegetable on every alternate day. Sardar Patel was suffering from aching teeth and when he was asked how he managed to chew the Jowari bread, he lightly said, "Oh, I break it up in water and get along splendidly". After some silence, he added that "one thing alone worries me, and that is that all the people in charge of the jail are Indians. It is through us Indians that they work this inhuman system. I wish they were all foreigners, so that I might fight them. But how could I fight our own kith and kin? (Doc.4).

Sardar Patel made it clear that the struggle for Independence which the Congress was waging in British India was for freedom of thirty-three crores of people including Princely States (Doc.5). He stressed for a complete National Government for India responsible to her people including defence forces and economic control. Jawaharlal Nehru nominated Sardar Patel to be the Acting President of the Congress in view of his impending arrest in October 1930. Sardar Patel after taking over made a whrilwind tour of the country, preached the massage of the Congress and laid stress on the boycott of foreign clothes. He also told his audience that the people did not want communal representation and seats in the Council. Their problem was hunger (Doc.6). Laying stress on Hindu-Muslim unity, he refuted the idea that Muslims were not taking part in the national struggle (Doc.7). Sardar Patel was, however, upset about the situation in Bengal, particularly instigation of the Muslims by the British (Doc.8).

It was during the Presidentship of Sardar Patel that the National Tricolour Flag was adopted after consideration at various levels by the Working Committee of the Indian National Congress on 2nd April, 1931 at Karachi. It was the unanimous view of the Committee that the colour of the flag should not bear any communal significance. However, many members felt that the flag with red and green stood for Hindu and Muslim communities, and later the white colour was added which was for the remaining communities of India. This was the flag under which the great National Non-Violent Struggle of 1930-31 started. Later on to give it a non-communal significance, red was substituted by kesari or saffron colour with charkha in the blue. Thus saffron represented courage and sacrifice, white—peace and truth, green represented faith and chivalry and the spinning wheel as the hope of the masses (Doc.9).

Though Sardar Patel was against Council entry, he supported the decision of the Congress to contest the election for the Assembly in 1934. As a disciplined soldier of the Congress Party, he accepted the decision of the High Command to fight the elections, and he said: "He would support any programme accepted by the Congress because he was against imperilling the prestige of the Congress at a very psychological moment like the present one by creating differences within the Congress ranks...". "Sardar was anxious that the unity in the Congress ranks should be maintained at all costs and every Congressman should implicitly carry out the Congress programme". He took a whrilwind tour of the Provinces particularly Bombay and Gujarat and exhorted the people to vote for Congress candidates and asked Bhulabhai J. Desai, General Secretary of the Congress Parliamentary Board to convey his message to the people of Bombay (Docs. 10, 11 and 12). Sardar Patel tried to explain to the people of *Ras* the significance of the forthcoming Provincial Assembly elections and urged them to vote for the Congress candidates. "The struggle has not ended, but its mode has been changed. The struggle for Independence never ends." Throughout his speeches during this period, his tone was that of reconciliation and not confrontation with the authorities. But he advised people not to resort to unlawful activities due to changes in Congress policy. However, at the same time he made it clear to the people that this was only a step forward for a long-drawn out battle with the alien Government for the emancipation of the country and people to be ready for more sacrifices to achieve Independence" (Docs. 13 and 14).

He argued that though they had postponed the Civil Disobedience Movement, the "fight between the people and the Government has not yet ceased" (Doc.15).

He stood for Hindu-Muslim unity and criticised the British Government for framing the communal award in order to create internal dissensions between the communities. He exhorted both Hindus and Muslims not to enter in quarrels. He held that "it was most irreligious to fight over mosques and gurudwaras and that such communal strifes were responsible for the country's subjugation" (Doc.16). "In fact God was not", he declared, "confined to mosques and temples only. He was all-pervading. The best way to see Him was to look within themselves" (Doc.17).

The British Government was quite concerned about the activities of Sardar Patel and was keeping an eye on him and in this connection the DIG Police, Bombay, informed the Special Secretary (Home), Bombay, in his secret letter dated 22nd March, 1935 that Vallabhbhai's tour was meant to take stock of the situation and to assess the line of policy the Congress should adopt in any anti-Government movement now under preparation in Wardha (Doc.18).

Sardar Patel exhorted the people to vote for the Congress whose "goal is Independence or "*Purna Swaraj*". However, the purpose of the Congress can be achieved only if in this campaign the Congress received an overwhelming support of the nation ... those persons who have been given right to vote should treat their right as sacred trust for the country". "To vote for the Congress is to vote for freedom; to vote against the Congress is to vote for slavery" he emphasised (Docs.19 and 20).

Sardar Patel was critical of the Government's policy of providing separate electorates for Harijans and Muslims. In this way he said "the Government wants to divide India into two separate parts. The Government is trying to defeat the Congress by the policy of Divide and Rule" (Doc.21). He was quite satisfied with the working of the Congress Ministries and in his speech at Haripur Congress, he particularly emphasised, "Communal trouble was frequent before the Congress assumed office but since the Congress assumption of office there was not a single instance of serious communal riots and those spoke volumes for the Congress ability to rule" (Doc.22).

Sardar Patel strongly refuted Jinnah's allegation of

repression of Muslims under Congress rule. In a statement of 11th December, 1939, which appeared in *the Hindu*, he termed these allegations as "wild, reckless and intended to endanger communal peace". He was sorry to note that though the Viceroy and the Governors were fully aware of the position, they refused to reply to these charges with which they were as much concerned as the minister due to the reasons best known to them.

Even Jinnah spurned the offer of Congress President Dr. Rajendra Prasad to submit the charges for investigation to an independent tribunal (Docs. 23, 24 and 25).

In a letter to Rajendra Babu on 16th October, 1939, Sardar Patel criticised appeasement of Jinnah. He wrote, "In my opinion, no further initiative should be taken by us... The last answer of Mr. Jinnah in reply to your letter puts the whole burden on him for further initiative. I think we were spoiling our case by making persistent approaches.... I have a strong conviction that there can be no settlement of the communal question till Mr. Jinnah feels that he cannot coerce the Congress" (Doc.26).

In his outburst over silence of the Viceroy and the Governors on Jinnah's baseless charges against the Congress Ministries Sardar Patel observed, "I have no desire to enter into a controversy with Jinnah on the eve of the meeting of the Congress Working Committee especially after the impossible stand he had thought it fit to take up in regard to the communal question but I feel it is my duty to the nation to draw public attention to the implications of Jinnah's latest statement.

"It is apparent from Jinnah's statement that he does not want any communal settlement.... His sole objective seems to be to keep up communal feeling at high tension. His insistence on the observance of the so-called day of deliverance is manifestly to exacerbate the prevailing animosity which many feel may lead to an outbreak of hostilities between the two communities" (Doc.24).

In his letter to Jawaharlal Nehru on 9th December, 1939,

he referred to the statement of Mr. Jinnah as nothing but an incitement to the Musalmans. He added, "Our people all over India will be irritated when they hear that you are meeting him after his provocative statements, we must end this situation as early as possible... ."

"I see that Sir Stafford Cripps is also meeting Messrs Jinnah and Ambedkar and some of the representatives of the Princes. I do hope that his round of visits will not again stir of dirt of muddy water of the under political ocean" (Doc.27)[1]

Later on when Sardar Patel was taken out in a procession on his arrival at Bhavanagar Praja Mandal Congress, it was attacked by Muslims near a mosque. In the clash, two persons were killed and one was seriously injured. However, the Sardar kept his cool and issued an appeal not to get excited over the situation and observe complete non-violence (Doc.28). Though Sardar Patel desired that there must be unity among different communities, he, however, considered it necessary". "If we want real unity then those persons who were behind such heinous acts should be found out and we should not leave them till they are remorseful for what they have done. They should not be given opportunity to think that we are fools and weaklings" (Doc.29). In spite of the attack on him at Bhavanagar by some Muslims, Sardar Patel asked Rajendra Babu for strong action against some Arya Samajists who were responsible for the murder of two Muslims at Sholapur (Doc. 30).

While the Congress leaders were greatly frustrated over the British Government's attitude of denying Indian people their aspiration of getting full freedom, they had at the same time included them in the World War-II which broke out in 1939 without their consent. The then Viceroy Lord Linlithgow declared India to be at war with Germany and did not care to consult Congress Ministries. This was resented by the Congress which made it clear that India could only cooperate in the war if she was declared an independent country. Sardar

Patel was bitterly critical of British. "It is strange that a country having one-fifth of the population of the world is made to join such a deadly war without its consent".

Adding further, he said, "the Congress wants independence for thirty-five crores. Liberty for the whole India". However, the British Government's declaration for India to join the World War-II without its consent, he said it was "derogatory to honour and prestige of India. It wants to suppress the Congress. This declaration is invitation to the Congress to fight" (Doc.31).

"We tell Englishmen that we are ready to fully cooperate with them. Even though we might not proceed further in our experiment of non-violence we are ready to side with you in war. Youngmen want an opportunity to receive military training. The legislative party of the Congress has again and again passed resolutions that army should be Indianised" ... "We are ready to forget all your past misdeeds. But I ask you even while dying you want to make a will and make arrangement for the future? We think that when our country is not independent, how can we try for independence of the world when we are slaves. If we help them without any clarification about the transfer of power, our chains will be more tight—our past experience is such. So what we talk is not about bargain but of clarification," he reasoned (Doc.32).

Sardar Patel was bitter that "imperialists talked sweetly, again and again negotiations were held. Gandhiji went to see the Viceroy again and again, but he got nothing which was acceptable. We kept enough patience because we did not want to harass the enemy when he is in difficulty. But now our patience is exhausted. It appears that the Empire has been showing its real nature. The Government at present is doing as if they want to divide, let it do so. But the nationalism which is deeply rooted will not be affected. At present they are busy getting opposite forces together with the aim of crushing the Congress".

Adding further, he said, "You have been riding on our shoulders for the last one fifty years, now get down. They say if they go what will happen to us? You ask us this question after ruling for two hundred years, then what you did all these years? It reminds me of an episode about a quarrel: The house owner is asked by the guard as to what will happen if he goes away? "I will learn how to guard". But this guard does not leave and threatens us again and again" (Doc.33).

Castigating the British Government for being non-commital, Sardar Patel said, "the Congress had said that if you sincerely desire our help then stop formation of Viceroy's Council and in its place form a National Government comprising representatives of the Congress, the Muslim League, the Hindu Mahasabha and all parties and some Englishmen can also be in it and let the Government be responsible to the people". ... But their proposal is to expand the Viceroy's Council comprising civil servants.... Their intention is not pure" (Doe. 34).

However, "In her hour of trial we did not want to remind her of her failings in respect of India, but at the same time we have not gone back a bit on any of our demands. We have made it quite clear that if our demands are accepted, our full and hearty cooperation would be at the disposal of Great Britain". Sardar Patel was emphatic that if the British Government accepted India's demand for freedom, "it is good, because it will be to their advantage and our benefit but, if they do not, we will be free to choose our own course, and we shall do so".

He further added, "There are people who sense danger in this move...., but big issues like the freedom of a vast country like India cannot be solved unless we are prepared to take certain amount of risk, and we are prepared to do so. ... Our support, if it is to be full and hearty, must come from the people of free India. Again we cannot help Britain so long as we are not free because all such help given would go to strengthen our bondage and we are not fools to allow this to happen" (Doc.35).

Meanwhile, war had taken an alarming turn so far as India was concerned due to the entry of the Japanese as an ally of the Axis powers against Britain. India came very near to the theatre of war in 1942.

Speaking before Nadiad (Gujarat) people, Sardar Patel said, "now the war has come to our doorsteps...Now we have to forget the differences between caste and caste, religion and religion, community and community and be united and shed fear" (Doc.36). Non-violence, he insisted, is alright for a limited field but not to meet external or internal aggression (Doc.37).

The Japanese forces took over Singapore, Malaya, Rangoon and Mandalay with lightning speed. Ceylon (Sri Lanka) was attacked and there was a danger of attack on India. Thus in 1942, India came very near to the theatre of war as there were air raids in Vishakhapatnam and Kakinada in April, 1942. The Japanese warships also appeared in the Bay of Bengal.[2]

Sardar Patel observed that the Congress is a unique institution. Crores of people are behind its back and hear its voice. "We have to fight with any power which tries to rule us. The Congress will fight with any invader. We do not want that one evil is replaced by another. We cannot choose between the bandits" (Doc.38). He exhorted people to join the nationalist forces and help the Congress. "Don't be afraid of death "... We have to learn one thing from Gandhiji and that is fearlessness", he told them.

The Allied powers were greatly worried over the fate of India. President Roosevelt of the United States and Chiang Kai-Shek of China put pressure on the British Government to come to some settlement with Indian leaders. Accordingly, Sir Stafford Cripps, a member of the British Cabinet, was deputed by the British Prime Minister, Mr. Churchill, to proceed to India to solve the deadlock.

Sir Stafford Cripps arrived in India (Delhi) in March, 1942 with a set of proposals. He held talks with the Viceroy and the members of his Executive Council, the Governors and then with Indian leaders of the main parties and communities including Mr. Gandhi, Mr. Jinnah and Pt. Nehru. His proposals embodied three main points:

(1) Immediately after the end of the war an elected body would be set up in India with the task of framing a new constitution. After fresh provincial elections the States would be invited to send representatives proportionate to their populations (from their lower House), with the same powers as members from British India.

The British Government undertook to accept and implement the new constitution subject to the condition:

(2) (a) Any province that was not prepared to accept the new constitution would retain its existing constitutional position, provision being made for its subsequent accession, should it so decide. His Majesty's Government would be prepared to agree with a non-acceding province to form a new constitution by a similar representatives process, and have the same status as the Indian Union itself.

(b) The signing of a treaty between His Majesty's Government and the constitution making body. The treaty would cover all necessary matters arising out of the transfer of power; it would provide for the protection of minorities in accordance with British undertakings, but would not restrict the power of the Indian Union to decide its future relationship with the British Commonwealth. Treaties with Indian States would have to be reviewed.

(3) However, Cripps also stipulated that during the war, the Viceroy's Council was to be reconstituted into an Interim Government of the party leaders. But the defence portfolio would be retained by the British.

Thus, as Hodson observes, the long-term policy was essentially that of the British Government, ...in provincial option was the key to the communal

> deadlock. ....A further point that was strongly but vainly made by official advisers was that a treaty could not provide for the protection of minorities unless it provided for British intervention on their behalf was necessary.
>
> Both the Congress and the Muslim League rejected these proposals. The Congress felt that the Cripps Mission's proposals were "to enlarge the gulf between the Congress and the Government, which they believed had finally demonstrated its refusal to part with the power" and insisted on the immediate *de facto* transfer of power to Indian hands, i.e. the Cabinet Government with powers and rejected the proposals.[3]

While the Congress was of the view that they would not compel any territorial unit to remain in an Indian Union against their will, they were keen to make every effort to create a common and cooperative national life and a strong national state. Hence, they rejected the proposals.

The Muslim League also rejected the proposals as they felt that the non-acceding clause was purely illusory and the creation of Pakistan was relegated to the realm of remote possibility.

The failure of the Cripps Mission, who obviously came to India to create American public opinion in favour of England, brought about distinct change in Gandhiji's mood. Rejecting the Cripps proposal Gandhiji called it a "*post-dated cheque on a crashing Bank.*"[4]

Thoroughly disappointed as well as disgusted with Cripps Mission's proposals, Gandhiji wrote to Horace Alexandar on 22nd April, 1942 that "Sir Stafford Cripps has come and gone. How nice it would have been if he had not come with that dismal mission. He, of all people, should never have come without having at least ascertained Jawaharlal's wishes. How could the British Government at this critical hour have behaved as they did? Why should they have sent proposals without discussing them with the principal parties? Not one single party was satisfied. In trying to please all, the proposals pleased none.[5]...

"I talked to him frankly but as a friend,...I made suggestions but all to no avail. As usual they were not practical. I had not wanted to go. I had nothing to say being anti-all wars. I was not present throughout the negotiations with the Working Committee. I had come away. You know the result. It was inevitable. The whole thing has left a bad taste in the mouth."

"My firm opinion is that the British should leave India now in an orderly manner and not run the risk that they did in Singapore, Malaya and Burma. That act would mean courage of a high order, confession of human limitations and right doing by India. Britain cannot defend India, much less herself on Indian soil with any strength. The best thing she can do is to leave India to her fate. I feel somehow that India will not do badly then. I must not argue this point if it is not obvious to you."[6] He argued that by their doing so India would not only regain her freedom but would at the same time avoid becoming a theatre of war between Britain and Japan.

Till now Gandhiji who had been against launching any mass movement during the war time, at the historic session of the All-India Congress Committee which met on 8th August, 1942 at Bombay gave the clarion call of *Quit India* to British Government and his countrymen to '*Do or Die*'—either free India or die in the attempt.

Of members of the Working Committee, Sardar Patel was an active supporter of the Quit India Resolution and the movement. He asked everybody to contribute according to their might in the Quit India Movement, started by Gandhiji. "If you do not, future generations will blame you ... do not have fear in your mind ... do not ask for programme ... no tax campaign, Civil Disobedience and such other battles which are directly or indirectly launched to break the Government machinery will be revived by the Congress. Railway employees will stop running the railways, postal employees will leave their jobs, schools and colleges will be closed and the entire machinery of the Government will not be allowed to function.... If all of you actively take part in the struggle then the struggle will end in four days and the Englishmen shall have to quit India...". We wanted even Government servants including the police to leave their jobs and join the movement as it was the big campaign for the liberation of India (Doc.39).

The Quit India slogan would be effective "if forty crores of Indian people asked one lakh Englishmen to quit India," he said. He further said that the Congress did not seek power for itself and would be satisfied if it was handed over to the Muslim League (Doc.40). Replying to a question whether the fight would be successful without the cooperation of the Muslim League, Sardar Patel replied, "I cannot say whether the Muslim League cooperates with us in this war but it is not right to say that Muslims are not cooperating because there are many Muslims in the Congress.... (Doc.41).

Jinnah described the Quit India Resolution "as black-mailing the British and coercing them to concede a system of Government and transfer power to that Government which would establish a Hindu Raj...".[7]

Assuring the Muslims, Sardar Patel said, "Let Muslims understand that this fight is not for establishing Hindu rule but to break the shackles of slavery". He criticised the Britishers for creating misunderstanding. They can also divide one community. Even amongst Hindus they drive a wedge between high class Hindus and Scheduled Caste Hindus" (Doc.42).

The "Quit India" movement of 1942 is a landmark in India's struggle for freedom. It was the last and, undoubtedly, the bitterest fight for freedom ever waged against the British in India. It surpassed all the earlier movements including the Great Revolt of 1857 in dimensions and intensity. The observations of the then Viceroy Lord Linlithgow are quite significant. "I am engaged here," wrote the Viceroy on 31st

August, 1942 to Prime Minister Winston Churchill, "in meeting by far the most serious rebellion since that of 1857, the gravity and extent of which we have so far concealed from the world for reasons of military security". It was spread over almost all the provinces from the Himalayas to Cape Comorin. The violent upsurge of the masses and their readiness to sacrifice everything for the emancipation of the motherland showed their grim determination to throw off the foreign yoke. It warned the British that they were not wanted in India and that "their belief that any section of the Indian people—the Muslims, the depressed classes or the states people—favoured continuance of their rule was a delusion."[8]

Commenting on Sardar Patel's role in the 1942 movement, *The London Times* observed, "Some leaders like Sardar Vallabhbhai Patel and other left wing members of the Working Committee put the impending mass movement upon the plane of revolt. They warned their audience that it will be necessary for them to face bullets and bombs which was as much to say that they were to create a situation that could be dealt with only by bullets and bombs" (Doc.43).

Wickenden, I.C.S., Judge in Central Provinces, who wrote the famous report on Quit India Movement summed up Patel's attitude as "anti-fascist and bitterly opposed to continuance of British rule". He further added that "there is nothing to indicate that he had pro-fascist or pro-Japanese tendencies" that he gave vent to the "most inflammatory words" (Doc.44).[9] As Sardar Patel said, "we do not want the change of master. No slave gains anything by changing his master. We have to be independent. Only Independent India can help in war" (Doc.45). At a press conference, Sardar Patel said that "the Movement would not be stopped even if there was a civil war or anarchy in the country". He preferred anarchy to slavery and expected a free India to emerge out of anarchy (Docs. 44 and 46).

The very next day (9th August, 1942), passing of the "Quit India" Resolution by the All India Congress Committee on 8th August, 1942, Gandhiji and members of the Working

Committee were taken into custody under the Defence of India rules. They were detained in Ahmadnagar Fort and at Aga Khan Palace, Poona. The Congress Committee was declared an unlawful organisation, the Congress headquarters at Allahabad were sealed up. All India Congress Committee funds were confiscated. Wholesale arrests of Congressmen began in every province and ordinance and New Defence of India Rule were issued immediately for official control on publication of newspapers. There were continuous spontaneous *hartals*. Peaceful and non-violent demonstrations were held. The whole of North Bihar, and Eastern District of Uttar Pradesh, Tamil Nadu, Andhra Pradesh, coastal areas of Orissa, Satara, Khandesh in Maharashtra and Bharoch in Gujarat played an important role in the struggle.

The Government used the most stringent measures to suppress the movement. Thousands of persons were arrested and imprisoned and a large number of people were killed as the police and Army resorted to firing.

Horace Alexander, contemporary British journalist and author of *India Since Cripps*, corroborates that it was "the repression let loose by the police that goaded to violent fury crowds that have intended to act quite peacefully."[10]

The Quit India Movement, in spite of its violence and intensity, did not succeed. The movement, however, succeeded in demonstrating that the people all over the country were ready to make all sacrifices for attaining freedom.

Winston Churchill, the then British Prime Minister, boastfully said that "what was at one time feared would become the most serious rebellion in India since the Sepoy Mutiny of 1857 fizzled out in a few months with hardly any loss of life"—obviously he meant loss of British life.[11]

The tide of war had turned in favour of the allies in 1944. Lord Wavell, who had succeeded Lord Linlithgow, released Mahatma Gandhi in May 1944. Gandhiji tried to solve the communal problem by holding discussions with Jinnah but his efforts failed. Sardar Patel was still under detention first in Ahmednagar Fort and subsequently in Yervada jail till June 1945.

On his release from detention of nearly three years, Sardar Patel returned to active political life. "My path is clear before me" he declared. "I want freedom, I am going to get it. Ten Englands cannot prevent me from getting it". No country could be kept in subjugation forever, he added (Doc. 47). In an interview with Associated Press of America on the eve of the meeting of the Congress Working Committee, Sardar Patel warned the Labour Government which came to power in the United Kingdom that India could "not wait long" for freedom and that the Indians themselves would take their country within five years if the British did not allow it earlier, he warned (Doc. 48).

Sardar Patel was critical of the Government for granting separate electorates to the Muslims with the intention of making them fight each other. "Today the League propagates that in the Congress, Hindus dominate. The Muslim League is shouting for Pakistan. Nobody is told what Pakistan is. It cries for the moon. The fact is that slaves have neither Pakistan nor Hindustan", he observed (Doc.49). He, therefore, exhorted Hindus and Muslims to make the country independent first by their joint efforts and decide the fate of India after the British left. He, however, felt that "if the British quit India, the difference between the Muslims and Hindus would disappear in ten days" (Doc.49 & 50). He was critical of Jinnah's partition cry for misleading Muslims (Doc.51).

As long as Linlithgow was the Governor General, the object of Linlithgow-Amrey*-Churchill** axis was to have indefinite continuance of British rule over India. The Hindu-Muslim difference came in as a handy pretext for denying independence to India. Lord Wavell who replaced Linlithgow foresaw that the British Government could not rule India for

*L.S. Amrey, Secretary of State for India.

**Winston Churchill, Prime Minister of Britain.

long after the war ended. Against the wishes of Churchill, he pressurised the British Government to agree to his proposal of holding the famous Simla Conference in June 1945 for having a responsible and representative Viceroy's Executive Council to satisfy them.

At the Simla Conference, Lord Wavell placed his plan of reconstituting the Viceroy's Executive Council. Besides himself and Commander-in-Chief (war) for the first time, he wanted to appoint Indian political leaders to all portfolios in his Executive Council (Home, Finance and Foreign Affairs except war) and to give equal representation to Hindus and Muslims. However, the Simla Conference ended in a failure, as the Congress and the Muslim League could not reach an amicable settlement. The Muslim League which claimed to represent the whole of Muslims of India insisted on nominating the Muslim members of the Executive Council. "They must be Leagurers", while the Congress asserted its national character and wanted to appoint at least one Muslim member. The talks failed.[12] In fact, "the League and the Congress had entirely different angles of vision. The idea of Pakistan and the idea of a united India were incompatible."[13]

The World War-II was over and in the elections in the United Kingdom, in 1945, the victorious Labour Party came into power with Clement Attlee as the Prime Minister in place of Winston Churchill. The Labour Party was committed to a policy to complete independence for India. As an urgency to the solving of the Indian problems, it ordered general elections in September, 1945 to the Central and Provincial Legislatures in India to test the relative strength of the political parties. The elections resulted in sweeping victory for the Congress in the General seats while the Muslim League won overwhelming majority in the Muslim seats. Elections to the Central Assembly were held first and then these elections were over by the end of 1945. The result of these elections showed a clear indication that the rift between the Congress and the Muslim League was now complete and deep-seated, and encouraged Jinnah in his negative attitude. On the other hand, it also showed the support which the country as a whole gave to the Congress. The Congress polled 91.3 per cent of the non-Muslim votes, while the League got 86.6 per cent of the Muslims votes."[14]

The British Government now decided to send a Mission of Cabinet Ministers to negotiate the final settlement. The members of the Cabinet Mission were Lord Pathick Lawrence, Secretary of State for India; Sir Stafford Cripps, President of the Board of Trade, and A.V. Alexander, first Lord of Admirality. The Cabinet Mission arrived in India in March, 1946. "The task of the Mission was to seek agreement with Indian leaders on the principle and procedure to be followed in framing a new constitution for an Independent India". For about a month it held meetings with leaders of the Congress, the Muslim League and other sections of public opinion. There was, however, no agreement among leaders of the two main political parties, the Congress and the Muslim League, on the formation of an interim Government and the setting up of a Constituent Assembly to frame a Constitution for India. The main difference between the two parties centred around the issue of immediate independence and maintenance of the unity of the sub-continent while Jinnah was reiterating the League's demand for Pakistan. Thus their proclaimed objectives were diametrically opposite. The rift between the League and the Congress continued to widen. "In the matter of a fortnight or so of the arrival of the three British Ministers, by 10th April, 1946, Jinnah convened a meeting of the Muslim League members of the newly elected legislatures; they passed a resolution reiterating the League's demand for Pakistan as including *Bengal, Assam, the Punjab, Sind, the North-West Frontier Province and Baluchistan*. In practical terms the resolution demanded the setting up of two constitution making bodies, one for Pakistan and one for Hindustan."[15]

Sardar Patel considered Jinnah's "Two-Nation Theory" as absurd. "Ridiculing the idea of two nations in one country, the Sardar said it would amount to the fact that the father may belong to one nation and his offspring to another.

"To this I would add that some may even belong to the category of No Man's Land—if the father belongs to one 'nation' and the mother to the other?" (Doc.52).

To preserve India's unity, the Cabinet Mission proposed a Federal Union of India embracing both British India and the States. The Union Government was to have an Executive and a Legislature constituted from British India and States representatives and was to deal with Foreign Affairs, Defence and Communications with powers necessary to raise the finances required for the above subjects. Any question raising a major communal issue in the Legislature was to be decided by voting by the majority of the representatives present and voting of each of the two major communities as well as a majority of all the members present and voting.

All subjects other than the Union subjects and all residuary powers were to vest in the Provinces (States).

States/Provinces were free to form groups with Executives and Legislatures and each group could determine the provincial subjects to be taken in common.

The constitutions of the Union and of the Groups contained a provision whereby any province could, by a majority vote of its Legislative Assembly, call for a reconsideration of the terms of the Constitution after an initial period of 10 years and at 10 years' intervals thereafter (Doc.53-Endosure).

The Cabinet Mission proposed the formation of an interim Government comprising the representatives of the Indian political parties. Sardar Patel seemed to have been favourably inclined to the Cabinet Mission proposal. As he wrote to Gopichand Bhargava in his letter of 26 May 1946, "There is only one Constituent Assembly for the whole of India. The idea of Pakistan has been reservedly condemned and rejected" (Doc.53). He also felt that with setting up of a Constituent Assembly and in an interim Government the Muslim League would no longer hold the power of veto and the Indian States would have to enter into treaties with the Constituent Assembly or interim Government (Docs. 54 and 53).

The Cabinet Mission also rejected the Muslim League's demand for Pakistan on communal grounds, because it would weaken India's defence, as Sardar Patel wrote to K.M. Munshi (Doc. 55).

In another letter to a friend Shri M.M. Gharekhan, he wrote, "The British Government have by their declaration made clear that they propose to leave this country and also propose to constitute a Constituent Assembly at once which will be free to frame its own Constitution of Free India without any interference from outside. An interim Government will be set up immediately to function during the interim period which, we hope, will in all probability function as a free Government, in fact, though it may not be so in law. This makes the way of India's Freedom absolutely clear. The great obstacle of the Muslim League holding the power of veto has once for all been removed. Undoubtedly, there are defects in the scheme but such defects are inherent in any scheme of compromise. Let us hope that the Constituent Assembly will be able to finish its business quickly and India will be able to take its place for the first time, after a long period of slavery, amongst the free nations of the world" (Doc.54).

Writing to his friend C.R. Reddy on 16 August 1946, Sardar Patel observed, "There have been considerable changes. The Congress President has been invited to form the interim Government and, for the first time, the British Government have (shown) the Muslim League its proper place. They have thus given proof of their *bona fides* and it is now for us to make or mar the future of India" (Doc.56).

In a subsequent letter on 1st June 1946 to G.V. Subba Rao, President, Andhra Swaraj Party, Bezwada, Sardar Patel wrote that "the Constituent Assembly would draft the Constitution passed by the Parliament for free India and would have to be accepted by the British Government ..." (Doc. 57).

Obviously thus Patel's acceptance was mainly due to the fact that the main demand of the Muslim League for Pakistan according to the plan was "buried for ever". In his letter of 2nd June 1946 to Nihchaldas Vazirani, Sardar Patel expressed his satisfaction: "Jinnah and the League had secured nothing for the Muslims after a struggle of five years against the Congress and after the spreading of so much communal bitterness. His main demand of Pakistan is buried forever. His demand for parity is not accepted. The Muslims in the Hindu majority provinces have lost weightage in the Constituent Assembly. They will be in a hopeless minority". This was the other important point which prompted him to accept the Cabinet Mission Plan (Doc. 58).

Replying to Sir Chimanlal Setalwad that Cabinet Mission proposal envisaged a "weak and emasculated centre", Sardar Patel assured him that nothing will be accepted which vouchsafed a weak centre. In another letter to the General Secretary, the Assam Provincial Congress Committee, Sardar Patel again stressed having a strong centre and "that there will be no question of division of the country". The Congress stands for a strong Centre (Docs. 59, 60 and 61).

On 10th July, 1946 Jawaharlal Nehru, who took over as Congress President (from Maulana Azad), stated at a press conference that the issue of minorities is a domestic problem and he would not accept the interference of the British Government. He also stressed the sovereignty of the Constituent Assembly to propound that it was free to make alterations in Plan.

Jinnah was livid and described Nehru's views as a complete repudiation of the basis on which the Cabinet Mission was based including all its fundamentals. Jinnah was bitter and exhorted his followers to resort to "*Direct Action*".

Sardar Patel was most unhappy with the developments because once again the demand for Pakistan was revived and in addition the Muslim League decided on "*Direct Action*". In a statement to the Press, Jinnah said on 18th August, 1946: "Pandit Jawaharlal Nehru would have been nearer the truth if instead of saying that there was lack of cooperation from the League, he had said the Muslim League was not prepared to surrender, and it would have been still more true if instead of saying that the Congress door of cooperation was set open, he had said that the Congress door was open to the Muslim League for abject surrender" (Doc.62-Enclosure).

Wavell who had earlier asked Nehru's opinion whether he should "invite Jinnah once more and persuade him", (Doc. 63) Jawaharlal declined.

Disturbed by all the developments Sardar Patel wrote to D.P. Mishra on 29th July, 1946, "Though the President (Nehru) has been elected for the fourth time, he often acts with childlike innocence, which puts us all in great difficulties quite unexpectedly.... He has done many things recently which have caused us great embarrassment.... It puts strain on us to set matters right" (Doc. 64). However, Patel praised Nehru for his burning passion for freedom and patriotism.

The Direct Action Day, observed by the League all over India on 16th August, 1946, led to "great killings" in Calcutta followed by massacres in Noakhali and terrible riots in Bihar and Uttar Pradesh as reprisals.

Pained at the happening, Sardar Patel on 16th August, 1946 writing to C.R. Reddy, observed, "The non-cooperation of the Muslim League has commenced and they are observing this day as their "*Direct Action Day*". The Congress, claiming to represent the vast majority of the people of India cannot afford to be weak or to fail to shoulder the responsibility of taking charge of the Government of the country, in spite of all difficulties that may have to be faced. If the British Government and the Congress play the game well, I have no doubt that we shall see India free sooner than many people imagine and neither the League nor any other group of people or interests, however strong or powerful, will be able to stop it" (Doc. 56).

In his letter to Sarat Chandra Bose of 24th August, 1946 Sardar Patel expressed great grief over the Calcutta killings. He added, "There will, I hope, be a fair, impartial and independent enquiry. It will take long for Calcutta to recover from the shock. I do not know what will happen to the Government during whose regime such disgraceful events have happened. In no civilised country such a Government should have a day's existence. But we are living in strange circumstances and we have to go through the ordeal" (Doc.65). Sardar Patel even advised people to defend themselves with violence, if necessary.

Addressing a mammoth meeting at Bombay, Sardar Patel reviewed at length the political situation in the country since the British Cabinet Mission's visit in April last. The Muslim League and its leader, Mr. Jinnah, said the Sardar, had threatened all the while that they would not rest content till Pakistan was achieved. The Congress had tried repeatedly to settle with the League but to no avail. Instead Mr. Jinnah has embarked upon the policy of "Direct Action" which ultimately culminated in country-wide bloodshed and anarchy. What had happened in Calcutta, Bombay, East Bengal and Bihar were the direct result of the policy pursued by the Muslim League. "Tracing the growth of communal rioting in the country," the Associated Press of America observed that Calcutta marked the real start" (Doc. 66).

At another mammoth gathering Sardar Patel observed that "tracing the attitude of Jinnah, it indicated its recalcitrant nature by saying that he was open to no compromise and adhered only to the idea of Pakistan. Mr. Jinnah believes, nay, insists, pointed out the Sardar, that only those Muslims who were in and with the League were Muslims in fact. All the other Mussalmans were not Mussalmans at all. Vallabhbhai made no comments on these statements, in fact, but left it to the listeners to draw their own conclusions and that made the point he was trying to make all the more telling.

"I do feel, however, that the Muslims outside the fold of the League, have now lost their force, or are rapidly losing it. Formerly we often read about protests from various sections of the Nationalist Muslim community. Their views may not have changed but their voice has temporarily gone. The elections dealt them a deathly blow, or at least it has put them in a state of coma."

"And Jinnah capped this advantage by insisting during the formation of the interim Government that the Congress shall have no Nationalist Muslim among its chosen representatives."

"Commenting on this unreasonable stand of the League leaders, Sardar Patel said that the Congress was anxious to protect the rights of the minorities—it has taken representatives of each of the minorities in its cabinet—and since the Nationalist Muslims could be considered such a minority, the Congress thought it a part of its duty to protect them by giving them representation" (Doc.52).

Sardar Patel reminded Sir Stafford Cripps in his letter of 19th October 1946 that when he (Cripps) was here he had cautioned him (Sardar) about the likelihood of communal trouble in India particularly in Bengal in case there was no settlement with the Muslim League and he (Cripps) had assured him that in Bengal "we have a Governor who would immediately put Section 93 into operation in case of any serious trouble" (Doc. 67). In his reply of 24th October to Sardar Patel, Cripps observed that "I realise very fully what a difficult situation you are all in and how terrible are the happenings in Bengal. It is, of course, quite impossible for us to judge from here exactly what is happening and why it is happening. It seems to us that firm measures are being taken to quell the riots and I hope they will be successful". Appreciating Sardar Patel's efforts in this direction he further added: "We are all very impressed by the way in which your team is tackling its most difficult job and I send you my very best wishes and may your patience not give out" (Doc.68)

Sardar Patel also wrote to Lord Wavell on 28th October, 1946: "I desire to bring up the question of Bengal before the full interim Government for immediate discussion and decision. I have been told by the Hon'ble Vice-President (Jawaharlal Nehru) that Your Excellency's view is that the problem of restoring peace and tranquillity in Bengal is your special responsibility and that the Government of India as such, i.e. the Governor-General-in-Council, cannot do anything to give relief to the people of that unfortunate province. It would, indeed, be a tragic paradox if we, who have undertaken the responsibility of the Government of India, should be powerless to do anything to terminate the reign of terror which prevails in East Bengal even according to the obviously minimised accounts of those responsible for allowing such a state of things to come into being under their eyes. The whole country is deeply agitated about the events as well as about our share for responsibility in the matter. And the question will have to be dealt with in the Legislative Assembly when Members will raise the question in some form or other. It will not be possible for us to deal with it as the former Government did".

"After an examination of the 9th Schedule of the Act and particularly Section 41 thereof, I find that I, as Member-in-Charge of Home Affairs, and each one of my colleagues is competent to propose measures to restore tranquillity in the large and spreading area involved in the present disturbed conditions of Bengal. Though under the letter of that Section, Your Excellency has power in your discretion to overrule our proposals, our understanding is that your Excellency will act in accordance with the collective advice of the cabinet." (Doc. 69).

To overcome Muslim League's fear Sardar Patel invited its leader Jinnah for a joint discussion on Cabinet Mission proposals and for heart-to-heart talk to sort out all problems. Warning them the Sardar observed: "Give up this approach, much can be done by love, but nothing by holding a pistol to our heads. You cannot get your object by threats. The Congress is not afraid." "If you are still keen on Freedom," Sardar Patel appealed to the League, come, let us sit together like two brothers and arrive at a settlement or let us refer our differences to arbitration and abide by the verdict; and let us jointly break this document (the cabinet recommendations). Sit with us and let us take freedom".

Turning to the political situation in India, Sardar Patel announced that 'our struggle with the British was virtually over. They had declared their intention to quit. All his life he had been a disbeliever in British intentions. But he was now convinced that they were prepared to leave.

"Falling into a serious vein, Sardar Patel said that 'Mr. Jinnah has been abusing him and the Congress, what was their fault. Mr. Jinnah claimed that the Viceroy had given him certain secret assurances and had gone back on them. The Viceroy said he had given no such assurances. Whoever was right, where did Congress come into the picture? The letter from the Viceroy announcing that he had given no assurance of the kind implied by Mr. Jinnah had been published long ago. Why then, did he wait all these days'?

"The reason Mr. Jinnah cited was that Pandit Nehru, the Congress President, had said something at Press Conference. This Mr. Jinnah claimed had given rise to a new situation....

"The Sardar referred to the statement of Mr. Jinnah that the initiative was with the Congress or the Government and said that the Congress had gone to his door hundreds of times. He had never once deigned to come to it. How could he expect the Congress to go to him, after the kind of speech he had made? He had abused and insulted the Congress. The Congress was not so helpless that it should go to him.

"On that footing no coalition was possible. There could be no coalition between two parties, one of which wanted to go north and the other to go south. The British were going anyhow. They could not afford to stay any longer. Indians would have to make India free and run the administration of a Free India. If there was agreement on that common ground, other things would come easy" (Doc.70).

Muslim League did not agree to join interim Government and, therefore, the British decided to hand over power to the interim Government to be formed by the Congress. Since the Muslim League did not agree to join the interim Government, the Congress decided to nominate five nationalist Muslim Members to the interim Government. These were Asaf Ali, Shafat Ahmed, Ali Zaheer, Fazlul Haq and Maulana Azad. However Maulana Azad was not willing to join as one of the five Muslim members and wanted to be accommodated from the Congress quota. "Sardar Patel did not agree to it as it would have given rise to fresh problems" (Doc.62). However, the

Viceroy did not agree to the inclusion of Fazlul Haq and Maulana Azad had no alternative but to accept Sardar Patel's proposal. (Doc.71)

The League sensing the setback it had suffered politically, changed its stance and agreed to join the Government while maintaining its opposition to participating in the Constituent Assembly.

Sardar Patel was happy that the Muslim League who had taken an oath in their convention at Delhi not to enter the interim Government till the principle of Pakistan was accepted were now anxious to join it in spite of the earlier pledge... (Doc.58).

Sardar Patel took strong objection to the provocative speech of Ghazanfar Ali before a gathering of students at Lahore stating that "we are going in the interim Government to get a foothold to fight for our cherished goal of Pakistan and I assure you that we shall achieve Pakistan". "In the interim Government, all our activities should be guided by two considerations, that is, to convince the Congress that no Government in India can function smoothly without the co-operation of the Muslim League and the League is the sole representative organisation of the ten crores of Indian Muslims. The interim Government is one of the fronts of the direct action campaign and we shall most scrupulously carry out the orders of Mr. Jinnah on any front he orders us". Disgusted, Sardar Patel wrote to Wavell "not to include his name (Ghazanfar Ali's) in the interim cabinet till he withdrew his speech" (Doc.72-Enclosure).

Sardar Patel also disclosed that it has been made clear to the Viceroy that if the League was to enter the Interim Government, it was to work as a team and not as a separate group. Secondly, they would enter the Interim Government only if they accepted the Cabinet Mission's proposals of May 16, 1946.

The Viceroy agreed with this position and said that the League too had accepted it. "Mr. Jinnah has often accused the British Government of bad faith and of double-crossing. It is now up to the Viceroy to settle accounts with Mr. Jinnah. We have nothing to do with the quarrel". At the same time he made it clear that as far as the Congress was concerned they were going to stick to their seats. "We will stay there, we will work effectively and we will function as cabinet", Sardar Patel said (Doc.73).

When the Muslim League declared to join the Interim Council, its main purpose, as explained by Ispahani, Jinnah's personal envoy to the U.S.A., "was to carry on the struggle for Pakistan within as well as without the Government."[16]

Mr. Jinnah agreed and for a time it was thought that the League's cooperation was certain. The Congress fears were however justified for it became evident in no time that the League had come with a determination to obstruct the hitherto smooth working of the Interim Government. "The League again went back on its word when Mr. Jinnah declared the League would not participate in the Constituent Assembly. Sardar Patel, however, declared: "The constituent Assembly shall meet on 9th December under any circumstance. It will be an insult to the members and those who elected them if it does not meet". He added that the Congress was determined to stay in office for all time to come".

Referring to London talks where Jinnah was invited, he observed that "by running to London Mr. Jinnah could not hope to bring Pakistan nearer. Threats of violence would not help him in any way. Only by coming to a settlement with the Congress could the Muslims expect to obtain a satisfactory solution of their legitimate demands. Sardar Patel deprecated the idea of the transfer of populations as fantastic and unpractical" (Doc.66). He further added, "the communal problem would have to be settled in India and by Indians themselves. The British have no place in this sphere and sooner they quit the scene the better it would be for all concerned". Emphasing further Sardar Patel observed, "we are on the verge of attaining complete freedom. It is for us to take it or throw it" (Doc.74).

Referring to the widespread disturbances, which in his

view, were the result of the political policy of the Muslim League, Sardar Patel said that the time had come for the people to defend themselves. "They can ask for Pakistan; they can ask for all India" he said. But this method would not pay. Poison would produce poison and the sword would ultimately have to be met by the sword. Therefore, he made on behalf of the entire Congress one last appeal to the League to desist from its present course and arrive at a peaceful agreement with the Congress" (Doc.73).

Sardar Patel also "appealed to the people to develop the spirit of self-defence instead of relying on the police and the military for help" (Doc.66). "Don't run away, don't weep, don't die in vain, but defend yourselves by all means whether violent or non-violent. Don't look to the help of police or military. Become sepoys of the country and form National Militia" said Sardar Patel. "Cowardice helps nobody. It only results in more innocent persons being killed", Sardar Patel asserted (Docs. 74 and 75).

The League refused to accept the convention of collective responsibility or the leadership of Nehru. In fact, the interim Government consisted of a Congress bloc and a Muslim bloc each functioning under separate leadership. The Viceroy also failed to persuade Jinnah to let the Muslim League join the Constituent Assembly.

Pained at the developments, Sardar Patel, in his letter dated 15th December, 1946 to Sir Stafford Cripps, one of the members of the Cabinet Mission, regretted the British Government's sincerity towards India. "With great difficulty, we were able to build a bridge between England and India by our joint efforts—and you know my own contribution. I regret to say that the sense of faith and confidence about the sincerity of Britain, that was created by our settlement, is fast being dissipated and the bridge is about to crack or collapse. You must have seen what Jinnah has said in London immediately after the debate. He swears by Pakistan, and everything conceded to him is to be used as a lever to that end. You wish that we should agree to help him in his mad dream. I am sorry to write to you in this strain, but I feel sad over the whole affair. You know "when Gandhiji was strongly against our settlement I threw my weight in favour of it" (Doc. 76).

Attlee now made a last attempt to bring the two parties together and on his instruction Lord Wavell proceeded to London with Jawaharlal Nehru, Liaquat Ali Khan, M.A. Jinnah and Baldev Singh for a discussion with His Majesty's Government. Sardar Patel did not accompany Nehru to London as he said "what is there? Every crucial decision would be taken here in India". "The London talks were futile. It would serve no purpose. I know that what the British Government will say. Oh? you are ruling in nine provinces out of eleven. Why can't you be a little magnanimous and concede the demands of the League? This attitude of the British Government is of that category which they adopted towards Hitler" (Doc.77). The London talks, as expected, failed to bring about any agreement. The British Government issued a statement on 6 December, 1946, stating that if the Muslim League did not join the Constituent Assembly, the new constitution would not be forced on the Muslims. This made the work of the Constituent Assembly ineffective, as all the seventy-four delegates of the Muslim League boycotted it.[17]

The deadlock was broken by Prime Minister Attlee's announcement of 20th February, 1947 that the British Government proposed to leave India at a date not later than June, 1947. Lord Mountbatten was appointed as the new Viceroy to take necessary steps for the final transfer of power. It was now apparent that leaders of the two political parties would not accept a compromise; partition of India became inevitable. Only Gandhiji and Maulana Azad still opposed it and Pandit Nehru said, "we saw no other way of getting our freedom....in the near future we mean...." Gandhiji in his paper *Harijan* wrote on 20th July, 1947, that "the British intervention had done the trick,"[18] and that Britain was leaving India as a cockpit between the two organised armies in pursuance of the policy of playing one community against another.

Mountbatten held discussions with leaders of the various political parties and announced his plan on 3 June, 1947. It accepted the principle of partition, if the Muslim majority areas so desired. It was also agreed that in case of partition, power would be transferred to the two successor dominions. British paramountcy over the Indian princely states would lapse and these states were urged to join either of the dominions. The plan was accepted by the Congress and the Muslim League. In accordance with the procedure laid down two commissions were appointed with Sir Cyril Radcliffe as chairman of both, to arrange the partition of Bengal and Punjab. The North-West Frontier Province and the district of Sylhet joined Pakistan after a plebiscite. The British Parliament passed an Indian Independence Act for transferring power to India and Pakistan as on August 15, 1947, and the Royal assent was given to it on July 18.[19] Thus India and Pakistan became independent dominions on 15th August, 1947. The Assembly assumed power in India at midnight session and it was at 1 A.M. that Sardar Patel the "old warrior" reached his home in Independent India and stretched his "weary limbs".

India's freedom was won at last but as the historian Dr. Tarachand writes, "It had brought with it severance of old ties of the cruel traumatic experience of the dismemberment of a naturally united country, the violent disruption of a vision which throughout history has served as a beacon".

Against the popular belief propagated by vested interests, Sardar Patel was a staunch believer in Hindu-Muslim unity. In one of his speeches on 5th January, 1947 he stressed that "if we want real Swaraj, Hindus and Muslims have to be united" (Doc.78). However, "his experience in office during the past year showed that it was impossible to do anything constructive with the Muslim League in. The League representatives during their continuance in office did nothing but to create deadlocks and their role was entirely an obstructionist one. Besides, as he had already once said, he found that all the Muslims, save for a few exceptions, engaged in all capacities in the Government were the Muslim League. Thus the riot had set in and it could not be permitted to prolong any longer except at the risk of a disaster for the whole country. Indeed at one stage, it obtained even now to some degree, things had become so bad that with the killings at Calcutta, riots spread all over and it became a perilous adventure for Hindus and Muslims to visit one another's localities. The economic life of the country was paralysed and there was little security of life or property.

The only way out of the sickening situation, the Congress realised, lay in the elimination of the third party, the British power. The British, on their part, had declared that they would quit in June, 1948. But the period was long. Also their statement promising to hand over power to the authorities in the provinces gave rise to a vigorous effort to dislodge the ministries in Assam, the Punjab and in the Frontier. The League succeeded in the Punjab. Even though they failed in the Frontier and Assam, the League movement caused great misery and bloodshed. In order to settle the issue immediately and prevent the slaughter of innocent people, the Congress decided to agree to the division of the country and demanded the partition of the Punjab and Bengal. This was no surrender to the League threats or a policy of appeasement (Doc.79).

Sardar Patel also observed that if the Muslim League insisted on separation, it would result in dividing Punjab and Bengal as otherwise coercion would come in and non-Muslims would be forced in Pakistan to quit and there would be a civil war (Doc.80).

Sympathising with the Sikh community who had suffered grieviously during the bloodbath of partition, Sardar Patel said "when we accepted partition, it was like our agreeing to have a diseased limb shorn off so that the remaining part may live in a sound condition. But before we could start the process of healing, events have overtaken us" (Doc. 81). "He made an earnest appeal to all Government officers to take all possible steps to evacuate the refugees from West Punjab by rail or road. In his statement of 3rd September 1947, he stressed the gravity of the situation in West Punjab "that imperilled the lives of millions of their countrymen on other side of Punjab and invoked them to instant call of duty for facilitating swiftest evacuation of the very forlorn and grief-stricken refugees from the place of variable hell to the abode of safety" (Doc.82)

Sardar Patel severely criticised Liaquat Ali Khan for the treatment of minorities in Pakistan and drew his attention to the plight of the refugees and his oft-heard assurances to the minority communities of Pakistan, adding "that value of these assurances is writ large on thousands of murders, abductions, forced marriages, burnt houses and maimed children, and the treatment of non-Muslim men, women and children leaving Pakistan in utter distress when they are being subjected to most harassing and humiliating experience. On the other hand, in India, over three-fourths of the country Muslims are following their normal avocation and showing no signs of leaving. They are living peacefully in their ancestral homes or on lands in complete protection of their lives and property vouchsafed to them by their Govemment" (Doc.83).

Sardar Patel emphatically denied that he and his colleagues agreed to the partition of the country either because of fear or out of a sense of defeat. Under the prevailing conditions in the country partition on the pattern was the best thing possible and he had no qualms about it. In a matter of weeks they had divided the country, the army, the services etc., and this indeed was a colossal task performed" (Doc.79).

Defending partition as an evil necessity, Sardar Patel observed "people say that Congress partitioned India. It is true. We have taken this responsibility after proper thinking and not because of any fear or pressure. I was a strong opponent of partition of India.* But when I sat in the Central

*See Annexure from I to VI.

Government I saw that from a peon to high officers all are infested with communal hatred. In such conditions instead of fighting and tolerating the interference of the third party, it is better to separate.

"We entered the Government after the genocide in Calcutta. There is much enmity between the two communities. In Calcutta, Lahore and Bombay wherever you go you will see that mini-Pakistans have been formed. No Hindu can enter a Muslim locality. No Hindu is able to stay in Rawalpindi. We saw that this problem will not be solved till alien the Government is here. When the British Government decided to abdicate power after one and a half years, in Assam, Punjab, Bengal, North-West Frontier Province—everywhere riots broke out and there were murders on a large scale. We asked the Britishers to leave early. Then, they said, "we will go if you mutually agree". So we decided to agree to the formation of Pakistan, but we demanded partition of Bengal and Punjab. We painfully took that decision. As a result the Government which was to transfer power in 1948 June decided to transfer it on 15th August, 1947. Army officers, etc. were also divided between the two countries".

"Even after partition seventy-five per cent of the total population is on this side. We have to uplift them. Today India is in difficulty. There is financial crisis. India was a debtor country. Now though it has become creditor it is not certain when Britain will return our money. Then what is the gain of being a creditor? (Doc.84)."

Sardar Patel further added that he would make no efforts to explain the responsibility of the Congress to divide the country. "We took these extreme steps after great deliberations. In spite of my previous strong opposition to partition I agreed to it because I felt convinced that in order to keep India united it must be divided now." "There should be peace in the country. To fight like wild animals, to stab a woman or a child passing on the road do not enhance the prestige of any community. Only peace will save us. We do not live in to satisfy anybody. ...Today we have an opportunity to unite India. Barring some part of Lahore and East Bengal we have now a golden opportunity to integrate India after one thousand years" (Docs. 79 and 84).

Again justifying partition, Sardar Patel stressed "partition of India became inevitable due to the Muslim League's attitude in Interim Government and the pro-Muslim League behaviour of Muslim Government officers". "Today the partition of India was a settled fact and yet it was an unreal fact. The partition, he hoped, however, removed the poison from the body politic of India. This, he was sure, would result in the seceding areas desiring to reunite with the rest of India. India was one and indivisible. One could not divide the sea or split the running of a river. The Muslims had their root in India. Their sacred places and their cultural centres were located here in India. I do not know what would they do in Pakistan and it would not be long when they would like to return" (Doc. 85).

During the All-India Congress Committee debate on June 2 resolution, Pandit Jawaharlal Nehru and Sardar Vallabhbhai Patel "bluntly told the Committee that the alternative before the Committee was either to accept partition or to be faced with complete balkanisation and anarchy" (Doc. 86). Sardar Patel informed Gandhiji also (on 1st February, 1947) about difficulties created by the League. "The League is now on warpath * Let us see what happens. It appears that kings are not going to behave well. Here many a time your advice is needed, but what can be done? We are doing what we think proper, but difficulties are mounting" (Doc.87).

"The Mahatma was an idealist, but he was also a shrewed judge of men. He too realised that it was impossible for the erstwhile champions of the Muslim League to become ardent nationalists overnight. Thus, while his plea for a change of heart on the part of the perfidious Muslims was perfectly valid, much more than that was necessary to ensure the desired

* Members of the Muslim League had joined the Interim Government, but they were not taking part in the deliberations of the Constituent Assembly (footnote of Doc.87).

result. The dictum that crime does not pay needed to be enforced with the utmost strictness. The Sardar's firm action alone fulfilled this requirement.[20]

Pandit Nehru while defending acceptance of partition also observed that "the Congress Working Committee also passed a resolution in favour of the partition of the Punjab into two administrative provinces. Partition was better than the murder of innocent citizens. After the resolution was passed, the Committee received numerous complaints from Bengal that Bengal also should be divided. The underlying principle in the case of the Punjab and Bengal was one and the same".

Agreeing with Sardar Patel, Nehru also said "the present, perhaps, is the most difficult period full of trials and tribulations. Today we have to shoulder responsibility. The first thing we have to do is to establish the Independence of India firmly and set up a strong Central Government. Having established a strong and stable Government all other programmes will not create much difficulty. The Congress has a heavy responsibility. You must bend all your energies to strengthen the Congress organisation. We have to face dangers, both external and internal, and if we are not strong we will go down" (Doc.88).

"Following Pandit Nehru, Sardar Vallabhbhai Patel, in a vigorous speech, at the All-India Congress Committee extended his full support to His Majesty's Government statement of June 3. Looking at the Cabinet Mission's proposals, in the light of his experience in the interim Government during the last nine months, he was not at all sorry that the State Paper had gone. Had they accepted the State Paper, the whole of India would have gone the Pakistan way. Today, they had 75 to 80 per cent of India, which they could develop according to their genius and make it strong. The League could develop the rest of the country.

The League Council, which met in camera, evidently nursed the ambition to capture the whole of India after August 15. It was the duty of every Congressman to work unitedly to make India strong, to build up an efficient army and strengthen her economic position". "The May 16 Plan, Sardar Patel said, no doubt gave them United India. The Congress agreed to it in spite of its shortcomings. But there was a snag in it. The Plan could not be executed if one or the other party withheld cooperation". "His nine months in office," Sardar Patel said, "had completely disillusioned him of the supposed merits of the State Paper. He had noticed that Muslim officials, right from the top down to the chaprasis, except for a few honourable exceptions, were all for the Muslim League! There should be no mistake about it".

"The May 16 Plan was gone and he was glad. That Plan left much room for conflict and bickerings. The Congress was opposed to Pakistan, but yet the resolution before the House assented partition, whether the All India Congress Committee liked it or not there was already Pakistan in action, both in the Punjab and in Bengal. Under the circumstances he would prefer real Pakistan because then they would have some sense of responsibility (Doc.89).

As chairman of the Advisory Committee on Minorities, Fundamental Rights, etc. Sardar Patel while submitting the reports to the Committee of the Constituent Assembly, congratulated various minorities viz. Anglo-Indians, Parsis and Christians who had abandoned claim for separate electorates and taken a correct perspective of the problems and helped in arriving at unanimous conclusions on many items. Sardar Patel felt that separate electorates further encouraged those separatist tendencies.

His mind went back to those days when the question of separate electorates was first discussed. Many eminent Muslims had recorded their view that communal electorates were a serious flaw in the body politics. Many Englishmen have also admitted that the country had to be partitioned today because of separate electorates. While referring to the Muslims, Sardar Patel said, "when Pakistan was conceded, at least it was assumed there will be one Nation in the rest of India and that there will be no attempt to thrust the "Two-

Nation Theory" here. It is no use saying we shall ask for separate electorates but will abide by your decision. We have heard this for many years and the result of this agitation was, they said, separate electorates or anything else was not sufficient for their protection. Therefore, they demanded a separate State. We said, "alright, take it, but for the rest of 80 per cent India you agree there shall be one nation" (Doc. 90.).

Sardar Patel in his letter to the British Officer Bozman dated 11th July, 1947 agreed with him that the division of India was unfortunate but somehow or the other they had no other alternative. "He nursed the hope that one day Pakistan would come back to India (Doc.91).

Recalling his address to a vast assemblage of men and women in Lucknow on 6th January 1948, he had blamed the Muslim League for propagation of the "Two-Nation Theory". "Today my mind turns back to those days when, in the city of Lucknow, the foundation of the "Two-Nation Theory" was laid. It was said that the Muslim culture and traditions were not akin to those of Hindus. They were a separate nation. Muslims of this city played an important role in fanning this theory. A few nationalist Muslims protested against it. They made common cause with the Hindus because both of them were perturbed at the advocacy of such a theory and raised their voice against it. But my Muslim League friends made a strong plea for separation. They only wanted separation and establishment of a separate State. Throughout the breadth and length of India, the Muslim League spread this doctrine of separation, and a major part of the Muslim youth also came under their influence. They accepted it as the whole truth".

In Calcutta, on August 15, they launched a "Direct Action" movement to give a direct blow to those who still did not believe in the "Two-Nation Theory", we then thought if there was to be a division of the country, let it be divided. Let them manage their own affairs and we will manage our own. We were then facing the problem of getting rid of the alien rule. So we accepted the division of the country" (Doc.95). He added that they considered division of the country as a lesser evil in view of the growing intensity of communalism (Doc.96).

On another occasion Sardar Patel said that "for several years, Gandhiji and I were in perfect agreement, however, when the time for decision on the question of India's Independence came we differed. He said, "I felt that we had to take Independence there and then. We had, therefore, to agree to partition. I came to this conclusion after a great deal of heartsearching and with a great deal of sorrow. But I felt that if we did not accept partition, India would be split into many bits and completely ruined. My experience of office of one year had convinced me that the way we were proceeding was heading for disaster. Gandhiji felt that he could not agree with this conclusion, but he told me that if my heart bore testimony to the rightness of my convictions, I could go ahead. Our leader whom he nominated as his heir and successor was with me. Gandhiji did not oppose us nor did he consent to what we thought was right and proper. Even today I do not repent for having come to that decision, though it was with a great wrench of the heart that we did so" (Doc.92).

In reply to a question asked in Calcutta why partition was accepted, the Sardar replied, "It is a long story but you should be able to appreciate matters better because Calcutta had tested the bitter experience of the League Ministry. Businessmen thought of leaving the city" (Doc.93). "I can tell you this", he further said, "if we had not accepted partition, India would have fallen into bits. Now that we have been able to salvage the major part of India and have been able to build it up into an extensive single unit, let us make it more powerful" (Doc.94).

Sardar Patel again justified the partition of India in his speech at Bombay on 30 October 1948.

"If we had not partitioned India, the consequences of what would have followed would have been much worse than actually taken place as a result of partition. At that time, we were quarrelling and fighting bitterly amongst ourselves. The third party was reaping the full benefits out of the dilemma in which we were placed and the situation in which we had landed ourselves. We have to pay the price for our liberty. It was then we decided that, if the foreign government undertook to leave as soon as possible, the price of partition was worth paying for. We suffered grievously as a result of partition. A limb was torn asunder and we bled profusely. But it was nothing as compared to the troubles that would have been in store for us and with which we would have had to put up. I have, therefore, no regrets for accepting partition. My experience of Government had convinced me that if we went on like the way we were carrying on, we would lose everything that we held precious"... (Doc. 97).

While addressing a public meeting at Rajkot, Sardar Patel again justified partition and said, "We had agreed to the partition of India", the Deputy Prime Minister went on, "for without that India would have been balkanised. Today we have consolidated the country "... (Doc.98) .

Nothing was dearer to Sardar Vallabhbhai Patel than the fullest protection of his motherland. And when Pakistan was at the height of its bellicose attitude towards the minorities in East Bengal and the beautiful valley of Kashmir, already locked in war, Sardar Patel, in his historic speech at Nagpur on 4th November, 1948, while calling upon people to realise their true duty to the nation amidst dangers to her security spoke with a thunder, "we are India's guardians and as long as we live, we are not going to tolerate all these dangers to our national existence". Here again, among the top leaders of the day, Sardar Patel was the first to issue a resounding threat to Pakistan that if Pakistan was bent on precipitous course to drive our Hindus from their homes in East Bengal it would have to compensate by parcelling out a portion of its territory to resettle lakhs of those unsettled" (Doc.99).

Replying to a civic address in Bombay on 16th January, 1948, Sardar Patel said, "...we have just heard people shouting that Muslims should be removed from India. Those who do so have gone mad with anger. At the same time, we have to sympathise with such people who have lost their dear ones and their valuables.... Anger rules their hearts and it turns their minds topsy-turvy. But we have to tolerate all this. However, so long as we are in the Government, we have to govern also. If we cannot act as trustees to the entire population irrespective of caste, creed or religion, we do not deserve to be where we are. I frankly ask myself; "are we to admit before the world that we are not fit to rule"? (Doc.100).

Addressing the Nagpur University students, Sardar Patel exhorted them to realise their responsibilities to prove worthy of the country's hard-won freedom forgetting the differences among all the communities residing in the country. "We are not going to do anything which would be contrary to our principle of justice for all communities—Hindus, Muslims, Christians, Parsees etc. "All communities have their proper place. Their religion is their concern" (Doc.101).

Sardar Patel was for preservation of all religions in democratic India. "The Government does not interfere in any way in the matter of religion". "But there are some," he said, "who in the name of religion encourage hypocrisy and public complain to the Government. So, for the welfare of the people we have to interfere". "Let us live as decent men—either Christians, Hindus, Muslims, Sikhs or Parsees. No religion prospers which is based on intolerance". No nation prospers unless that nation has character, he stressed (Docs. 102, 103 and 104).

He further said, "I am a frank man, our principle of justice is for all communities—Hindus, Muslims, Christians, Parsees etc. All communities have their proper place." I say bitter things to Hindus and Muslims alike, at the same time, I maintain, as I have said a number of times, that I am a friend of Muslims. If Muslims do not accept me as such, they also act like mad men. They do not seem to understand the right or wrong..." (Docs. 100 and 101).

Sardar Patel praised the majority of the Muslims for settling down peacefully and assured them full protection so far as their lives and property were concerned. He added no better proof of this could have been given them than by the steps we took to guarantee their safety in the city of Delhi itself (Docs. 105, 106). We willingly agreed to keep their houses vacant against the return of those who had fled to Pakistan, although a large number of homeless refugees were at our hands.

The work of restoration of mosques, which has been virtually completed, and the one-way traffic of the return of refugees from Pakistan are sufficient testimony to the peaceful and amicable relation which prevailed in this country. High posts both in the army and civil service as well as in public life continue to be shared by them...". Sardar Patel continued: "In return for all this, the Government does not expect from the Muslims anything more than what it demands from other communities, namely, a complete and unquestioned loyalty to their State..." (Doc. 107).

"Replying to those Muslims who still demanded separate electorates and reservation of seats, Sardar Patel said that having worked for the partition of the country and for a free homeland they should go there to enjoy the fruits of that freedom, leaving this country in peace. There was no place for them in India" (Doc. 108).

He further stressed that "we have achieved something by making India more united today than it was at any time during the past several centuries. We should unite more, but that requires a determined effort. In such united India, Muslims should feel as secure as the rest of the population. For this, however, Muslims will have to change their outlook. They must forget the lesson of the "Two-Nation Theory" which has been taught to them" (Doc.100)

His speeches and action were a strong repudiation of the charges levelled against him that he was anti-Muslim. In his speech at Nagpur on 5th November, 1948 Sardar Patel had observed that "all communities—Hindus, Muslims, Christians, Parsees, etc.—were like brothers and the Government would not think in terms of one community or another"

(Doc.101). Reiterating that though India was a land of a variety of religions, cultures, traditions, habits and languages, yet throughout history it has evolved a synthesis of harmony and oneness which has been the admiration of the world and the secret of its preservations. We have to live up to this precious heritage and demonstrate to the world that while religions, habit, thought and languages may divide, the country unites us" (Doc. 109).

Referring to the conference of Nationalist Muslims in Lucknow, Sardar Vallabhbhai Patel said that "it was surprising that 70,000 Muslims had collected in Lucknow but they did not say a word about what Pakistan was doing in Kashmir". So as a friend of Muslims, I want to say a word and it is their duty now to sail in the same boat and sink and swim together. I want to tell you very frankly that you cannot ride two horses. Select one horse whichever you like best. Those who want to go to Pakistan can go there and live in peace. Let us live here in peace to work for ourselves" (Docs. 95, 110).

Sardar Patel warned the Hindu Mahasabha and RSS that "they must understand that the Government of India cannot tolerate any challenge to peace and tranquillity in the State". He stated that every loyal Muslim must be treated as our brother and anyone who thought he was at liberty to trouble the Muslims, then the freedom was not worthwhile (Doc. 111).

Lord Mountbatten who tookover as the last Viceroy of British India after Lord Wavell, recognised Sardar's greatness. He highly praised Patel's statesmanship as a stern realist and a true "statesman of vision and realism, with (his) both feet firmly on the ground". He wrote to Sardar Vallabhbhai Patel on 14th August, 1947: "It was, indeed, fortunate that a statesman of your vision and realism should have been associated with all the discussions on the 3 June Plan and with all the subsequent vital and delicate negotiations with the States.... future generations will appreciate the full effect of the wise policy you have followed" (Doc.112).

The Sardar, who held Mountbatten in high esteem for his understanding and sympathetic attitude towards India, reciprocated: "The history of the six months of your Viceroyalty comes to be written, it cannot but accord to you the major share of the credit for the manner in which the manifold difficult tasks have been accomplished and for the transformation which has been made in Indo-British relationship during these fateful months. "In fact, what you have achieved in the way of friendship and goodwill merely emphasises what the long line of your predecessors have missed as a result of studied aloofness and failure to take into confidence leaders of public opinion" (Doc. 113).

Happy at the decision of the Labour Government to replace Wavell with Mountbatten, Patel had written to Sir Stafford Cripps on 28th February, 1947 expressing the hope "that with the new Viceroy the process of transfer of power may proceed smoothly and rapidly" (Doc. 114).

In his reply Cripps assured Patel: "I am sure you will like Mountbatten enormously as I do and respect him. He is very advanced in his views as you will find and you will like him too". Striking a personal note, Cripps added: "You must take care of yourself because you are terribly precious to India just now in these last final months" (Doc. 115).

To Lord Ismay, Chief of the Staff of Lord Mountbatten (from March to November, 19) who thanked Sardar Patel for his kindness during his stay in India, Patel gave a parting shot: "You have been singularly fortunate (and I somehow feel in that circumstance India has also been lucky) that you came to India with Lord Mountbatten and thereby were able to see at close quarters how India reacted to the final gesture which your people made to us. You have also seen how we faced perhaps the most difficult task that was ever set to any country's government. You have also witnessed the manner in which the country as a whole and the administration have accustomed themselves to the great and vital change from foreign rule to self-government. *It is now for you to convince your old chief whether you have had to deal herewith men of straw or with men of substance*—I am sure, if you could succeed in doing something to remove such misapprehensions as exist among the Conservative Party, and particularly its gifted leader, about men and affairs in India, you would be rendering a signal service not only to this country but also to your own; for I genuinely feel that in the continued friendship and goodwill between our two countries lie the interests of both". "You have yourself seen how that friendship and goodwill burst forth when the psychological opportunity came on 15 August. It is now for your statesmen and the country to capitalise that friendship and that goodwill and not to let these be smoothered by old controversies in their new form" (Doc.116).

REFERENCES

[1]Mr. V.B. Kulkarni in his book writes, "In view of the British obstinacy on the issue of India's freedom, the Congress has withdrawn its ministries and was in no mood to co-operate with the Government and Viceroy Linlithgow increasingly turned to Jinnah.

"The way was thus made clear for Jinnah to come closer to the British Government and to secure for himself and his party much more than he had even dreamt of winning. His correspondence with the Viceroy, embodying his rapidly mounting demands, began on November 5, 1939, in his letter of that date, he asked the British Government not to make any declaration about the future of India except with the approval of the two major communities, i.e. Hindus and Muslims.

"It was this fact, more than anything else, which emboldened the Muslim League to adopt the famous partition resolution on March 23, 1940 as its Lahore session.

"It is evident from the Linlithgow-Jinnah correspondence that the British Government spared no efforts to foster the growth of separatism in the country as a counterpoise to the forces of nationalism represented by Gandhi and the Congress".

"The Indian Triumvirate" Edited by V.B. Kulkami, Bharatiya Vidya Bhavan, Bombay, 1969, pp. 161 and 164.

[2]Quit India Movement (Books for Millions), edited by P.N. Chopra, Publications Division, Ministry of I&B, Govt. of India, 1987, p. 6.

[3]The Great Divide (Britain-India-Pakistan)—with An Epilogue Covering Events—1947-1985, edited by H.V. Hodson, Oxford University Press, Karachi, pp. 96-97 and 105.

[4]A New Advanced History of India, Edited by P.N. Chopra and others, Prentice-Hall of India (P) Ltd., New Delhi, 1996, p. 622.

[5]Quit India Movement (British Secret Report, Secret Evidence—Part-1), edited by P.N. Chopra, Thomson Press (India) Ltd., 1976, p. 217.

[6]Ibid.

[7]The Great Divide (Britain-India-Pakistan), with An Epilogue Covering Events—1947-1985, by H.V. Hodson, Oxford University Press, Karachi, 1969, 1985, pp. 106.

[8]Quit India Movement (British Secret Report, Secret Evidence-Part-1), Edited by P.N. Chopra, 1976, Thomson (India) Press, p. 01.

[9]Historic Judgement on Quit India Movement" Justice Wickendons Report, edited by P.N. Chopra, Konark Publishers, New Delhi, 1989, pp. 234-238.

[10]Quit India Movement (Books for Millions)," edited by P.N. Chopra, Publications Division, Ministry of I&B, Govt. of India. 1987, p. 11.

[11]Ibid, p. 14.

[12]Lord Wavell himself admitted in his Journal "my efforts to bring better understanding between the parties have failed and shown how wide is the gulf". Though Maulana Azad in his "India Wins Freedom" (Bombay, l959, pp. 106-107) appreciated Wavell's effort and genuine desire to open a new chapter in the relations between Congress and the Government. In a letter to Lord Wavell he said that by calling the Simla Conference, Wavell had rendered India and the Government of Britain a service which had few parallels in history and that the new possibilities of Indo-British friendship were due to that step",—Wavell. (The Viceroy's Journal) by Penderel Moon, London, Oxford University Press, Delhi-Karachi, 1973, pp. 149-150, 155, 157 and 158.

[13]The Great Divide (Britain-India-Pakistan), with An Epilogue Covering Events—1947-1985, edited by H.V. Hodson, Oxford University Press, Karachi, p. 125.

[14]Sardar Patel's Select Correspondence-1945-50, Vol. 1, by V. Shankar, Navajivan Publishing House, Ahmedabad, p. 8.

[15]Sardar Patel's Select Correspondence—1945-50, Vol. 1, by V. Shankar, Navajivan Publishing House, Ahmedabad, p. 92.

[16]India's Struggle for Freedom (Books for Millions), Edited by P.N.Chopra, Publications Division, Ministry of I&B, Govt. of India, 1984, p. 67.

[17]India's Struggle for Freedom (Books for Millions) edited by P.N. Chopra, Publications Division, Ministry of I&B, Govt. of India, 1984, pp. 67-68.

[18]Ibid, p. 68.

[19]Collected Works of Sardar Vallabhbhai Patel, Volume-XI, edited by P.N. Chopra, Konark Publishers (P) Ltd., New Delhi, 1997, p. x.

[20]The Indian Triumvirate—A Political Biography of Gandhi-Patel-Nehru, edited by V.B. Kulkarni, Bharatiya Vidya Bhavan, Bombay, 1969, p. 215.

1

Bombay Government to Government of India Indicating Vallabhbhai Keeps Grievances in Reserve to Launch Satyagraha

Collected Works of Sardar Patel

IOL & R MSS.Eur. F-150/2

17th January, 1930

(Extract)

SECRET

Copy handed to Viceroy

Telegram No: S.D.82 dated the 17th January, 1930

To
Home, New Delhi

....
....

It is considered essential that any overt steps taken in pursuance of the Congress resolutions whether for non-payment of taxes, extensive picketing of liquor shops or otherwise, and including any active movement of Youth Leagues, should be met and checked immediately, whether before or after 26th January. In regard to such activities this Government would not place much reliance on prosecutions under the ordinary criminal law which, besides being rarely possible or successful and almost always unedifying, come too late to prevent such movements from gathering strength or to restore prestige lost by allowing people to conduct openly revolutionary propaganda in public.

A civil disobedience or no-tax campaign may at any time be launched in parts of Gujarat where Congress workers have been carefully preparing the ground for years and are ready to act. There are present indications of such a campaign in *Matar*, and Vallabhbhai Patel has been careful always to keep a few grievances in reserve for a fresh satyagraha campaign in Bardoli whenever politically expedient.

....

....

The Bombay Government therefore considers it essential to have a plan of action ready as soon as such a situation develops anywhere, and require the fullest powers to take the initiative only against any unlawful organisation and to give the protection to law-abiding persons throughout... .

BOMBAY SPECIAL

2

Bombay Government Explains to Government of India Circumstances Leading to Vallabhbhai's Arrest

Collected Works of Sardar Patel

Home Department (Special): MSA

8 March, 1930

SECRET

TELEGRAM

From ... Bompol, Bombay

To....Polindia, New Delhi

Desp. 8th March, 1930, 1.30 A.M.

CLEAR THE LINE

Vallabhbhai Patel arrested near Borsad today and subsequently convicted and sentenced to 3 months' imprisonment and Rs. 500 fine under following circumstances. On hearing Vallabhbhai was proceeding to incite villagers of manufacture salt. District Magistrate issued notice under section 42 District Police Act prohibiting him from making speeches for one month, and informed Government.... Government immediately telegraphed to hold up order if not already served and, if served, to cancel it at once. Shortly afterwards wire received from District Magistrate stating "Vallabhbhai arrested, no excitement", followed shortly by wire reporting conviction and sentence. District Magistrate informed that Government accept situation and asked to keep Government informed of developments and to take no similar action against others without referring for orders.... District Magistrate had been in close consultation with Government regarding land revenue agitation in Kaira and was aware that precipitate action of any kind not contemplated. Vallabhbhai now at Sabarmati Jail. Further wire just received from District Magistrate strongly urging to stop Gandhi's procession on 11th. Will wire opinion tomorrow. Please inform Garrett.

3

Jawaharlal Feels Arrest of Vallabhbhai Means "India in Thick of Fight for Independence"

Collected Works of Sardar Patel

THE TRIBUNE
12 March, 1930

Sardar Vallabhbhai Patel's arrest and conviction[1] is a significant and happy omen. It means that we are in the thick of the fight, we shall miss his wise counsel: but his undaunted spirit and determination, which made Bardoli famous in India, will radiate from the walls of Sabarmati Jail, and create an all-India Bardoli. It is clear that other prominent Congressmen will soon follow Sardar Vallabhbhai Patel and Gandhiji may also be arrested before long.

I suggest to all Congress committees and other organisations and individuals that Gandhiji's arrest should be followed immediately by an *all-India hartal* to demonstrate our deep respect for, and confidence in, our great leader and our determination to follow him. I hope that all institutions that sympathise with the struggle for freedom will close their doors that day and the whole country will demonstrate again that it stands for the independence of India.

1 He was arrested at Ras on 7 March, 1930 and immediately sentenced to three months' imprisonment and ordered to pay a fine.

4

Mahadev Desai's Interview with Vallabhbhai in Jail (10 March 1930)

Collected Works of Sardar Patel

YOUNG INDIA
12 March, 1930

(Extract)

I had the honour in company with Prof. Kriplani to have the *darshan* of the Sardar in Jail. His first word and his last was that he was never happier in his life than at the present moment ......

'But joking apart let us know how you are being treated'.

'Just like an ordinary criminal. I am perfectly happy'.

'Don't the new Jail Rules apply to you?'

'The Superintendent knows nothing about the new rules, and they refused to give me a copy of the Jail manual'.

'But let us know something about your appointments and your associates.'

'Well I am in a cell which is locked up for the night at about 5.30 P.M. on weekdays and 3.30 P.M. on Sundays. I was afraid I might not have sleep on the first day, but then there has been no difficulty. I have been sleeping like a log. But I do wish they allowed us to sleep outside in this hot weather. I think our friends who were here in 1922 were all allowed to sleep outside'.

'And food?'

'As good or bad as one can expect to get in jail. Don't

bother about food. I assure you I can live on air for three months', he said, again bursting into a loud laugh.

But we pressed him for details. *Jowari gruel* was given in the morning, but he did not take it for fear of getting dysentery, and then *Jowari roti* and *dhal* or *roti* and vegetable every alternate day. 'The *gram roti* is good encugh for a horse', he added. He was suffering from aching teeth and asked him how he managed to chew the *Jowari* bread. 'Oh, I break it up in water and get along splendidly. I tell you, you need not worry yourself about my food'.

'And do you have a bed to sleep on, or a light?'

'Neither. They have given me a blanket, and Bhagvad Gita and Tulsi Ramayana. If I was given a light I should be able to read at night which is impossible at present.'

'You want anything else to read?'

"*Ashram bhajanavali* (hymn book) is all that I want. The three should suffice for the brief period of three months'.

'And your associates?'

'Ordinary felons. Ours is called the juvenile ward, though there are in it older people than myself. They are from all parts of the country and have come in for all sorts of crimes. Our three friends from Jalalpur, sentenced for picketing, were for a day with me, but they were removed'. Dangerous because familiar company, I suppose;'

......

He gave me a list of things that he wanted including a soap and his shaving tackle. 'No razor allowed', said the Superintendent, 'but we shall allow you a shave'.

'I know what kind of a shave you will give me,' said Vallabhbhai.

But here the jailor interrupted the Superintendent with evidently better knowledge of jail rules. He said: 'In this case, sir, razor might be allowed, provided he does not keep it with himself. We shall give it to him when he wants'.

'Quite all right', said Vallabhbhai. 'But why not give me

a razor and allow me to shave the others? There will be some work to my credit'. And even the little parts of that inhuman machinery called the jail department could not help creaking with laughter. But they are jealous of their inhumanity, and soon repair the mistake if even they blunder into humanity. So the jailor added: 'You may have your soap, but it should not be scented soaps' And again the jail gate rang with laughter.

As we were leaving the Sardar said: 'Don't worry about me. I am as happy as a bird. There is only one thing over which I am rather unhappy'. And he was silent for a moment. The Jail Superintendent and the Jailor looked curiously at each other.

We also wondered what it might be. 'It can't be said', said the Sardar still tantalizing us. But we insisted.

"Well", said the Sardar, 'one thing and one alone worries me, and that is that all the people in charge of the jail are Indians. It is through us Indians that they work this inhuman system. I wish they were all foreigners, so that I might fight them. But how could I fight our own kith and kin?'...

5

Vallabhbhai Stresses Need for "Fight for Independence" in British India and Princely States[1]

Collected works of Sardar Patel

HOME DEPARTMENT (SPECIAL) : MSA
24 July, 1930

(Extract)

It is said that when the movement is going on in the British Raj, the subjects of the Native States should not take part in it. I don't understand who can separate them, so, come what may, but the subjects of the Native States and that of British

Raj are but one. None can separate them and if any Native State or Officers of the Native States attempt in that direction, that attempt is in vain. The movement for Independence which is going on in British Raj is a campaign for freedom of 33 crores. In those 33 crores, native princes also demand freedom because the thing is that we are more independent than the native states that are slaves. We want to do away with the slavery of these 33 crores, none can make divisions in them. Few officers are making such attempts—these attempts are foolish.... This is a change in era and none can stop that. What is going on in all sides of India today, none can stop. They may break heads by lathis or kill by bullets. That is all the work of God. God will stop it. None can stop it. Whatever hardships we have to bear are inevitable. You should not be afraid of hardships.... You might be afraid of being beaten, that Government will hang you, that Police will beat you with lathis. I tell you not to be afraid of lathis. You should not be afraid to lose your life because He who can take our life is sitting above. No one is authorised to take the life of another. He alone has kept the power of taking life with Himself.... The Working Committee of the Congress is held unlawful. Tomorrow other committees might be held unlawful. Five of us might be sitting in a house, more than five of one family might become an unlawful assembly. Come what may, what matters? What are they going to do to us? None can frighten a man who is fearless. So one ought to be fearless.....So I tell you all be brave, the pages of history of Gujarat are being written for the first time. All India believes that good work is being done in Bombay and Gujarat. While Government say that it is slacking in those places, may God therefore give you sufficient sense and sufficient power and may He bless you.

1 Government version of Vallabhbhai's speech in Kaliawadi, Jalalpore Taluka on 24 July, 1930.

6

Vallabhbhai Condemns Plea for Communal Representation
Collected Works of Sardar Patel

BOMBAY CHRONICLE
25 February, 1931

Sardar Vallabhbhai Patel said lectures and *darshans* helped neither the people nor the country. What was wanted was solid work. As long as a single yard of foreign cloth remained in the country, it blocked the progress of India's freedom. The speaker was convinced that merchants would never give up selling foreign cloth, as long as there were buyers for it. The remedy lay with the people in giving up foreign cloth altogether.

"Let those who talk of communal representation and seats in the council come with me to rural India where there was no communal problem to solve. The only problem that faced that part of India was the problem of hunger and of bread. The last fifteen years of Mahatma Gandhi's work had been to solve the problem of bread for the masses and today the country has realised that the problem could only be solved through Khaddar. We therefore give you notice, as long as we live we will make it impossible for people to sell foreign cloth in India."[1]

1 Speech at Delhi on 23 February, 1931.

7

Sardar Patel Praises Muslims for Their Role in Freedom Struggle

Collected Works of Sardar Patel

BOMBAY CHRONICLE
1 August, 1930

Sardar Vallabhbhai Patel, Pandit Madan Mohan Malaviya and Mr. T.A.K. Sherwani addressed another mammoth meeting on Thursday night held at the Dongri Maidan (Bombay) under the auspices of the Congress Muslim Party. Dr. Rajab Ali Patel presided. The meeting was attended by thousands of Muslims and was representative of all sections of the Muslim community. A number of local Muslim leaders were present in the meeting.

Sardar Vallabhbhai in his speech refuted the idea that Muslims were not taking part in the national struggle.

Pandit Malaviya spoke for about an hour and laid great emphasis on Hindu-Muslim unity. He surveyed India's political history of the last three thousand years and showed how India had lived peacefully and prospered during the Hindu and the Muslim periods and how the British rule had brought about communal disunity and economic ruin.

Mr. T.A.K. Sherwani also delivered an important speech on the position of Muslims in the national fight.

8

Vallabhbhai to Gandhiji on Worsening Situation in Bengal

Collected Works of Sardar Patel

(Extract)

SARDAR SHRINO PATRO-4

21 September, 1931

RESPECTED BAPU,

The situation in Bengal continues to worsen. From Sengupta's speech it is clear that the British instigated the Muslims. The Liberals[1] have appointed a non-official committee. We hear that the Government has asked the Police Commissioner to suppress the whole thing. British traders in Calcutta have asked the Government to arrest Sengupta. Sengupta on his part has challenged the Government to arrest him. When all this was going on there was firing on the prisoners in Jail, leading to two deaths and injuries to a score of 25 of prisoners. The feelings of the Hindus in Bengal have been inflamed because of this.

......

In Bengal, Subhash Babu has resigned the Presidentship of the Bengal Congress Committee.

That is how things are at present and we are continuing our work, but you need not worry about it. What happens at your end would be known in a few days. Whether it is the darkness (of despair) or light (of hope) everybody would know. The situation here remains unchanged; it has not deteriorated, nor has it improved.

Respectfully yours,
Vallabhbhai

Mahatma Gandhi,
Camp: London

1 The Leaders of the Liberal Party.

9

Congress Adopts 'Tricolour' as National Flag Under Presidentship of Sardar Patel

Collected Works of Sardar Patel

AICC PAPER
8 August, 1931

To
The President
All India Congress Committee

Sir,

At a meeting on the Working Committee of the Indian National Congress held on the 2nd April 1931 at Karachi, the following resolution was passed appointing a Committee of seven persons to examine the objections to the existing flag and recommend a flag for the acceptance of the Congress: "Whereas the National Flag now in vogue has gained a popularity by usage and convention and whereas objection has been taken to the three colours in the Flag on the ground that they are conceived on a communal basis, the Working Committee hereby appoints the following as a Committee for the purpose of examining the objections and recommending a Flag for the acceptance of the Congress. The Committee shall have the authority to take such evidence as it may consider necessary and to send its report and recommendations to the Working Committee on or before the 31st July 1931."

1. Sardar Vallabhbhai Patel,
2. Maulana Abul Kalam Azad,
3. Master Tara Singh,
4. Pandit Jawaharlal Nehru,
5. Principal D.B. Kalekar,
6. Dr. N.S. Hardiker, and

7. Dr. B. Pattabhi Sitaramayya (Convener).

Soon afterwards the following questionnaire was prepared by the Committee and circulated widely:

1. Is there any feeling amongst any group of people or community in your province, in regard to the design of the National Flag, which in your opinion should be taken into consideration by the Committee?
2. Have you any specific suggestions for making the Flag more popular?
3. Is there any defect or drawback in the design now in vogue which you consider demands attention?

The various Provincial Congress Committees were addressed directly and the public were approached through the press, while the members of the All India Congress Committee were individually addressed by the A.I.C.C. office. In response to this questionnaire eight Provincial Congress Committees, namely, Andhra, Bihar, Bombay (City), Karnataka, Sind, Tamil Nadu, Utkal and U.P. and fifty individuals and the Executive Committee of the Central Sikh League have sent up memoranda. Although the time fixed for the receipt of replies expired on 1st June, they continued to be received till 5th July.

A meeting of the Flag Committee was convened during the sittings of the Working Committee in Bombay (from 7th July forwards). Two sittings were held on the 8th and 9th July. On the first day all the members attended the meeting and on the second all but Maulana Abul Kalam Azad. We had the advantage of Sardar Sardul Singh's presence at both the sittings. We felt that no oral evidence was necessary.

The task before the Committee was recognised to be both difficult and delicate. There was a consensus of opinion both in the Committee and in the public that responded to the questionnaire *that the colours of the Flag should not bear any communal significance*. While it is true that the Congress never countenanced any communal interpretation of the colours of the Flag, the fact remains that when it was originally conceived the two colours chosen, namely, red and green, were selected on this basis and stood for the Hindu and Muslim communities, and later the white colour was added, being meant to stand for the remaining communities of India... .

Yours obediently,
Vallabhbhai Patel,
Abul Kalam Azad
Tara Singh
Jawaharlal Nehru
D.B. Kalelkar
N.S. Hardiker
B.Pattabhi Sitaramayya
(Convener)

AICC Resolution

The following are some of the important resolutions passed by the meeting of the AICC held in Bombay on the 6th, 7th and 8th August, 1931:

II. National Flag

The A.I.C.C. confirms the following change in the National Flag recommended by the Working Committee:

> "The Flag to be three-coloured, horizontally arranged as before, but the colours shall be saffron, white and green in the order stated here from top to bottom with the spinning wheel in dark blue in the centre of the white stripe: it being understood that the colours have no communal significance, but that saffron shall represent courage and sacrifice, white, peace and truth, and green shall represent faith and chivalry, and the spinning wheel the hope of the masses. The proportions of the flag shall be length to breadth as 3 is to 2."

10

Sardar Patel to Support Congress Decision on Council Entry: Refuses to Criticise Socialists

Collected Works of Sardar Patel

BOMBAY SENTINEL
14 July, 1934

(Extract)

After coming out of Nasik Road Jail.....

In an exclusive interview given to the Sentinel representative who travelled with him, Sardar Vallabhbhai Patel said: "More than anything else, the Congress needs unity in its rank today. To my mind, this is not the time when we should quarrel over small differences. It would be unfair to those two burnt their boats in their loyalty to the Congress, if we do not put up a united front"... .

When asked to give his views on the Patna decision regarding Council Entry, ... the Sardar said that he would support any programme accepted by the Congress because he was against imperilling the prestige of the Congress at a very psychological moment like the present one by creating differences within the Congress ranks.

Continuing, the Sardar said that if the Congress were to be divided at the forthcoming session of the Congress on the question of Council entry, he felt that it would be very unfortunate. He thought that no genuine Congressman would find any difficulty to implicitly carry out the programme of the Congress, although there might be changes in the policy.

Asked if he approved of Council Entry programme, the Sardar said that he had never approved of the Council Entry programme, but he was not prepared to say as to what he would do before he discussed and consulted with his colleagues ... he was definite about one thing and that was that he would support any programme of the Congress, if it meant saving the prestige and honour of the Congress.

......

In this connection Sardar Patel said that the Congress needs more of unity within its ranks, than it did at any time before. He felt that differences of opinion should not divide the Congress at present as it would be unfair to those who have burnt their boats in their loyalty to the Congress. Every Congressman should implicitly carry out the Congress programme as a matter of discipline... .

11

Sardar Patel Asks People of Bombay to Accept Government Challenge and Return Congress Candidates to Assembly with Thumping Majority

Collected Works of Sardar Patel

BOMBAY CHRONICLE
16 July, 1934

(Extract)

The first public utterance of Sardar Vallabhbhai Patel at the Congress House compound on Sunday evening, after his release from jail, was a fervent exhortation to the people of Bombay, and particularly the Congress Socialist Party, to make the ensuing Congress session a complete success and avoid split in the Congress ranks.

Proceeding Sardar Vallabhbhai said that while he was in jail many political changes had taken place, but the fight for freedom once started would never cease till the goal was reached... It was well-known that he was a staunch opponent of Council entry but now that the Congress had decided on that programme he would loyally abide by the decision. It was no use questioning the step that had already been taken by the Congress. The people themselves were responsible for creating a situation which necessitated the step. If the situation was different then nobody would have dared to talk of Council Entry.

"Now the issue was a clear-cut one. Having decided to contest the elections it was now their duty to see that they captured the Legislatures. Their prestige was at stake. Government had thrown out a challenge and Congress had accepted it. It was not the time to consider whether they had taken the right or the wrong step. Exercise your votes to the fullest extent and see that as many Congressmen as possible are returned to the legislature. Then come to me and I will show you the way", that was his advice to them.

......

He reiterated that those who had faith in the Council Entry Programme were bound by their loyalty to the Congress to support the Congress candidates and then having fulfilled their duty they could join the Sardar and he would show them the way.

The success or otherwise of the Congress candidates at the ensuing elections had tremendous significance. Failure to sweep the polls would mean a justification of the Government's repressive policy and the justification of the incarceration of Mahatma Gandhi... .

12

Bhulabhai Desai Urges People to Elect Congress Candidates to Assemblies as Requested by Vallabhbhai

Collected Works of Sardar Patel

BOMBAY CHRONICLE
21 July, 1934

(Extract)

The announcement that it has been decided in consultation with Sardar Vallabhbhai Patel, the Congress President, that Congress candidates will contest for both the seats in the Legislative Assembly from the Bombay City constituency in the ensuing elections, was made by Mr. Bhulabhai J. Desai, General Secretary of the Congress Parliamentary Board, just before his departure from Bombay to Madras by the Madras Mail on Friday night.

......

... In all constituencies we have enough Congressmen to choose from. I must at the same time state that there is such sincere co-operation that whichever Congressman is selected ultimately he will have the support of those who might have been selected in his absence... .

13

Sardar Patel Advises People Not to Resort to Unlawful Activities Due to Change in Congress Policy[1]

Collected Works of Sardar Patel

HOME DEPARTMENT (SPECIAL) : MSA
25 March, 1935

(Extract)

Addressing a public meeting at Godhra...

Sardar Patel said that "I am very glad to meet you all after a long time. You have presented me with an address but this is not the time to give addresses nor it is the time for me to accept such addresses. A time will come when India will be an independent country and then I will welcome such addresses. As long as we are slaves there is no value of such addresses. At present we are fighting for Swaraj and our fight will continue till we gain our desired object. We know that it is very difficult to get Swaraj . To get Swaraj we shall have to sacrifice a lot. We are not going to get Swaraj by going to jail or by receiving *lathi* blows or by sacrificing a few acres of land. Swaraj will be imminent if you all follow the doctrines of Mahatma Gandhi".

Mahatma Gandhi has repeatedly requested you to wear

khadi and not to use foreign articles, but you seem to pay no attention to this advice. If you act according to his advice, I assure you that we would get Swaraj within a week. We fought with the Government for 4 (four) years and Government also realised that it was no use harassing us. I must say that you fought with the Government with full vigour and strength. But at the end of 4 (four) years we had to give up the idea because we were tired, we had no strength left to us. Now it is time for us to regain our lost strength and when we acquire new strength we shall again continue our fight for Swaraj. Our fight for independence will never stop. But the method of fighting has been changed. When the Congress saw that you were not prepared to sacrifice more, that you had no faith in your leaders, it changed its programme of work. Now the policy of the Congress is to gain Swaraj by sending our men to the Assembly. Formerly Government had the idea that people had lost their faith in Congress, but at the time of the election when you supported our candidates Government knew the strength of the Congress. I thank you all for supporting our candidates during the election, but your duty does not end there. By giving secret votes for our candidates you have performed one duty. Now our duty is to give open votes for the (Congress, i.e. you should wear the uniform of Congress (khadi). Prepare cloth at your own houses and wear it. Do not wear khadi which is prepared in mills, but always wear hand-woven khadi. By doing so you will be able to give bread to your starving brothers and sisters. British people want to rule over us because they want to continue their trade with India. They want to strengthen their trade with India and to do that they play all sorts of games with us. We are fools that we don't understand their tricks and thus they take away our gold from India. Thus day by day we are becoming poorer and they grow fat at our own expense. As long as the British remain in India we are not going to be happy. When we will be independent like other countries then only we will be able to flourish our trade and thus be happy. A time will come when the British will have to give the reins of the kingdom in our hands and they shall have to go back from where they had came and according to me that time is now imminent. The British are very powerful, no doubt, they have guns, cannons, rifles, army, navy and police and the British Empire is supposed to be the strongest in the world. Still there will be a time when it shall see its downfall... .

1 Government version of Sardar Patel's speech at a public meeting held at Godhra on 25 March, 1935. About 2000 persons including about 300 women and 300 children attended the meeting.

14

Vallabhbhai Exhorts People to be Ready for More Sacrifices to Achieve Independence

Collected Works of Sardar Patel

GUJARAT SAMACHAR
18 July, 1934

Sardar Shri Vallabhbhai sent following special message for the readers of Janmabhoomi:

"I have come out after a long sentence of two and half years. I have yet to learn much, observe a lot and want to have a dialogue with a number of people. I am, therefore, not prepared to say anything at present. In my absence, a great upheaval has taken place. Many new ideas have been found and many a party have been organised, but there is no reason for us to get panicky nor get embarrassed.

We should welcome the new ideas as well as new parties, if they are helpful in leading us nearer towards freedom. If they prove hindrance to our goal of achieving freedom, we should not hesitate to leave them. No nation has achieved freedom easily without paying its price. Though we should be proud of our penance and sacrifices, our sufferings appear too meagre in comparison to other nations who have sacrificed both for achieving and sustaining their freedom. Those who think that we have not gained anything in relation to our sufferings are mistaken.

The present manifestation of awareness and self-respect are the culmination of our sacrifices. We have therefore absolutely no reason to become pessimistic.

Seize one path and realise the goal of concentrating on that path only is a prime necessity today. This necessity for becoming united had not arisen earlier. This is no time for discussion on trivial matters and mount up the differences of opinion. It is very necessary for us to leave our differences behind and work unanimously. Time is far away for sharing the fruits amongst ourselves. Substantial achievement is still far away.

"There shall be no obstacles to our achieving freedom if we move unitedly with a oneness as we did during the last four years. I am confident that we shall not go astray after making such large and lofty sacrifices. Everything will be alright if you continue to have faith in the Congress. There is no reason for pessimism".

VALLABHBHAI PATEL

15

Vallabhai to Balubhai Asking Him to Remain Firm and Not Partake in Celebrations of King's Birthday

Collected Works of Sardar Patel
Home Department (Political): NAI

BOMBAY
20 March, 1935

(Enclosure)
[of Gandhiji's Letter (in Gujarati) to Sardar Patel]

WARDHA 3
18 March, 1935

BROTHER VALLABHBHAI

It is difficult to give advice. It seems Balubhai had

committed himself to some extent. If prayers are offered, why not sweets be distributed. Can there be only one and the same condition regarding the free grant and the monetary grant. There is no distinction in the demand of the Government.

Whatever it may be, Balubhai should consult friends and if all are one, should say as under:

The fight between the Government and the public has not yet ceased. The celebration of the anniversary is not in connection with any private individual, but is for the kingdom of the King. To partake in such celebrations of the realm whose policy of administration we condemn, would mean paying the price for pedantry. The Civil Disobedience is postponed. The Government can get things done by issuing any orders. But there will be many who will not be prepared to obey such orders of their own sweet will. Such occasions should hardly be celebrated by force by the Government. We are not out to wound the feelings of anybody. So the Government should not force and we will not create any mischief. Those who desire may take part in the celebration. The Government should not write to the Municipality and *vice versa*. The Municipality according to my opinion cannot take part even though some concessions are granted at this juncture. Balubahi cannot touch the big question. This is my ordinary opinion. How am I to know what turn is necessary looking to the Ahmedabad atmosphere. Advise Balubhai as you think best.

Blessings from "Bapu"

16

Sardar Patel Assures Hindus Congress Would Safeguard Their Interests[1]

Collected Works of Sardar Patel

THE TRIBUNE
10 October, 1935

(Extract)

"My message is the message of the Congress and to act on it is to strengthen the Congress which is engaged in the struggle for country's emancipation from foreign yoke,".... Refuting the allegations brought against the Congress by the Nationalist Party, the Sardar said that in the hands of the Congress the interest of the Hindus were as safe as of other communities... .

Condemning the communal tension prevailing in the country, particularly at Lahore, the Sardar held it responsible for the unrest and political retrogression. He held that it was most irreligious to fight over mosques and Gurudwaras and that such communal strifes were responsible for the country's subjection... .

1 Sardar Patel's speech at Jullundur on 8 October, 1935.

17

Sardar Patel Advises Punjabis to Avoid Communal Fighting[1]

Collected Works of Sardar Patel

THE HINDUSTAN TIMES
5 October, 1935

(Extract)

Responding to an invitation of the Congress Parliamentary

Board, Sardar Patel arrived here (Jullundur) this morning...

At both the places the Sardar addressed mass meetings, in support of Raizada Hansraj, and strongly condemned communal bickerings in the Punjab pointing them out as the great obstacle to national progress, and ultimately to the attainment of Swaraj. Recalling the Jallianwala Bagh tragedy and the vow taken by them on the Ravi Bank, in December, 1929, to strive for complete independence... . Continuing he said that in no other province religious teachings were so much misapplied for creating unrest as in the Punjab. In fact God was not, he declared, confined to mosques and temples only. He was all-pervading. The best way to see Him was to look within themselves. He exhorted the masses, consisting mostly of peasants, to steer clear of communalism, and organise themselves so as to safeguard their interests against exploiters. He also stressed the use of hand-spun khaddar and other articles produced in villages... .

1 Speeches at Rurka Kalan and Bhag in Phillaur tehsil of Punjab on 3 October, 1935.

18

Shillidy DIG Police Bombay to Bristow Special Secretary Home Bombay Showing Concern at Congress Regaining Prestige Among Farmers of Gujarat on "Frost Relief" Issue

Collected Works of Sardar Patel

HOME POLITICAL (SPECIAL): MSA
22 March, 1935

(Extract)

MY DEAR BRISTOW

I have had occasion to watch the recent activities of Vallabhbhai Patel and other Congress leaders in Gujarath (sic) in their work of rehabilitating Congress prestige and submit now for the information of Government a general appreciation of the situation as it appears to us.

2. The object of Vallabhbhai's tour was apparently to survey and take stock of the whole situation: what the people still thought of Congress, what grievances they nourished against Government or Congress, and generally, what line of policy Congress should adopt in any new anti-Government movement now under preparation in Wardha. It is significant that immediately after his tour, Vallabhbhai went straight to Wardha. He is reported to be due back soon in Gujarath (sic) complete no doubt with orders.

3. The damage done by the frost has given the Congress workers a very timely and useful excuse for activity. Congress stock was rather at a discount, nor was there any tangible grievance to be exploited against Government. Evidence is not wanting to show that Morarji Desai and his co-workers are out to impress the peasants that thanks to Congress pressure Government have now sanctioned this "frost relief" of assessment: not only that, these same workers are out to see that every peasant gets the last possible anna out of Government. Peasants are being encouraged to bring their cases to the Congress workers for scrutiny to prevent them being "done down" by revenue officials. Further, it is intended apparently not to spend any of the Peasant Relief Fund till after every possible rupee is extracted from Governments then again Congress will magnanimously pay out what Government have "unjustly" refused to sanction. Heads—Congress wins: Tails—Government loses.

4. Efforts are being made at the same time to belittle the Government's action. Confidential orders have been issued by Collectors, so it is whispered around, to raise the annawari as high as possible, so reduce the amount of relief to be paid. This, it is argued, is but natural on the part of Government whose finances are by no means affluent. The action of all Revenue officers is therefore subject to very close observation: Government may thus receive complaints on this score.

5. The recent restoration of some Ashrams and buildings

will, it is feared, assist the Congress workers in their work among the villages. Hitherto their style was rather cramped: it was the old story—the foxes had holes and the birds of the air had nests, but the Congress worker had nowhere to lay his head. Further activity in the villages, whether under the direct aegis of the All India Village Industries Association or otherwise, may be anticipated with comparative certainty... .

Yours Sincerely,
G.G. SHILLIDY

C.H. Bristow, Esquire, ICS,
Secretary to the Government of Bombay,
Home Department (Special),
Bombay.

19

Vallabhbhai, Chairman, Congress Parliamentary Committee's Appeal to Nation to Elect Congress Candidates

Collected Works of Sardar Patel

BOMBAY CHRONICLE
7 July, 1936

The following appeal has been issued on behalf of the Congress Parliamentary Committee:

"It was decided by the Lucknow Session of the Indian National Congress that elections to the Legislatures under the New Constitution should be contested on behalf of the Congress. The Working Committee of the Congress accordingly constituted the Parliamentary Committee to organise the elections on behalf of the Congress".

... "it is the duty of the Committee to secure the election of the Congress candidates by over 30 million voters. This task can be performed only if the entire Congress organisation in the country is mobilised and the active support of the general public is secured:

The country knows what the Congress has stood for during all these years of struggle and sacrifice. Our goal is Independence or *Purna Swaraj* and those, and only those, who are pledged to this vow and for the struggle for attaining it, can be set up on its behalf.

The All-India Congress Committee will be issued the Election Manifesto in due time, and suitable candidates will be selected, whose duty it will be to carry out jointly the Congress policy in the Legislatures. The purpose of the Congress can, however, be achieved only if in this campaign the Congress receives an overwhelming support of the nation. The Public, and particularly those persons who have been given the right of vote, should treat their right as sacred trust for the country.

The Congress has proved its worth not by words, but by deeds and by suffering, and an appeal is made on its behalf to the nation for all possible support in the fullest measure, so that it may achieve its high objective".

VALLABHBHAI PATEL
CHAIRMAN
RAJENDRA PRASAD
GOVIND BALLABH PANT
SECRETARIES.

Notes: All Communications intended for the Congress Parliamentary Committee should be addressed to the Secretaries, Congress Parliamentary Committee, Congress House, Girgaum, Bombay.

20

Sardar Patel Unhappy Over Internal Squabbles in Tamilnad Congress, Asks Self-seekers to Leave Party

Collected Works of Sardar Patel

BOMBAY CHRONICLE
21 December, 1936

(Extract)

......

Referring to the elections, Sardar Patel asked the people not to worry themselves about controversial issues and said: "If Congress found that office-acceptance would help the cause of Indian freedom, it would not hesitate to accept it. But, if it was harmful the Congress would reject and there was enough time to consider it".

Uttering a warning to Congress candidates, Sardar Patel said: "If any of the Congress candidates joined us in the expectation that Congress will accept office, I must tell them that they should drop out and there is time yet to do it as dates for nomination have not been fixed in Madras".

He exhorted the voters of Trichy (Trichinapally) to give the same lead as in the last Assembly elections by returning all Congress candidates and concluded saying: "To vote for Congress is to vote for freedom: to vote against Congress is to vote for slavery".

21

*Sardar Patel Exhorts People of Surat to Vote for Congress Candidates. Refutes Rumours about Differences Between Gandhiji and Nehru**

Collected Works of Sardar Patel

Home Department (Special): MSA
(Extract)

SURAT
26 July 1936

To
The District Superintendent of Police,
Surat.

Sir,

......

Among prominent persons was Sardar Vallabhbhai Patel,

addressing people of Surat. Sardar Patel told them in Gujarati, ... At present the aim of the Congress is to capture legislatures and thus carry on the struggle for Independence. The Lucknow Congress also resolved to capture the legislature. At present many newspapers published different views on this subject. I request you all to be firm minded and not to be misguided by false reporters. At Present our attention should not be directed towards anything else but Council entry. That should be our goal at present. The legislature has two parts: One Council and Second Assembly. The representatives for the Assembly have to remain in the Assembly for five years and those for Councils for nine years. Hence if unfit and disloyal representatives enter the legislature they will ruin the interest of the country. Hence I appeal to you to give your votes for Congress candidates......

... In Surat district there are five seats. There is separate electorate for the Muslims. There are two seats in the Assembly from Surat, Broach and Panch Mahali district. Here also the Muslims are given separate electorate. We should try our best to capture all the five seats of these districts.... Those who have sacrificed their everything for the country, those who have proved themselves to be loyal and faithful to the country will get admission there. Title holders and rich persons are no more wanted in the legislature. They have not done and are not going to do any good for the country by entering the legislature. As we have been determined to capture the legislature we should see that no outsider manages to enter the Councils or the Assembly. Because the outsider will work against the Congress and thus the Congress will have to suffer. You should not give a single vote to those who are not Congress Candidates... .

...Under such circumstances we may lose some seats in these two provinces. Also there is separate electorate for the Muslims and the Harijans etc. *In this way the Government want to divide India into separate parts. The Government is trying to defeat the Congress by the policy of divide and rule.* At this stage what is the duty of Gujarat? From Gujarat only

Congress candidates should enter the legislature and none else. In short, Gujarat should have hundred per cent result at the time of election.

The Government have tried their best by adopting various measures to crush the activities of the Congress in this connection but the Congress is bold enough to say at this stage that the majority of the candidates in the legislature will be from Congress party.

...So, I appeal to you all once again to help the Congress. May God bless you (claps)...

Remarks:

The speeches of Vallabhbhai J. Patel and Kanayalal Nanabhai Desai were not at all seditious nor objectionable. The speech of V.J. Patel created good impression upon the public.

I beg to remain,
Sir,
Your most obedient servant,
P.C. SHROFF
P.S.I,C.I.D, Ahmedabad.

* Government version of Sardar Patel's speech at Surat Sahr Samiti held on 26 July, 1936.

22

Sardar Patel's Resolution Deploring Interference of Governors in Ministerial Work Endorsed by CWC

Collected Works of Sardar Patel

HINDUSTAN TIMES
21 February, 1938

(Extract)

"In this hour of crisis, I appeal to you to pass this resolution, the most important resolution of the Congress which has been prepared after most careful consideration and deliberations and thus demonstrate our national solidarity. We may have our differences, but on this issue I want you all to stand as one man and give a proper reply to the challenge thrown at the Congress".

......

Continuing Sardar Patel observed, "Communal trouble was frequent before the Congress assumed office but since the Congress assumption of office there was not a single instance of serious communal riots and this spoke volumes of the Congress ability to rule". Despite all these facts and repeated assurances by the Congress Ministers about the maintenance of law and order the Governor-General's interference could only mean one thing, namely, that he was anxious to raise some issue to get the Congress Ministers out of office. We are not going to play into the hands of the British Government... .

23

Sardar Patel Refutes Jinnah's Allegations of Repressions of Muslims Under Congress Rule

Collected Works of Sardar Patel

THE HINDU
11 December, 1939

Sardar Patel has issued the following statement regarding Mr. Jinnah's suggestion to Muslims:

Ordinarily I would not have concerned myself with Jinnah's appeal to the Muslims to celebrate the so-called 'day of deliverance'; but in this case, when he has concentrated his attack on what he terms "the Congress High Command" and has invited his community to a course of conduct likely to stir up communal strife. I, as the Chairman of the Parliamentary

Sub-Committee, would fail in my duty if I did not refute the unfounded allegations made by Jinnah in the appeal and the draft resolution.

The country is, by now, familiar with Jinnah's vague allegations which are growing everyday in their extent and vagueness. But when the Muslim League, through the Pirpur Committee, first made definite charges against the Congress Ministries, I instructed them to enquire into each allegation and submit a report. These reports, which in all cases were published by the respective Provincial Governments, showed that the charges were entirely unfounded. When the Congress asked the British Government for a declaration of their war aims and their immediate application to India, Jinnah again returned to the charges of oppression in general terms against the Ministries. Dr. Rajendra Prasad, the President of the Congress, thereupon, offered to submit the charges, if specified, to an independent Tribunal for inquiry, but Jinnah spurned the offer, stating that he had placed the charges before the Viceroy. But before the Viceroy could speak, we have his latest outburst in which his community and the world in general are invited to accept his unsupported assertions as proved facts.

I am constrained to characterise these allegations as wild, reckless and intended to endanger communal peace. When the Congress Ministries took office, as Chairman of the Parliamentary Sub-Committee, I instructed the Ministries scrupulously to respect the rights of the minorities. Grievances of a communal nature were carefully examined by the Ministries and in several cases re-examined by the members of the Parliamentary Sub-Committee. Furthermore, every Premier, at my instance, had invited his Governor unhesitatingly to intervene in matters affecting the rights and interests of the minorities, whenever the Governor felt that the action of the Ministry was not correct.

When Jinnah recently made the charges, I again instructed every Premier to invite his Governor's attention to them as they also affected him, and I was informed that the Governors considered the charges as unwarranted. The Governors, though invited to contradict, however, could not possibly do so at the time for reasons of constitutional propriety. But I have no doubt that they must have submitted their reports to the Viceroy. Had the Governors taken the view that there was any substance in those charges, they would have certainly drawn the attention of their Ministers to the same and I am absolutely confident that before no fair judge could Jinnah establish a single charge made by him against any Congress Ministry or against the 'Congress High Command'.

It is unfortunate that even now the Viceroy and the Governors, for reasons of their own, do not reply to these charges with which they are as much concerned as the Ministers. The Ministers accepted office at the request of the Governors and went out of office voluntarily for a nobler cause, and their record of work has been highly spoken of by all British statesmen, the Viceroy and the Governors. I, therefore, consider it unjust to them that their fair name should be allowed to be exposed to such unmerited calumny.

What motive Jinnah has in issuing this appeal when he and Jawaharlal Nehru are about to meet in order to explore the possibilities of a settlement, it is difficult to see. But if what Jinnah says is his confirmed view, many will be driven to the conclusion that he has no desire to see that the negotiations are brought to a successful end. It is humanly impossible to carry on any negotiations with self-respect unless this highly offensive statement is withdrawn. It is also inconsistent with the dignity of a great national organisation like the Congress to negotiate under the threat of such a country-wide communal demonstration.

24

Sardar Patel Indignant Over Silence of Viceroy and Governors on Jinnah's Baseless Charges Against Congress Ministries

Collected Works of Sardar Patel

THE HINDUSTAN TIMES
16 December, 1939

Sardar Vallabhbhai Patel, Chairman of the Congress Parliamentary Sub-Committee, has issued the following statement to the Press:

"I have no desire to enter into a controversy with Jinnah on the eve of the meeting of the Congress Working Committee especially after the impossible stand he has thought it fit to take up in regard to the communal question but I feel it my duty to the nation to draw public attention to the implications of Jinnah's latest statement.

"It is apparent from Jinnah's statement that he does not want any communal settlement, although he says he is willing to discuss the question with Pandit Jawaharlal Nehru. His sole object seems to be to keep up communal feeling at high tension. His insistence on the observance of the so-called day of deliverance is manifestly intended to exacerbate the prevailing animosity. It may well lead to an outbreak of hostilities between the two communities. The draft resolution for the proposed meetings is a hymn of hate based on unspecified unproved, if not disproved, charges against a band of selfless public servants whose good work has been highly appreciated by the Secretary of State, the Viceroy, the Governors and the Indian masses. To persist in such a course is proof positive that Jinnah is bent upon fanning the fire of communalism.

"When Babu Rajendra Prasad offered to refer the matter to arbitration, he had in mind a brief inquiry occupying a fortnight or at the most a month during which the inquiry into the specific representative charges which Jinnah was asked to formulate would be over. It was assumed by the Congress President that the findings of the inquiring authority would be given swiftly, thereby paving the way for national unity and a united demand for a declaration of Britain's war aims and their immediate application to India.

"The rejection of the Congress President's offer for such swift easy and unobjectionable method of dealing with this unpleasant affair shows the direction in which Jinnah's mind is working. If he meant business, Jinnah would not ask for the impossible. His long experience of public life should have shown him that the British Government would never agree to what amounts to a direct impeachment of the Viceroy and seven provincial Governors. Perhaps that is the very reason why he has put forth this demand.

"According to Jinnah, the British Viceroy and the Governors are fellow-conspirators in the tyranny practised by the Congress over the Muslims. If that were so, he may as well have asked for an International Commission. If a person like the Chief Justice of India is not good enough in the eyes of Jinnah, no other British Judge is likely to be acceptable.

"I can only say that I am amazed at the conspiracy of silence on the part of the Viceroy and the Governors. Jinnah's attack is as much against them as against the Congress. The League has openly charged with dereliction of duty and defiance of the King's Instruments of Instruction. They know that the charges are baseless. Apart from failing to help the cause of justice and exposing the Congress Ministries to a false and malicious campaign of abuse and vilification, they are, by remaining silent owing to narrow ideas of constitutional propriety, doing grave injury to themselves and to their professions of impartiality between the Indian communities. There would be an end to this mischievous campaign if they come out with the truth and tell the world that they have never felt the occasion to invoke their special responsibility for the protection of the legitimate rights of the minorities against the inroads of the Congress Ministries.

"In his statement, Jinnah has cited instance of Congress tyranny and oppression. They are the national flag, the singing of Bande Matram and the teaching of Hindi. As he has specified these complaints, they must be the main grievances for which he wants an inquity. If he had graver charges than these against the Congress Ministries, he would not have failed to mention them first. Does Jinnah seriously suggest that a Royal Commission is necessary for the investigation of such charges? This is enough to show that he has no case".

25

Sardar Patel Unhappy Over Silence of Governors on Charges Levelled Against Congress Ministries by Muslim League

Collected Works of Sardar Patel

THE HITAVADA
17 January, 1940

(Extract)

......

Inaugurating the proceedings of the conference, Sardar Patel gave a brief review of the political developments in the country. He asserted that the present deadlock was capable of solution only if the Congress demand for a declaration of India's freedom and the convocation of Constituent Assembly were acceded to. The Congress could go back to office tomorrow if it so chose, but it would not do so until and unless its demand had been met.

......

He expressed pain at the silence of the Governors with regard to the charges levelled against the Congress Ministries by the Muslim League. If only the Governors spoke the truth, he said, the League would be exposed... .

26

Sardar Patel to Rajenbabu Criticising Appeasement of Jinnah

Collected Works of Sardar Patel
Rajendra Prasad Papers

11 CHAUPATY SEA-FACE
OPP. TILAK STATUE, BOMBAY
16 October, 1939

MY DEAR RAJENDRA BABU,

I have received your letter of the 13th October. On the question referred to in your letter my opinion is that we should ignore Press reports. Sir Sikandar could have written to Maulana Abul Kalam Azad whom he met at Delhi last time or to Gandhiji with whom he has easy access. In my opinion, no further initiative should be taken by us. The last answer of Mr. Jinnah in reply to your letter puts the whole burden on him for further initiative. I think we are spoiling our case by making persistent approaches, but in this matter Maulana Saheb's advice must be the last word. I have a strong conviction that there can be no settlement of the communal question till Mr. Jinnah feels that he cannot coerce the Congress.

Yours Sincerely,
VALLABHBHAI

Babu Rajendra Prasad,
Sadaquat Ashram,
Dighaghat, Patna.

27

Sardar Patel Unhappy Over Nehru's Meeting with Jinnah

Collected Works of Sardar Patel
AICC Papers

ALL-INDIA CONGRESS PARLIAMENTARY
SUB-COMMITTEE
9 December, 1939

MY DEAR JAWAHAR,

I have received your letter of the 7th December together with a copy of Mr. Jinnah's letter to you of the 4th. After having written that letter to you he issued that amazing statement which is nothing but an incitement to the Musalmans. He has issued another statement yesterday which is also offensive. I am glad that you are coming over here on the 14th. Our people all over India will be irritated when they will hear that you are meeting him after his provocative statements. We must end this situation as early as possible and I am glad that you are meeting him before the Working Committee meeting. I am going to Ahmedabad tomorrow for the meeting of the Provincial Executive, but I will return back to Bombay on the 14th morning.

I see that Sir Stafford Cripps is also meeting Messrs Jinnah and Ambedkar and some of the representatives of the Princes. I do hope that his round of visits will not again stir of dirt of muddy water of the under political ocean.

Yours Sincerely,
VALLABHBHAI PATEL

Pt. Jawaharlal Nehru,
Allahabad.

28

Sardar Patel's Procession Attacked by Muslim Goondas at Bhavnagar

Collected Works of Sardar Patel

THE HINDUSTAN TIMES
15 May, 1939

(Extract)

One person was killed and another seriously injured as the result of a clash which occurred between a huge procession of Muslims and a large crowd which received Sardar Vallabhbhai Patel, who arrived at 9 o'clock this morning to preside over the fifth session of the Bhavnagar Praja Mandal Conference.

Sardar Patel was being taken in a procession. As soon as they reached a mosque, a Muslim procession came on the scene and the clash occurred.

The Conference authorities decided to abandon their procession and Sardar Patel was taken to his destination under police protection.

The police brought the situation under control and made over a hundred arrests in the mosque.

Sardar Patel has issued an appeal to the public not to get excited over the situation and observe complete non-violence.

Public funeral for Bachubhai Virji Patel, who was fatally injured, has been arranged, and a complete *hartal* is being observed in the city... .

...The city observed complete *hartal*.

Sardar Patel issued a statement immediately regretting the incident in the morning and requesting the people not to lose their balance in the midst of provocation, but carry on the programme peacefully.

29

Sardar Patel for Erecting a Memorial to Bachubhai and Nanabhai Who Were Killed in Attack by Muslim Miscreants at Bhavnagar

Collected Works of Sardar Patel

SARDAR PATEL KE BHASHNON
16 May, 1939

(Extract)

I desire that there must be unity between different communities. But if we want a real unity then persons who are behind such heinous acts should be found out and we should not leave them till they are remorseful for what they have done. They should not be given opportunity to think that we are fools and weaklings. Some might tell us to forget what has happened, but that advice is like asking you to believe that day is night and night is day.

Those people who shelter the killers, hide them, or are sympathetic to them are also equally dangerous and you must think whether to continue being friendly with them. You have to think about the risk to continue putting your heads on the hoods of the serpents.

I am an enemy of cowardice, I do not want to be with cowards.

If the state and the authorities wish that it is better to forget such incidents and if we ignore such incidents then there is danger in future that such incidents will happen with more intensity. So we have to arrest the culprits and find out the gangs of conspirators. The good of the state lies in uprooting such dangerous elements. We have to be ready to do our duty whether the state does its duty or not.

This incident is a serious warning to the people and the ruler of Bhavnagar. We have been given a notice that now onwards we cannot sleep soundly with a confidence that everything is alright. We can't ignore such a warning.

It is our duty to know the times and prepare for self-defence. This is the time when criminals are moving in all the directions. If we give them grounds to believe that we are cowards then anti-social elements will be able to move freely. ...

In this country, in British India as well as the native states, I have been encouraging progressive and democratic forces. So this was an attack on me. It was not an attack on an individual but it was an attack against the forces which I have been supporting. But the person who attacked is a fool. The string pullers and plotters who are behind him should be traced.

What happened on the first day of the conference is forgotten and if there is a danger of such incidents not happening in future then communal unity will recede very far. Today the question is of your safety, when such incidents happen, you cannot actively conduct your business or follow your normal routine. For that there should be an atmosphere of security and confidence.

You have always to be awake and alert. I wish that you should be ready to receive the blows not like* a coward but like a brave person and if necessary you must be prepared for more sacrifices. Those of you who have been witness to these incidents or those who can help the police in investigation should boldly come forward to help the police publicly... .

* Sardar Patel's speech at a public meeting in Bhavnagar on 16 May, 1939.

30

Sardar Patel to Rajenbabu Endorsing Strong Action against Arya Samajists Responsible for Murder of Two Muslims At Sholapur

Collected Works of Sardar Patel

Rajendra Prasad Papers
(Extract)

PURUSHOTTAM MANSION
OPP. OPERA HOUSE, BOMBAY
22 May, 1939

DEAR RAJENDRABABU,

......

Since the Hyderabad agitation commenced the Arya Samajists have made Sholapur as their base and have been sending all their *jathas* through that centre. The Bombay Government have been put to considerable strain on this account. Yesterday when their procession passed through a *masjid* there was some small quarrel and immediately the Arya Samajists came with knives from their camps and killed two Muslims and wounded several. We cannot allow such gun-powder and fire continuously so close together and the Bombay Government have taken today strong action in Sholapur ordering the removing of all the Arya Samajists from Sholapur. It will create some trouble for us, but we cannot afford to be weak in the handling of such communal situation.

......

Yours Sincerely
VALLABHBHAI

Babu Rajendra Prasad
Camp: Ranchi (Bihar).

31

Vallabhbhai Assures Congress's Preparedness to Face All Odds[1]

Collected Works of Sardar Patel

SARDAR PATEL KE BHASHNON
3 September, 1940

(Extract)

It is strange that a country having one-fifth of the population of the world is made to join such a deadly war without its consent.

You say that your aim is pure. If you are fighting for high ideals, great principles then say so. We want to know that. But did not get direct reply. From what they spoke it can be deduced that for the reconstruction of Europe, both Britain and Germany are fighting . This is a war to show how the whites can control the world except Europe and America. That is the stinking smell that we get from their announcements.

We were fighting with you. Now you are fighting with other countries; then you put an end to our relations.

They say here there are many religions, so many castes and communities. They do not unite. They are unfit to govern. For twelve months they kept on saying this and played the cat and mouse game.

Congress wants independence for thirtyfive crores. Liberty for the whole of India. Congress does not fight so that some Congressmen might get some post. It is not our business to see that some two or three men get the jobs of five thousand rupees per month.

This declaration is derogatory to the honour and prestige of India. It wants to suppress the Congress. At this time Congress hopes that crores of people will heartily support it. The declaration is invitation to the Congress to fight.

......

Congress will see that patriotism is not destroyed by the Government. Congress is not going to lie low when such efforts are being made.

Are we yet to suffer? After having been ruled for two hundred years, we are not able to stand on our feet. We will suffer whatever is inflicted on us for that responsibility will be yours.

We are not against Englishmen. This is not a question of particular community or individual. This resolution opposes imperialism. We have been fighting imperialism before Nazism was born. When both are fighting what are we to do? Do we watch those forces fighting with each other? If two evils fight let them fight. But one evil is in our home.

......

In 1930-32 we could prepare for struggle. In that struggle government was less brutal. But in this struggle, do not expect any mildness towards us. Suddenly a struggle will be thrust on us... .

1 Speech delivered at Surat on 3 September 1940.

32

Vallabhbhai Feels An Independent India would be a Better Ally of British in War[1]

Collected Works of Sardar Patel

SARDAR PATEL KE BHASHNON

18 July, 1940

(Extract)

......

Gandhiji says that Congress, for the last twenty years, has adopted non-violent methods. If we abandon that road we will be in danger. Our condition is different. It is good if we go to that extent. But we have not the capability to combat internal disorder and external aggression, if we can it is best... .

We tell Englishmen that we are ready to fully co-operate

with them. Even though we might not proceed further in our experiment of non-violence we are ready to side with you in war. Young men want an opportunity to receive military training. The legislative party of the Congress has again and again passed resolutions that army should be Indianised... .

As a principle, it is good that if we believe in universal love we should help England unconditionally. But if I do that I shall have to renounce the world. I cannot inspire such love even in my family. In contrast, nobody except Gandhiji has developed such extensive love, therefore, whole world bows to him... .

We are ready to forget all your past misdeeds. But I ask you even while dying you want to make a will and make arrangement for the future? We think that when our country is not independent, how can we try for independence of the world when we are slaves. If we help them without any clarification about the transfer of power, our chains will be more tight—our past experience is such. So what we talk is not about bargain but of clarification.

1 Speech delivered at L.D. Arts College on 18 July, 1940.

33

Vallabhbhai Holds Both British and Hitler Responsible for War[1]

Collected Works of Sardar Patel

SARDAR PATEL KE BHASHNON
8 September, 1940

(Extract)

......

World is heading towards destruction because heaps of sins are accumulated. Europe is also experiencing fratricidal war similar to ours. Though it is far away, but it is nearing us, because our country is a party. We do not know when it will reach here, but the fact is that it is approaching very fast... .

When the war started we asked the empire "You declared that India is a partner in the war without consulting us, but now you explain to us as to what is war aim so that we may understand as to what is selfishness and we may take steps accordingly". We did not get a direct reply. In the meantime both the parties started publicity campaign. Germany complains of injustice having been done to it and so Germans are fighting to undo the wrong done to them. This was the tone of German radio.

But the empire did not give a direct reply to our query. Imperialists talked sweetly, again and again negotiations were held. Gandhiji went to see Viceroy again and again, but he got nothing which was acceptable. We kept enough patience because we did not want to harass the enemy when he is in difficulty.

But now our patience is exhausted. It appears that empire has been showing its real nature. Government at present is doing as if they want to divide, let it do so. But the nationalism which is deeply rooted will not be affected. At present they are busy getting opposite forces together, with the aim of crushing the Congress... .

... We demanded that national Government should be formed at the centre. Anglo-Indian newspaper like *Statesman* said that if there is any political wisdom in the British Empire it will accept the offer of the Congress, because Congress never put such an offer and in future it will never put such an offer. Now Congressmen can say that "Britishers missed the bus".

...You have been riding on our shoulders for the last one fifty years, now get down. They say if they go what will happen to us? You ask us this question after ruling for two hundred years, then what you did all these years. It reminds me of an episode about a quarrel: The house owner is asked by the guard as to what will happen if he goes away? "I will learn how to guard". But this guard does not leave and threatens us again and again.

......

When the sword is hanging on its head even then empire says that we cannot govern because there is disunity amongst us and so it cannot forsake its moral responsibility. The thing behind the curtain of this moral responsibility is dangerous. Britishers do not name the parties, vested interests. From behind the curtains it appears that when the power, which is in great difficulty, speaks like this then there might be some heavenly suggestion. For us it is proper to watch the consequences. We have not to be dejected. We have to keep vigil. When these people refuse to concede anything, it might be to our advantage. That might be the wish of God.

What are we to do under these circumstances? We should live amicably. We should unite. Such difficult times might come when we will fight against each other which is dangerous for India. Let British Government make efforts to divide us, but we have to eradicate vengeance and enmity. The fields of native states are nor battlefields? The field of battle is in India. You have simply to implement Congress programme... .

1 Speech delivered at a public meeting in Vadhwan on 8 September, 1940.

34

Vallabhbhai Castigates British Government for Not Making Its War Aims Clear[1]

Collected Works of Sardar Patel

SARDAR PATEL KE BHASHNON
9 September, 1940

(Extract)

After Congress Session, Congress has passed resolutions,

and it is clearly stated that Nazism and Fascism are destroyers of democracy. Democracy does not accept these '*isms*'. Congress believes that these isms are going to cause damage to the world. Congress has declared this not after the war was declared but prior to it... .

......

Congress had said that if you sincerely desire our help then stop formation of Viceroy's Council and in its place form a national government comprising the representatives of Congress, Muslim League, Hindu Mahasabha and all parties and some Englishmen also be in it, and let that Government be responsible to the people. You have simply to say that when the war ends then the constitution, framed by constituent assembly, which will have representatives of all the provinces, will be signed by you. But they did not accept any proposals and continued repeating what they had been saying. Their proposal is to expand the Viceroy's Council comprising civil servants. They want us to join the war efforts... .

Their intention is not pure...

Now they ask us that if they are defeated and enemies come here what will happen to us? They are getting nervous and it is difficult to answer this question. Though they were here for two hundred years we are sorry that they have to ask us this question. We say "You don't worry. After staying here for two hundred years if you have to ask this question, then leave by the first available transport. We will manage our affairs.... Let whatever happens to us but you ask your hearts as to what will happen to you, when you lose India after two hundred years? Your real agony is about that.

1 Speech delivered at the public meeting in Ahmedabad on 9 September, 1940.

35

Sardar Patel Reiterates Demand for Complete Independence In Order to Elicit India's Support for British War Efforts

Collected Works of Sardar Patel

HINDUSTAN TIMES
16 September, 1940

(Extract)

"The resolution which Mr. Rajagopalachari has just placed before you is a short one—perhaps the shortest passed by the Committee since the war broke out. There is no reference in it to the failures of the British Government to meet the Indian demand for freedom nor any criticism of it... .
..."looking to the present position of Britain. In her hour of trial we did not want to remind her of her failings in respect of India, but at the same time we have not gone back a bit on any of our demands. We have made it quite clear that if our demands are accepted, our full and hearty co-operation would be at the disposal of Great Britain. The question whether our demand will be accepted or not does not matter much, as it suites us both ways. If the British Government accept it, it is good, because it will be to their advantage and our benefit, but if they do not we will be free to choose our own course, and we shall do so".

The Sardar added: "There are people who sense danger in this move and feel that we will be taking great risks if this resolution is passed. No doubt there is a certain amount of risk in it, but big issues like the freedom of a vast country like India cannot be solved unless we are prepared to take certain amount of risk, and we are prepared to do so. When we met at Wardha in September last, we thought that it would be a long war and there would be a stalemate for pretty long period, but the rapid developments during the last two or three months have changed the face of the war and we have to take stock of the fact that the entire Nationalist press of the country had approved the Delhi decision that the country is behind us. I can understand the position of those who do not want to give any thought to this until freedom is achieved, but in that case we need not make any demand from Britain either. There are people who talk of moral support. Britain, placed as she is at present, has no value for moral support in the same way as Mahatma Gandhi's appeal to every Briton had no value in the eyes of the Englishmen. But it is precisely in this frame of mind that Britain may feel the need of coming to a settlement with us. There is no question of bargaining in it. Our support, if it is to be full and hearty, must come from the people of a free India. Again we cannot help Britain so long as we are not free, because all such help given would go to strengthen our bondage and we are not fools to allow that to happen"... .

36

Sardar Patel Feels People's Unity as the Greatest Weapon Against British Oppression[1]

Collected Works of Sardar Patel

SARDAR PATEL KE BHASHNON
9 March, 1942

(Extract)

......

Now the war has come to our doorsteps. Such a huge population, one-fifth population of the world, their weapons were taken away. Since last two hundred years we have not been allowed to keep weapons. So we are also habituated to go to police station even for the minor events. But now its police stations are not going to be there.

...So try to learn how to defend yourselves. You can't to be brave if you do not shun the fear to death. ... Now we have to forget the difference between caste and caste, religion and religion, community and community and be united and shed fear. This is not the time to sit in a shade and work. Follow the instructions of Gandhiji. Strengthen the unity in the village.

1 Lecture given in Nadiad on 9 March, 1942.

37

Sardar Patel Reaffirms Faith in Non-violence in a Limited Field But Not to Meet Internal or External Aggression

Collected Works of Sardar Patel

THE HINDUSTAN TIMES
20 July, 1940

"Nobody should imagine that there is any split in the Congress Working Committee or that the Congress Working Committee is going to be separated from Mahatma. Gandhi. Nothing can separate us," declared. Sardar Vallabhbhai Patel... .

...He added: "We have worked together nearly 25 years and if even today Mahatma Gandhi were to ask us to follow him we would put our faith implicitly in him and unhesitatingly accept his advice, but he had asked us to take the brave decision not in our individual capacity but as representatives of the great national organisation whose aspirations and objectives are the independence of this great country, and the Working Committee would not be true to itself if it did not recognise its limitations".

Proceeding, Sardar Patel said: "Our heart is indeed after the great ideal of non-violence which, under the inspiring leadership of Mahatma Gandhi, we have practised in the limited field, but we must confess that we as representatives of our constituencies are not capable of the task of shouldering the responsibility of meeting external attacks or internal disorder with non-violence. The resolution of the Working

Committee is a sincere offer of help which the British people can appreciate. It is a test of their sincerity in their relations with India".

"If the British Government want the hearty co-operation of this country they must make it possible for the people to be ready to take their proper place in the changing world and discipline themselves for the responsibilities which they will have to shoulder".

38

Sardar Patel Optimistic About Formation of Congress Government After the War[1]

Collected Works of Sardar Patel

SARDAR PATEL KE BHASHNON
26 January, 1942

(Extract)

The whole world is going to catch war hysteria, in a way is already caught. You do not think that you are not concerned with war. It is like a piece of wood in burning fire which is at the end, which thinks that would not be burnt but it gets burnt in the fire.

......

As the war comes nearer and nearer, government gets more and more nervous and side by side the anti-social elements become more and more active. The Government machinery is getting loose day by day. Government has not enough power or means to get control over the situation and this loose machinery and cracking government is going to fall in the lap of the Congress. You have to understand this.

......

The war is such that it might destroy the whole world. I do not know whether this is the last fight or we shall have to fight again. Gandhiji says that the wars will stop when the world gets wiser... .

Our ancestors used to spine while sitting at home... .

Swaraj means that the villages became self-dependent and do not depend on outside help for their safety. Spinning wheel is the centre of constructive programme. There should not be a situation when tons of cotton is grown but there is shortage of cloth. So every village should have enough of cotton.

......

Lazy and pleasure seeking people do not deserve Swaraj. One who is not satisfied by getting enough for himself but makes effort to see that there is nobody in the village who is hungry only can bring Swaraj.

Congress is a unique institution. Crores of people are behind its back and hear its voice. We have to fight with any power which tries to rule us. Congress will fight with any invader. We do not want that one evil is replaced by another. We cannot choose between the bandits.

1 Lecture given in Bardoli Swaraj Ashram on Independence day on 26 January, 1942.

39

Sardar Patel on Aims and Objectives of Gandhiji's Call to British to Quit India[1]

Collected Works of Sardar Patel

SARDAR PATEL KE BHASHNON

26 July, 1942

(Extract)

When the war began Congress Working Committee passed a resolution though India has been dragged into the war without the consent of the Congress. We are ready to forget past record of the Government if aims of war are clearly stated. Congress can think of supporting the war. Many a time we demanded that. The matter was discussed in Parliament also but result was big zero.

After that A.I.C.C. session was held at Poona. The Congress was accused of having faith in non-violence and accepts the leadership of Mahatma Gandhi, so Congress support has no value. Congress and especially Mahatma believed that we must see as to which side is more moral and give a moral support to that side. But the Government did not want moral support, it wanted help in military equipment and recruits in the army. So in the Poona meeting of A.I.C.C. having decided to differ from Gandhiji, but on condition to differ, if the government desired strengthening the army, then even parting company with Gandhiji. We can tell people but it can happen only when people feel that this land is theirs, so that we may be able to open our mouth before the public. We meant that Government should immediately form a national cabinet. But we did not get any reply. So Congress decided that if it maintains silence, it will lose its identity.

Thus when Congress was ignored we felt that the empire did not care for us at all. So we resolved to express our moral protest and gave full powers to Gandhiji to launch a struggle. It had moral effect on the entire world. Then the empire lost their vast territory of Singapore, Malaya and Burma. Ceylon was attacked and there was a danger of attack on India. So in order to see whether the government came to its senses we decided to postpone our moral struggle.

Then British empire sent its representative Sir Stafford Cripps to India. He was a friend of many a Congressman, so they and many other people felt that he was a man of progressive ideas and so the intention of the government should be pure in sending him and it wanted some compromise and so we decided to think over the proposal which he brought with him and we authorised Maulana Azad to negotiate with him and present before the Working Committee his talks with Cripps but Cripps felt that a meeting with Congress leaders should precede meeting Gandhiji because Gandhiji was the guiding spirit of the Congress. So

Gandhiji was invited by a wire. Gandhiji informed that he was of no use, because he was against any violent war and he had separated himself from the Congress, yet if Cripps insists he would come to meet him.

Thus Gandhiji went to Delhi. There what he saw was nauseating and his soft feelings for Britishers and the Government evaporated. He plainly told Stafford Cripps, if a thoughtless person like Amrey had brought such proposals then he would not have been surprised but he was considered to be a friend of India as well as Russia and a man of progressive ideas. So why did he bring such proposals? Why did he come to inflict such a sinful blow on India?

Then Gandhiji left but Congress, in order to independently examine Cripps' proposals and clearly know what they were, negotiated deliberately for full fifteen days. Initially Cripps talked sweetly. He also said that Viceroy would rule like a constitutional monarch of England, Congress also asked him to sidetrack his other proposals like partition of India and the merger of native states and wanted to know as to what he immediately proposed to do because why talk about the future. When British Government proposed to give independence to India, because it might be that in future they might not have anything in their hand to give. So talks about that could be held when the time comes. Congress wanted to know if he proposed to give something at present on the basis of which people could be persuaded to help war efforts. All those days he talked sweetly and on last day he wrote a letter to Maulana Azad that as Congress had demanded national government it had reversed its stand which it had taken during the talks but really it was he who had gone back and levelled a false charge against the Congress.

So Gandhiji was exasperated. Thereafter All India Congress Committee session was held at Allahabad. ...When Working Committee met at Allahabad Gandhiji expressed his opinion that intentions of the empire seemed to be of a doubtful nature, so it was our duty that we should tell our rulers that for their good and our good they should quit India but this was something new.

......

I have told you that the Working Committee has passed a resolution. We were ready to sidetrack Gandhiji and non-violence and wanted to help. But as soon as Cripps brought the proposals of British Government, Gandhiji told us to give up all hopes of compromising with the Government. Understand the full implication of his asking the Britishers to quit India. Everybody knows that there is going to be an invasion. Not ninetynine but 99.75 per cent people of this country say let this devil go, we do not mind if another devil comes. So much poison is there in the minds of people against Britishers. When people hear about the victories of Germany or Japan, they rejoice. Nobody has heard about Britishers victory... .

Russia is fighting. We admire its courage. It fights because the people know that they are fighting for the freedom of their country, but for whom should India fight? We are not independent. So Gandhiji asks Britishers to quit India.

They can stay on one condition. Their army might stay here but our independence should be intact. They can stay here by signing a treaty with us. The treaty should be of the type which they have with America and China. They can stay here in a way that they have established relations of love with Russia. They cannot stay here as ex-rulers.

......

What will be the condition of India if it is attacked? They say that the responsibility of defending India is their sacred duty, but we do not believe it. They had a similar responsibility of defending Burma. They utter only one sentence that final victory is theirs but we are apprehensive as when that last war will be fought.

America also says loudly that war will not be won if India is not free and Britishers want to turn this land into a battlefield in order to keep their empire in the eastern hemisphere alive. Our land can be turned into battlefield only when our country becomes free, and only then we will be able to help other countries in giving their freedom. But when Churchill returned from America after signing the Atlantic Charter he said something about India. We have been able to know his evil intention.

......

In Wardha Working Committee it was decided that if we had to repulse the attack, we could do it only if we were free. *Japan Radio*, day in and day out, says loudly that they do not want even an inch of our land and they are fighting in order to drive out the foreign rulers. Some of our people have joined them. They say that it is a matter of patriotism Subhas Babu is also there but we are not to be led away by Japanese propaganda. We should not also believe that Moscow will come and make us free.

So Congress has decided that it does not require anybody's help and asked Britishers to quit India silently. But they won't leave India quietly. From the time resolution was passed, its newspapers have raised a hue and cry and showered abuses on us. They say that they want to defend the country but which country? If they wanted to defend then who opened the gates for the enemies to enter? Because they could not retain Burma, attack on India became easy.

Those people who are enemies of our liberty are here and they are real fifth columnists. American Journalists threaten and the mouthpiece of the Labour party *Daily Herald* advises that they would not help us if we do something. But I ask as to when they have helped and what kind of help were they to give? In the year 1930, Labour party sent Gandhiji to jail and held Round Table Conference.

Ramsay Macdonald who gave communal Award, which gave an impetus to communal tension, was a leader of Labour Party. This is the reason why we tell the Britishers to quit India.

Yet if they want our help they have to come to their senses. Forty crores of Indians know how to fight with nine crores of Japanese people and they also know how to die. But today we get suffocated from all sides and have forgotten how to die, but once we get open air, then if nothing else we will realise how to die.

......

... Gandhiji has already written. He says, "Quit India for your own good, for the good of India. I say this as your friend". Whether they go or not we have to defend ourselves.

Gandhiji has said that he will neither remain in jail nor will allow anybody to remain in jail. This war is not going to last long. We want quick remedy. We want to be free before the Japanese invade India. The rulers can run away, but where are we to go? People from Burma escaped and came here. Out of them how many Indians die? Where is their defence machinery? How many Burmese people asked you to return? They do not want to leave India and they want to take Indians to Burma and fight. We see how much Indians are loyal to you. Gandhiji also knows their mentality. It is slavish mentality. People of independent country have one thing in mind—to drive foreigners out and not to allow others who try to enter. Therefore, Gandhiji will show us the way towards quick fight. Gandhiji has plans regarding the struggle and he is going to reveal his plans to us. At that time you will be put to test. If the people hide indoors then we will not only lose prestige but our independence also.

When Gandhiji at the age of seventyfive is ready for self-sacrifice how can we sit quietly gossiping? Gandhiji stayed here for twenty years. He taught us the hymn of independence and you raised the slogan "Victory to Gandhiji". When will you get such a golden opportunity? Who else has been born in this country who has taught us to die for independence in the last two hundred years? Today when we have Gandhiji with us we have not to miss this golden opportunity. There might be calamities of various types but it is better to die a martyr's death than to die like flies.

People ask us as to how to fight. Let every man and woman behave as if he or she is the citizen of an independent nation.

He or she has to know that for that courage is required. There is risk but the risk of invasion is much greater. This is the war time. If we sit aside during the times of war then those who have been fighting will distribute the world amongst themselves. Today India can divert the current of war. There is no end of war except India's independence.

......

Everybody has to contribute according to his or her might in the struggle started by Gandhiji. If you do not, future generations will blame you. Those who have been appointed in the Viceroy's Executive Council know that they have been there because of the sacrifice of Congress? Bravery of Indian soldiers is being praised but why they do not think that if the soldiers of India rotting in slavery can fight so bravely then soldiers of free India will fight more bravely.

Such an opportunity will not come again. Do not have fear in your mind. Do not miss this golden opportunity. Let the rulers not say that Gandhiji was all alone. He has launched the struggle at the age of seventy-four and he had taken the burden on his shoulders. So, we can demand your contribution. Time may arrive or not but you have to be prepared for highest sacrifice. Do not ask for programme. All the programmes beginning with the agitation against Rowlatt Act, till the individual satyagraha are to be implemented in the struggle which we are to launch. No-tax campaign, civil disobedience and such other battles which were directly or indirectly launched to break the Government machinery will be revived by the Congress. Railway employees will stop running the railways, postal employees will leave their jobs, telegraph offices will not be allowed to function, Government servants will leave their jobs, schools and colleges will be closed and entire machinery of the Government will not be allowed to function. All of you shall have to co-operate in these activities. If all of you actively take part in the struggle then the struggle will end in four days and Englishmen shall have to quit India. Even if the Government arrests all the workers, all Indians are Congressmen and as such they will carry on the struggle. Everybody shall have to be ready when called upon to fight, then independence will knock at our door.

1 Speech delivered at the public meeting attended by about a lakh of people in Ahmedabad local board on 26 July, 1942.

40

"British Should Quit and Power Might Be Handed Over to Muslim League, If Necessary" : Vallabhbhai[1]

Collected Works of Sardar Patel

26 July 1942

Vallabhbhai Patel, who presided over a meeting of the Gujarat Congress at Ahmedabad on 26th July 1942, asked the workers not to wait for any programme as all the tactics including strikes, no-tax campaign, etc., which were tried from 1919 to 1942 would be implemented during the struggle which would not be restricted to the Congress, but Kisans, students and other non-Congress bodies were free to join it. It was better to die fighting the battle for freedom than to die after being completely ruined. Referring to "Quit India" slogan, he said that it would be effective if 40 crores of Indian people asked one lakh Englishmen to quit India and further said that the Congress did not seek power for itself and would be satisfied if it was handed over to the Muslim League. He expressed the opinion that members of the Local Self-Government Bodies and Government servants, including the Police, would be asked to leave their jobs and join the movement as it was the big campaign for the liberation of India.

1 P.N. Chopra, *op. cit.*, pp. 247-48 (Quit India Movement-British Secret Report)

41

Sardar Patel on Programmes and Modus Operandi of Quit India Movement[1]

Collected Works of Sardar Patel

SARDAR PATEL KE BHASHNON
28 July, 1942

(Extract)

Replying to Journalists' queries Sardar Patel explained:

Q: What type of ensuing struggle will be?
A: All the previous struggles had limited objective but the struggle which will start soon will not have any limited objective. This time the ill-feeling and the poison which is in the minds of people is unprecedented. The present condition of our land has been created because of war. Looking to the handships of the people and their sufferings there is reason to believe the people will wholeheartedly join the struggle.

......

Q: Suppose all the leaders are arrested simultaneously then what will happen?
A: When leaders are arrested, new leaders will emerge from the people. Time and situation create new leaders. Those leaders in England who were ruling England before the war were toppled as soon as the war was started and new leaders have emerged. In any country at any time struggle for independence has not stopped for the dearth of leaders. In India also struggle will continue.
Q: The people who could not oppose the rioters will they be able to resist government atrocities?
A: There is difference between a riot and freedom struggle. If in the riots people were disappointed, there is no reason to think that in the whole country people will not act... .
Q: Is there any possibility of country-wide strike in impending struggle?

A: There is every possibility of countrywide strike in the impending struggle and there should be strike. All the programmes from 1919 struggle onwards are included in this struggle. It will end only when Englishmen quit India.
Q: Mahatmaji asks Englishmen to Quit India, is it practical?
A: It is practical. In no country foreigners can stay permanently. So Gandhiji's asking them to quit is quite practical. When we have to freedom of any kind, when India is in danger, then India can get the power of defending itself only if the Britishers quit.
Q: Will Englishmen quit by our simply telling them to do so?
A: In Congress there is no fool who believes that Englishmen will quit by telling them to do so. That is why we are going to launch a big struggle. If the people fully co-operate in the struggle, then it will be known whether Britishers quit or not.
Q: They talk of giving full independence to India after the war, so is it not proper to wait?
A: After the war started last offer was Cripps's offer. There is not a single dishonest and fraudulent offer uptil now. In that plan there is an intrigue to permanently stay here even after the war. That offer is responsible for this decision of the Congress. If there had been no danger of invasion on India in immediate future, we would have waited. But the danger which is threatening us, India should have the full power to combat it. Englishmen are fighting not for defending us but for consolidating their rule here. If they are fighting for defending India, then they should not find it difficult to accept the proposal of the Congress.

......

Q: Are there any messages sent to the Congress for starting negotiations?
A: Congress cannot have any compromise in the hope of getting independence at a future date. Britishers want to prepare Indians for defending themselves against foreign invasion. We cannot agree to it in the hope of brighter future. India can prepare itself only if immediately India is declared independent. If India is declared independent then only India

can he ready to join hands with allies and fight against Germany and Japan. But there is no place for negotiations regarding the freedom of India.

Q: Sir Tej Bahadur Sapru has suggested convening of a Round Table Conference, what do you think about it?

A: Such Round Table Conference cannot solve such problems. It is an open secret that Government has been able to consolidate its position by the policy of divide and rule, and making us fight each other. If government calls Round Table Conference, then our experience will not be different from the Round Table Conference, which were held before.

Q: You say that everybody should work as if he is independent. Will you clarify it?

A: A slave does not know how to work as a free man. If a slave understands the gravity of being a slave then it will refuse to behave like a slave and if an Indian behaves like that British rule will terminate.

Q: Will free India fight violently or non-violently?

A: Free India will fight in a manner which is convenient. If a majority of Indians want an army, they will be free to keep an army. Everybody has right to get independence even by violent means. Those who are wedded to non-violence will fight non-violently. Of course, their sympathy will be with the army of free India.

......

Q: Will the fight be successful without the co-operation of Muslim League?

A: I cannot say whether Muslim League will co-operate with us in this war but it is not right to say that Muslims are not co-operating because in Congress there are many Muslims. If you want one example you can see from the statement of Khan Abdul Ghaffar Khan that in North West Frontier Province mass struggle is to be launched and there the entire province is full of Muslims.

Q: Why Congress does not make any preparations for such a big struggle? How will you be able to fight?

A: We are preparing for the last thirty years. What more

preparations need to be made?

Q: When the struggle is started what will happen to local institutions like municipality or local board?

A: After an announcement about the struggle is made, we cannot hide ourselves behind those institutions. Those who will not join the struggle will run those institutions and if they cannot run the institutions those will be closed. Why think about that now?

......

Q: If India is granted freedom, then in what way India can help the Government in war?

A: If India is independent then it can manufacture arms within big factories.

Q: India has not enough arms, who will lend arms?

A: Just as Chinese Government supply arms to China similarly India will be supplied arms by the Indian Government. If these people are fighting for democracy, then let them introduce democracy in India and then they will receive our co-operation. If India is independent then, as allies keep their army in other countries, similarly they can sign a pact with India and keep their armies here. The army which stay here cannot be our masters. Those armies if they live in a country as independent then there might be quarrel but if they stay as friends then they live peacefully. In England also there is American army which is there as their friends... .

Q: In a recent statement Sir Stafford Cripps has given a valid threat regarding our struggle. What have you to say about it?

A: Everytime when a struggle is to be started such threats are being given and yet struggle goes on.

Q: What can people of native states do in the struggle?

A: The Kings have signed a treaty with government. If people of native states have enough strength they will also launch a struggle. Congress does not ban such a struggle. And Kings are also not free. They also want freedom. So why be afraid of them? A free India will decide about the status of rulers of native states when the time comes. The people of native states also have to fight as other people fight.

Q: Even if there is internal fighting and lawlessness during the struggle, will the struggle continue?
A: There might be mutual fighting and lawlessness during the struggle. Unfortunately if that happens even then struggle will continue. Between slavery and lawlessness we shall have to choose lawlessness. Even after lawlessness independent India will emerge. But if India chooses slavery it will not be able to rise for ever.

1 Replies given to journalists in Ahmedabad on 28 July, 1942.

42

Sardar Patel's Appeal to Students to Join Quit India Movement

Collected Works of Sardar Patel

SARDAR PATEL KE BHASHNON
19 July, 1942

Here there are communal disputes. If you want to know the history of the disputes read the book *Communal Triangle* by Achyut Patwardhan. It will tell you how foreign power made the communities to fight each other and it continues to do so. The resolution which was passed in Wardha states that till there is foreign rule in India the communal disputes will not be settled. The rulers say that they want to quit India but only when Indians unite. I tell them that it does not behove them to say so. When two brothers are fighting if a third person who is an outsider comes and tells them "You two brothers fight and unite, till then I am sitting in your house". Will that be proper? That person should be slapped and thrown out.

Let Muslims understand that this fight is not for establishing Hindu rule but to break the shackles of slavery. We will come to understanding after achieving independence. Only then our slavery will be abolished. If we hope that Hindus and Muslims will come to understanding before achieving independence is a false. We are not going to come to understanding by the rifle of the Britishers. They are sitting here to see that we do not come to some understanding.

Let Britishers make us quarrel according to their heart's content. They can also divide one community. Even amongst Hindus they drive a wedge between high caste Hindus and scheduled caste Hindus.

It is surprising that when they have lost major part of their empire and when they are on the point of losing India even at such a time they, sitting at a distance, are yet so arrogant. How can that be tolerated? Today if people who profess different religions come to an understanding then they will find some other excuse.

......

After Quit India resolution, India is frowned upon by nations of Europe and America. The newspapers of England and America are vociferous in expressing their anger. Even by paying thousands of rupees and by trying hard to give some place to India they would not have devoted number of columns to India as they are doing today; though these columns are full of abuse.

Congress by passing this resolution has put their democracy to test. We also will be put to test as to whether we really want independence or not.

If we want to succeed in that test Gandhiji says that we have to make the struggle speedy and short.

Impending revolution will be so great and so speedy that every individual, big or small, high or low, has to take part in it. If all of us take part, then it will be a befitting reply to the columnists of the foreign newspapers. If very few people are with the Congress, then why so much anger, so much shouting and so much uneasiness? If handful of people are with Gandhiji in this struggle, then there is enough space for those few in jails. But they know very well that this fight will be unprecedented.

Now some people say that at the present help the allies unconditionally ... When a world war had started before twenty years, then American President Wilson had said that Germans are like Kansa and so after they are defeated the principle of self- determination would be applied to all the nations. So Indians were overjoyed and helped the war unconditionally. At that time unanimously a resolution was passed in central Legislative Assembly granting hundred crores of rupees for war. It was passed in one sitting. So much fraternity was witnessed. At that time British rulers had also said that as soon as war is terminated India will be granted independence.

War ended. President returned home. Those people told him that he was living in the world of imagination and the principle of self-determination was impractical. Then Rowlatt Act was passed which was an atrocious act. Those who tell us of help them now and they will grant us independence afterwards will get other from of Rowlatt Act.

At the time the consequences of helping the Government were Jallianwala Bagh. People were ordered to crawl in the lanes of Amritsar.

Therefore, we say that we do not want to be duped again. After deep thinking and weighing all the sides we have passed the resolution. Now we are not going to hear plea of England or America.

Those who are sitting in Viceroy's Council say that we should have accepted Cripps' proposals. Shri M.S. Aney....utterances have surprised me because he believes in undivided India. Now he goes to Poona and advises us that we should have accepted Cripps' offer. So, how does he want Pakistan? Once cannot talk both ways. Firoz Khan Noon says that Congress wants to turn India into a Hindu Kingdom. One can understand his saying so. But Congress says Britain to hand over entire country to Muslims but Britishers have to quit. This exposes them, because this demand of the Congress does not leave anything for Muslims to complain anything, but if they want to say that Britishers should stay here and arrange in a way which is entirely beneficial to us then it is a different thing. We do not know if Muslims want Britishers to stay here to protect Pakistan. Shri M.S. Aney has said that Cripps' offer was worth accepting, then he should clarify whether he would accept division of India.

You have to give a fitting reply to those who say that students are not with the Congress. You all will no doubt pass resolution to that effect but you have to see that you actively participate in the struggle. After the Wardha resolution is passed by the AICC you have to respond to what Gandhiji asked you to do. At that time if you try to weight the sides then future of the country is bleak. ...

Britishers had promised to defend Malaya, Singapore and Burma but we have seen what they have done. That is the reason why Congress says that Britishers won't be able to protect us; and those who have some sense also say so.

American mission had came here. It also said that in India production of goods at present is what it was in pre-war days. It has not increased. This is not the fight of human beings, it is fight of machines. In India there are no machines. Why do they not give machines. There is sea on three sides of India, when there is such a vast ocean yet in India not a single ship is being built. What is the reason? At the most on the sea coast one will find fish catching boats. Allow us to build ships and produce things we need, say the owners of Scindia Company, but the rulers are not interested.

This war is in the air also. Here hundreds of aerodromes are being built for flying in the air but has any aeroplane manufacturing factory been started? One of us had opened a factory where readymade parts of aeroplanes were imported from America, joined here and thus aeroplanes made ready. It was given permit after two and a half years. That also only one-third parts were of the Government and the state. That factory also went into liquidation. Wagons and railway lines also have disappeared from some places.

They ask us to help war efforts but in order to help young-men require thousands of rifles which are not supplied. If they want help they should supply rifles. Who refuses? But they do not trust us. They are afraid that if they supply rifles they will be used against them.

Let them give up power and be friendly with us and see

how much help is being given by India. We are forty crores. will cope with seven crores of Japanese. Let them stand on one side and see what happens but they say that we are not capable of defending ourselves. We are fit only to be slaves and that only of theirs and of none else. This indicates their evil intention.

When Trincomalee was bombed they fled from there and also advised people to run away. They have made full preparation for running away but where are we to go? They say they want to defend India. India can be defended only by independent India. We are confident about it. That is the reason why we tell them to quit India. As such they talk of quitting when the war ends but why not quit now?

Today in our country they do not allow us to start factories which can be called veins of the country because they know that if a small country like Japan can be industrial and create trouble then what India with forty crores of people would do? If they allow us to start factories then how can they take away raw material from here and sell us finished goods. They, in their country, produce grain which can last only for eight weeks. When that is consumed let them chew coal and iron. This is their condition. So how can they quit India? Even now they want to fleece India.

Therefore, Gandhiji says to them to quit India. As soon as struggle starts you put your books on book-shelf or book-cases, lock them. If principal asks you to continue study tell him that as soon as struggle is over you will continue studies.

43

London 'Times' on Sardar Patel's Role in 1942 Movement[1]

Collected Works of Sardar Patel

12 November, 1942

The *Dawn* in its issue of 12-11-1942 quoted *The London*

Times in which the following extracts occurred:

> The demonstrations have been widespread but perhaps less widespread than had been feared. The Punjab, Sind, the North West Frontier and Assam have been scarcely affected and in all the great tract of India ruled by the Princes, only Mysore and Baroda have produced incidents. In both these States the Congress influence is strong..... It may be taken for granted that Gandhi's use of the words upon rebellion with reference to his impending movement probably exercised a great deal of influence on the character of the demonstrations. There is evidence that in the country districts particularly many people took these words literally. Some leaders like Sardar Vallabhbhai Patel and other left wing members of the Working Committee put the impending mass movement upon the plane of revolt. They warned their audience that it will be necessary for them to face bullets and bombs which was as much as to say that they were to create a situation that could be dealt with only by bullets and bombs. These orators particularly addressed themselves to students who were not particular about their methods and were joined by all these elements which favoured political violence as an opportunity for loot.

1 P.N. Chopra, *op. cit.*, p. 332.

44

Wickendon's Assessment of Sardar Patel—Anti-Fascist and Bitterly Opposed to Continuance of British Rule[1]

Collected Works of Sardar Patel

13 June, 1942

We have quite a different picture of Vallabhbhai and of all the Working Committee members he gave the most vehement support to Gandhi. He approved of Gandhi's draft resolution sent to Allahabad declaring as it did Britain's incompetence and inability to defend India and preventing Indians even from defending it themselves; there might be some chance of defence if the British withdrew. Later on, according to the notes, he placed himself in Gandhi's hands feeling that he was instinctively right in all critical situations; he agreed with the draft except that any pro-Fascist suggestion might be removed. I think that sums up Patel's attitude right till the time he was arrested. His was a bitter opposition to Britain amounting to hatred and anything was better than that Britain should be allowed to stay. He shared Gandhi's defeatism and saw no prospects of saving the country if things continued as they were. He at least thought there was a chance to resist Japan if they were allowed to go about it with their hands free; there is nothing to indicate that he had pro-Fascist or pro-Japanese tendencies. The satisfaction with which he greeted Gandhi's resolution was expressed probably in the cynicism which Kanji Dwarkadas found in him. If it had to come to a change of masters, he did not think the British were any better than the Japs; that is the expression of his hatred for Britain. The extent of his support to Gandhi is revealed by the Nagpur report of 13th June, 1942, which states that he had written to Gandhi on behalf of those supporting the resolution insisting on a movement and threatening resignation of himself and his similarly minded colleagues from the Working Committee if no settlement was reached favouring a movement. The letter was written in the first half of June when the talks with Nehru's group were going on. We know that this was not an idle threat, though I doubt whether it influenced Nehru's and Azad's decision. According to the full report on the Wardha Working Committee meeting, he was opposed to delay and thought a movement might have been launched immediately after the departure of the Cripps Mission as the most fitting expression of what the country thought of the proposals. After the Wardha resolution had been passed, Vallabhbhai Patel threw himself heart and soul into building up the maximum enthusiasm for the movement in the Bombay Presidency. Though there is a number of reports in the secret evidences, they give but a small idea of his tireless activity. The most significant information comes from Ahmedabad where he spent several days in the last week of July; it will be remembered that Ahmedabad was one of the most seriously disturbed places in the country. It is significant that in this area, which was notorious for its turbulence, he spent so much time. The Ahmedabad people had always proved themselves devotees of violence, and, therefore, there is no difficulty in believing that Patel encouraged them towards violence and not non-violence. Soon after his arrival on 25th July, 1942 he told the people that nothing would stop the movement and that Gandhi would not show his disapproval of violent incidents? He expected Congressmen themselves, however, to observe non-violence. Presiding over a meeting of the Gujarat Congress Committee on July 26th, he told them the campaign would include everything that had been tried in previous campaigns and there would be no restrictions upon anybody joining it. He said it was better to die fighting a battle for freedom than to die after being completely ruined. He did not care to whom the Government was handed over as long as Britain cleared out. The next day there is a report of a private meeting in the Congress House at Ahmedabad. He then gave vent to the most inflammatory words of which we have knowledge:

> If all the leaders are arrested tomorrow and there is no time to meet you again, you should carry on the programme set forth before you by Gandhi from 1919 to 1942. Die but do not fall back. In this struggle, if instances like Viramgam occur or the railway line is removed or an Englishman is murdered, the struggle will not be stopped. If the scorched earth policy is sought to be pursued here, as in other countries, allow it to be carried out. Face it boldly, even at the cost of violence. Carry this message to every nook and corner of Gujarat. You should put aside the constructive programme now and be ready to carry out Gandhi's firmans. Acts of violence even of the type of Chauri Chaura will not stop the movement. Congressmen of course must act strictly within the limits of non-violence, even if Gandhi and other leaders were arrested before the meeting of the A.I.C.C.?

To press conference on July 28th he was naturally more restrained, though he said that the movement would not be stopped even if civil war anarchy ensued; he preferred anarchy to slavery and expected a free India to emerge out of anarchy. It was at Ahmedabad too that he addressed a meeting of the Rational Students' Union on July 29th and told them that the struggle would be short and swift and would be finished within a week—a statement remarkable enough to be mentioned by Gandhi in his final speech. Undoubtedly if the movement was to be so swift then violence was essential. Throughout all his speeches, he played upon Britain's incapacity to defend the country and the manifold injustices for which she was responsible. According to a consolidated report of his activities, he addressed as many as nine largely attended public meetings in Gujarat, with audiences which sometimes exceeded 20,000. Surely Chandra Kant was speaking the truth when he said that the Bombay people after the arrests had only Vallabhbhai Patel's speeches to act upon and they followed his programme; they lost their temper and committed acts of sabotage and arson. We have to remember too Kanji Dwarkadas's second set of notes corroborated by his letter to B. Shiva Rao dated 27th July 1942. He had been speaking with Vallabhbhai Patel again and had been told that the idea was to drive the British completely out of India and that everything short of physical violence would be permitted. There can be no reason to doubt this information.

Two instances of railway sabotage are given, one of which connects Vallabhbhai Patel with the sabotage through a certain Jainti Lal Chhotelal Patel who is described as his personal follower. The information is supposed to have been given in a confession during the trial. I have mentioned instances elsewhere of addresses he gave to students calling upon them to join him in the movement.

Coming to Bombay, he is specifically named along with by Giani Mehr Singh as being present at the secret meeting of the Working Committee at which sabotage was decided upon. There are two interesting pieces of evidence which seek to cast the main responsibility for the sabotage programme upon Patel himself. One comes from Jai Chand Vidyalankar, who relies for his information upon Algu Rai Shastri, M.L.A. of the United Provinces, whom he met on August 14th or 15th. According to him, Sardar Patel had dictated the sabotage programme an hour or so before his arrest and the arrangements for dissemination were made through a Gujarat worker. Jai Chand speaks of another incident attributed to Patel which convinced him that Algu Rai Shastri was telling the truth. I need not give the details here, but it had connection with the United Provinces and showed Patel advising use of force. The second piece of evidence comes from the C.P. report relating to discussions among detenues in the Jubbulpore Jail, quoting Kaka Kalekar. The latter said that, though Gandhi was aware the movement might take the form it did, it was actually started in that form by Vallabhbhai Patel who was in favour of open rebellion. Sabotage plans were made known to a selected few by Vallabhbhai Patel just before the arrests and instructions, though intended to be drawn up by Patel, were actually issued by his men. These two statements stand alone, widely separated in place and time, but they gain value because they can have no connection with each other. Even if there is exaggeration, they could only have their basis in the violent propaganda which Patel had been conducting and which must have been well-known to Congressmen as a whole.

In his speech to the A.I.C.C. session on July 7th Patel saw no hope of any settlement with Britain, and the opportunity had come for the people to fight for their own independence just as the Russians and Chinese were fighting for theirs. It was an opportunity which might not come again. The fight would be tough, but he wanted it to be short and swift; there was to be no jail going. It will be remembered he left unuttered certain additions to the forms of civil disobedience which had been used in the past. He said the object was to free India before the Japanese came and to fight them if they did. All this makes up, I think, a very clear and consistent picture of Patel as dominated by his hatred of Britain, his acceptance of

Gandhi's guidance and putting everything he had into the movement in the hope of expelling Britain from the country. He was convinced of Britain's defeat and saw at least some prospect of resisting Japanese invasion and domination of the country, whereas there appeared to be none if Britain remained. It is not surprising, therefore, that he was the advocate of violence and sabotage as all the reports show. It is likely that he had a more personal part in the actual issue of instructions of sabotage than any of the other leaders.

1 T. Wickendon's assessment of Sardar Patel as member of the Working Committee in P.N. Chopra, *op. cit.*, pp. 196-200.

45

Sardar Patel Asserts Attainment of Complete Independence As Ultimate Goal[1]

Collected Works of Sardar Patel

SARDAR PATEL KE BHASHNON
25 June, 1942

(Extract)

......

Generally it is customary in India to have one thing in mind and express quite the contrary. Everybody wishes that this empire is destroyed. People do not openly say so but in their mind it is quite the opposite. They rejoice when the enemy of Britain is victorious. But that is not good. We do not want the change of masters. No slave gains anything by changing his master. We have to be independent. Only independent India can give help in war.

Viceroy says form National Front here but he also says that India is not one nation, but there are two nations: Hindus and Muslims. Then how can national front be constituted?

......

This land is wonderful. Whenever there are ups and downs, one pious soul defends. Today greatest of the great person in the world is Mahatma Gandhi. Today our country is highly esteemed in the world because of him. If we do not act on what he says we are fools.

...So, our first task is to achieve independence and for that everybody should be ever ready.

1 Lecture delivered at Vadilal Sarabhai Hospital, Ahmedabad on 25 June, 1942.

46

"Movement Not to Stop Even If There Was a Civil War or Anarchy": Vallabhbhai[1]

25 July, 1942

After his arrival in Ahmedabad, Vallabhbhai Patel is meeting Congress workers from the different parts of Gujarat and Kathiawar, and advising them to be ready for the Congress call.

Vallabhbhai is reported to have said, during his talks with some people, that the struggle would start soon after the AICC meeting was over, that it would not stop even if there was a civil war or anarchy in the country, and that it would shake the whole world. It would be carried on by the masses even if all the leaders were arrested by the Government, at the end of the AICC meeting. The Congress would not interfere if some people lost their temper and took dangerous and drastic steps against the Government during this struggle, nor would Gandhi show his disapproval in that connexion. Congressmen would certainly observe non-violence during the struggle, but others were not bound by that rule.

1 P.N. Chopra, *op. cit.*, p. 245.

47

Sardar Patel Castigates Government for Bengal Famine and Deplores Apathy of People

Collected Works of Sardar Patel

BOMBAY CHRONICLE
28 June, 1945

(Extract)

An earnest plea for a moral revolution in the Congress and the country was made by Sardar Vallabhbhai Patel, in a brief talk to Congress workers at the Jinnah Hall...

......

"My path is clear before me," he declared. "I want freedom. I am going to get it. Ten Englands cannot prevent me from getting its. No country could be kept in subjection forever," he added.

......

During the three years he had stayed in jail many things had happened, things which had never happened before. They constituted a black chapter in the history of British rule in India. Many events happening outside had caused sorrow to himself and his fellow prisoners. But nothing had grieved them so much as the famine in Bengal. It was strange that the people did not struggle against the calamity;... They died tamely and passively....

The responsibility of Government authorities, both British and Indian, was great. But that of others was no less great. It was a matter of shame that while people were dying, others were found trading on death and making money out of it.

......

Turning to the August resolution Sardar Patel said that many people said that the August resolution was wrong. He would tell them that such people were mad. If they had not passed the resolution the Congress could not have continued with honour. They had suffered much on that account. But the Indian National movement was like a rubber ball. The harder it was hit the greater its rebound. The sterner the repression the greater its subsequent growth and development.

......

Referring to British friends of India and their appeals Sardar Patel said that every Viceroy who came to India claimed to be her friend. There was not one in the long list of those who ruled over India, who admitted that he was her enemy. The last Viceroy was not only a friend of India he was a particular friend of Gandhiji.

To all those friends Sardar had only one thing to say. What India wanted was freedom. She wanted to be as free as her friends... .

48

Sardar Patel Warns Labour Government that India Could Not Wait Long for Freedom

Collected Works of Sardar Patel

BOMBAY CHRONICLE
12 September, 1945

(Extract)

......

In an interview with the Associated Press of America on the eve of the meeting of the Congress Working Committee, Sardar Patel stated that the Congress was waiting to see whether the new Labour Government would come forward with a proposal. Pending that, he predicted that the Congress would make no new move. He intimated that endless waiting was not planned. Asked specifically whether he had in his own mind any time limit for India to obtain independence, Sardar Patel said: "We will not wait long".

Reminded that the new Labour Government could

normally expect to remain in office for five years, he was then asked whether India would take matters into their own hands if no acceptable offer appeared within that time.

"We will certainly settle affairs before five years," he declared.

......

Sardar Patel, the iron-handed organisational Executive in the Congress, has been one of the bitterest fighters against continued British control in India and his bitterness towards it appeared not to have abated in the slightest. He was critical of the conduct of the Simla Conference at which the British offered to set up an 'interim' Government with Hindus and Muslims represented on a fifty-fifty basis. He was equally critical of the current procedure looking towards holding elections in India.

......

He reiterated his long-held belief that the British do not seriously intend to permit India to attain self-Government or win freedom and cited the recent conference at Simla as added proof. He declared that Lord Wavell went to London on his trip preceding the present one with an agreement already reached between the Congress and the Muslim League for setting up an 'interim Government. Under its terms the two groups would have parity on the Viceroy's Council. Instead of accepting this arrangement, Sardar Patel said the British had attempted to split the Muslim League by substituting its own proposals.

These proposals called for including Muslims from the Punjab Unionist Party on the Viceroy's Council as well as League Muslims, that was the arrangement offered to the Muslim League at Simla, he said, and they refused to accept it. Patel insisted that this demonstrated that the British did not really wish to see the two rival parties in India come to an agreement... .

49

Let Hindus and Muslims Decide Fate of India After British Leave[1]: *Vallabhbhai*

Collected Works of Sardar Patel

SARDAR PATEL KE BHASHNON
24 September, 1945

(Extract)

After a long time we meet without any hindrance or ban on meetings. Ban orders have just been withdrawn and so it is possible to address such a huge meeting.

......

Government have granted separate electorates to the Muslims with the intention of making us fight each other. Today League propagates that in Congress Hindus dominate. Muslim League is shouting for Pakistan. Nobody is told what Pakistan is. It cries for the moon. The fact is that slaves have neither Pakistan or Hindustan.

In northern India where Pakistan is to be created the Muslims of that region and the Muslims of Punjab and North-West Frontier Province do not want Pakistan but all this will be decided afterwards. India is a slave country. Let Hindus and Muslims of the country by their joint effort make it an independent country. After Englishmen leave India, this is a question of 10 days, and it will be immediately solved.

Congress has the power of the people. Today Englishmen might be behaving in a different way, but that will not make any change in the power of the Congress or people. It is a fact that till India becomes independent there won't be any peace in the world and nobody will have peace.

We have to prepare ourselves for the election. We want to create such an atmosphere that nobody can dare to stand for election against the Congress. From Bombay Quit India message was given and in Bombay we have decided to contest the elections. So I need not say anything to Bombay. This is limited franchise and our institutions are yet not declared lawful. Our workers are in jail still we want to show to the world through these elections that people are with the Congress.

This is the time for preparations of fresh struggle. Who can say what kind of future struggle there will be, but we have to make preparations from today for that struggle. I am going to come to you to get votes from Bombay and to enrol Congress members before that I make this clarification.

Vandematram.

1 From the speech delivered at Shivaji Park, Dadar, in public meeting on 24 September, 1945.

50

Freedom of India Essential for Freedom of World : Vallabhbhai

Collected Works of Sardar Patel

BOMBAY CHRONICLE
25 September, 1945

(Extract)

......

Sardar Vallabhbhai Patel who presided at Monday's meeting at Bombay expressed gratification that after three years some of the restrictions imposed on the activities of the Congress had been removed by the Government and they were in a position to meet the masses again and address them. It gave him great pleasure to see such a multitude of men and women gathered in the maidan. He was specially overwhelmed by the response which the women of India had offered at every step. And just as in the present instance, he saw the tremendous wave of enthusiasm and resurgence of a new vitality all over the country.

Any doubts which the Working Committee members

might have entertained while they were behind prison bars were dissipated when they saw firsthand after their release the tremendous enthusiasm of the country. During their absence the people of India had not bowed their head passively to the repressive laws of an alien government, but had made a colossal effort to implement the 'Quit India' resolution of August 1942. He could not speak too highly of the courage, the fortitude and the heroism of the common people of the country when they were left leaderless and disasters, like famine, Government highhandedness and terrorism confronted them.

After referring to the Simla debacle, Sardar Patel said that it was wrong to think that the Congress had retracted from the 'Quit India' resolution or that the struggle had ended. After three years, he said, they were invited at Simla for a settlement. But the attempts to arrive at an agreement proved fruitless. Settlement or no settlement, he entertained no doubt whatever about the ultimate success of the Congress in achieving the freedom of the country, for their claims were based on right and justice. When they asked for the freedom of the country nobody could tell them that they were asking for something which was wrong. For this purpose they relied on absolute non-violence and their strength was in the righteousness of their cause. The present war had taught a lesson not only to the vanquished but to the victors as well. For if one country invented the atom bomb, the likelihood was that in course of time some other country would devise something even more deadly. But India and the Congress entertained no such fears as the most deadly missile in their armoury was non-violence.

Referring to the advent of the Labour Government in England, he said that whichever Government came into power in Great Britain, it made no difference whatever to India. For they all believed in the same old imperialist policy. "Several of our colleagues are still in jail and for us the fight for freedom is not yet over," he said.

... In India, even the blind could see what the people wanted and that was the freedom of the country for which the Congress was fighting... .

In Bombay, ... Some of the Muslims here were of the opinion that the victory of the Congress meant the creation of Hindu Raj. Therefore, they wanted Pakistan. But what this Pakistan was nobody had taken the trouble to define; perhaps even those who clamour the loudest for it do not know what it is all about. They might ask the Congress to give them the moon but neither the Congress nor anybody could fulfil their impossible demands. So long as India was a slave country how could anybody give anyone else their Pakistan or Hindustan? The irony of it was that the Muslims of Bombay clamoured the loudest for Pakistan while those of the North-West Frontier Province, the Punjab and other so-called Pakistan areas were the least vocal in this respect. Such an issue could only be decided when India became free and not so long as Indians were not masters in their own homes. If the British quit India the differences between the Muslins and Hindus would disappear in ten days.

Concluding, he said that freedom of India was essential for the freedom of the world and there would be no peace and no unity in the world so long as India and other nations in Asia were in bondage. He assured the gathering that the day India became free the Congress wouid have fulfilled itself and there would be no need even for its continued existence.

51

Patel to Jamshed Mehta Feels Muslims Misled by Jinnah

Collected Works of Sardar Patel
Sardar Shrino Patco-IV

POONA
20 September, 1945

DEAR BROTHER JAMSHED,

Received your letter dated 5th. Your wire was also

received. I have given your letter to Bapu and he has read it.

Communal problem has become most complicated. There is not a single indication that it will be solved. Nobody wants India to be partitioned. But a big bulk of Muslims are misled and is playing in the hands of British Empire. It hampers the progress of the nation and is injurious for both. Yet it appears that for the present they won't realise. Unfortunately all indications lead us to think that fratricidal war is our fate.

In Congress there is no group which is in favour of partition.

I can understand your heartfelt agony.

VALLABHBHAI'S VANDEMATRAM

Shri Jamshed Mehta

52

Sardar Patel Ridicules Jinnah's Two-Nation Theory as Absurd

Collected Works of Sardar Patel

BOMBAY CHRONICLE
5 December, 1946

(Extract)

The expression "sea of human faces" could never be better applied than to the mammoth crowd that gathered on the sands of Chowpatty last Sunday to see and hear Sardar Vallabhbhai Patel for the first time since he became the Home Member of the Interim Government.

......

The President of the B.P.C.C. gave a short and stirring welcome to the leader—and then the Leader himself began, in low tones at first, which made us doubtful whether he could be heard all round, but he warmed up, never to a pitch of frenzy, never to any impassioned appeals of high emotional value, never to reckless impulsiveness—he warmed up "coolly" and let his wit and ridicule score the points for which others rely on emotion and temper.

Vallabhbhai does not believe in "Direct Action". His speech had no direct hits. He did not call Jinnah this or Wavell that. Serenely he traced the history of the Congress-Muslim League relationship through the labyrinth of the British proposals, but his cold and calculated treatment of the subject was embellished by his hooks of wit and ridicule which, I am sure, even those against whom they were aimed would have enjoyed, if they had a sense of humour.

I know it sent the mammoth assembly tumbling into helpless laughter. The funnier part was the fact that while cracking his humour, Vallabhbhai himself remained perfectly serious.

He did not indulge in long-winded sentences, but in short stoccato hammer-blows which were so camouflaged that they had their effect without their appearance. It is not possible to retain in the translation the beauty of the original, but I will try to recapture some of the most salient features of his speech.

Tracing the attitude of Jinnah, Vallabhbhai indicated its recalcitrant nature by saying that he was open to no compromise and adhered only to the ideal of Pakistan. Mr. Jinnah believes nay insists, pointed out the Sardar, that only those Muslims who were in and with the League were Muslims in fact.

All the other Mussalmans were not Mussalmans at all. Vallabhbhai made no comments on these statements of fact, but left it to listeners to draw their own conclusions and that made the point he was trying to make all the more telling.

I do feel, however, that the Muslims outside the fold of the League, have now lost their force, or are rapidly losing it. Formerly we often read about protests from various sections of the Nationalist Muslim community. Their views may not have changed but their voice has temporarily gone. The elections dealt them a death blow, or at least it has put them in a state of coma.

And Jinnah capped this advantage by insisting during the formation of the Interim Government that the Congress shall have no Nationalist Muslim among its chosen representatives.

Commenting on this unreasonable stand of the League leader, the Sardar said that the Congress was anxious to protect the rights of the minorities—it had taken representatives of each of the minorities on its Cabinet—and since the Nationalist Muslims could be considered such a minority, the Congress thought it a part of its duty to protect them by giving them representation.

Vallabhbhai made us laugh again when he talked of the two-nation theory. His way of putting it was exquisite. Ridiculing the idea of two nations in one country, he said it would amount to the fact that the father may belong to one nation and his offspring to another.

To this I would add that some may even belong to the category of No Man's Land—if the father belongs to one "nation" and the mother to the other;

Vallabhbhai next dwelt for a while on the League leader's declaration of Direct Action (*Seedhi Chot*) and all that it meant and brought—destruction, disaster, distortion, dishonour.

He wished that Mr. Jinnah would attempt to achieve his ends by peaceful ways to which Congress were ever willing to respond. Noakhali, Bihar, the slaughter of innocents, the stabbings in the back, all these atrocities are no solution to India's problems. Sane thinking alone by both the parties would bring results of peace and prosperity.

He did not condemn the British for any foul play, but he was definitely opposed to the Congress taking part in London talks now proceeding. The original decision of the Congress not to do so was fully justified as the matter was now entirely between the British and the League. The Congress had agreed to the arrangements proposed by the British. The Congress meant to carry them out. Now it was up to the British to live up to them.

The Constituent Assembly, due to meet on Monday, Vallabhbhai sounded determined, WOULD MEET ON MONDAY, no matter what happened, no matter who attended or who did not. The work must go on without any more planned procrastination... .

53

Cabinet Mission Proposals Recommendatory, Final Decision with Constituent Assembly

Collected Works of Sardar Patel

SARDAR'S LETTERS—MOSTLY UNKNOWN-IV

NEW DELHI
26 May, 1946

MY DEAR DR. GOPICHAND,

I have received your letter of the 17th inst.

There is no communal settlement at all and the Congress resolution of 1929 has no application. The Cabinet Delegation has made certain recommendations for the consideration of the Constituent Assembly.[1] It is open to the Constituent Assembly to accept or reject them. These proposals may not be acceptable to the Sikhs; and, therefore, it is for them to approach the Cabinet Delegation for necessary changes.

There is only one Constituent Assembly for the whole of India. The idea of Pakistan has been reservedly condemned and rejected. The group assemblies are not constituent assemblies in any shape or form. The provinces are free to do whatever they like, and, therefore, there is no reason to be afraid of.[2]

It is true that in the Frontier non-Muslims get no seat and no right of electing a member to the Constituent Assembly but the Muslims in Orissa have also been similarly treated as the principle of population basis has been accepted uniformly. Therefore, one cannot say that there has been injustice in this matter.

Yours Sincerely,
VALLABHBHAI PATEL

Dr. Gopichand Bhargava,
Lahore.

1 See Enclosure.

2 From Cabinet Mission Statement: "19(viii). As soon as the new constitutional arrangements have come into operation, it shall be open to any Province to elect to come out of any group in which it has been placed.

Such a decision shall be taken by the new legislature of the Province after the first general election under the new Constitution".

Enclosure

(The Cabinet Mission's recommendations for the framing of Constitution for All-India)

We recommend that the constitution should take the following basics form:

There should be a Union of India, embracing both British India and the States, which should deal with the following subjects: Foreign Affairs, Defence and Communications, and which should have the powers necessary to raise the finances required for the above subjects.

The Union should have an Executive and a Legislature constituted from British India and States representatives. Any question raising a major communal issue in the Legislature should require for its decision a majority of the representatives present and voting of each of the two major communities as well as a majority of all the members present and voting.

All subjects other then the Union subjects and all residuary powers should vest in the Provinces.

The States will retain all subjects and powers other than those ceded to the Union.

Provinces should be free to form Groups with executives and legislatures and each Group could determine the Provincial subjects to be taken in common.

The constitutions of the Union and of the Groups should contain a provision whereby any Province could, by a majority vote of its Legislative Assembly, call for a reconsideration of the terms of the Constitution after an initial period of 10 years and at 10-yearly intervals thereafter.

54

Sardar Patel on Cabinet Mission Proposals

Collected Works of Sardar Patel

SARDAR'S LETTERS-MOSTLY UNKNOWN-IV

NEW DELHI

20 May, 1946

DEAR FRIEND,

I have received your letter of the 18th inst.[1]

I have received numerous letters from friends who have expressed the same sentiments and appreciation of the work that has been done by the Cabinet Mission at this critical juncture of our history.

You must have seen from the declaration of the Prime Minister (Attlee) that the paramountcy is to disappear altogether. This means that the Political Department will also go. The Indian States will have to enter into treaties individually, directly with the Constituent Assembly or with the Interim Government. Thus the long, complicated and secret working of this all-important Political Department is about to close.

The British Government have by their declaration made it clear that they propose to leave this country and that they also propose to constitute a Constituent Assembly at once which will be free to frame its own Constitution of Free India without any interference from outside. An Interim Government will be set up immediately to function during the interim period which, we hope, will, in all probability, function as a free Government in fact, though it may not be so in law. This makes the way of Indian freedom absolutely clear. The great obstacle of the Muslim League holding the power of veto has once for all been removed. Undoubtedly, there are defects in the scheme but such defects are inherent in any scheme of compromise. Let us hope that the Constituent Assembly will be able to finish its business quickly and India will be able to take its place, for the first time, after a long period of slavery, amongst the free nations of the world.

The heralding of Freedom will throw open avenues of service all-round and we have not enough men for the tremendous constructive activities that will have to be taken up. Young men with ability, experience and willingness to serve will indeed be in demand and if any occasion arises for utilizing your services, I will certainly remember your offer.

Yours Sincerely,
VALLABHBHAI PATEL

Shri M.M. Gharekhan
Bombay

1 From M.M, Gharekhan's letter: "History has been made at the anvil of the Mission's talk. In it you have contributed a good deal. With the better counsel prevailing among our other countrymen the drawbacks could be replaced by sounder and simpler provisions".

55

Sardar Patel to Munshi Over Rejection of Pakistan

Collected Works of Sardar Patel

SARDAR'S LETTERS—MOSTLY UNKNOWN-IV

NEW DELHI
17 May 1946

MY DEAR MUNSHI,

I have received your telegram of the 17th inst. Thank God, we have successfully avoided a catastrophe which threatened our country. Since many years, for the first time, an authoritative pronouncement[1] in clear terms has been made against the possibility of Pakistan in any shape or form. The continuous threat of obstruction to progress and the power of veto from obstructionist elements have been once for all removed. The withdrawl of British Power in India is no more in doubt and we are free to shape our own destiny without hindrance or interference from outside. We are now on the eve of accomplishing our life's work and if we can finish it quickly, nothing would stop us from achieving our final objective.

Yours Sincerely,
VALLABHBHAI PATEL

Shri K.M. Munshi,
Camp: Matheran.

1 See Enclosure.

Enclosure

(Pertinent Extracts from Cabinet Mission's Statement of 16 May, 1946 disfavouring partition of the country)

...The setting up of a separate sovereign State of Pakistan on the lines claimed by the Muslim League would not solve the communal minority problem; nor can we see any justification for including within a sovereign Pakistan those districts of the Punjab and of Bengal and Assam in which the population is predominantly non-Muslim, Every argument that can be used in favour of Pakistan, can equally, in our view, be used in favour of the exclusion of the non-Muslim areas from Pakistan. This point would particularly affect the position of the Sikhs.

We, therefore, considered whether a smaller sovereign Pakistan confined to the Muslim majority areas alone might be a possible basis of compromise. Such a Pakistan is regarded by the Muslim League as quite impracticable because it would entail the exclusion from Pakistan of: (a) the whole of the Ambala and Jullundur Divisions in the Punjab; (b) the whole of Assam except the district of Sylhet; and (c) a large part of western Bengal, including Calcutta, in which city the Muslims form 23.6 per cent of the population. We ourselves are also convinced that any solution which involves a radical partition of the Punjab and Bengal, as this would do, would be contrary to the wishes and interests of a very large proportion of the inhabitants of these Provinces. Bengal and the Punjab each has its own common language and a long history and tradition. Moreover, any division of the Punjab would of necessity divide the Sikhs leaving substantial bodies of Sikhs on both sides of the boundary. We have, therefore, been forced to the conclusion that neither a larger nor a smaller sovereign State of Pakistan would provide an acceptable solution for the communal problem.

Apart from the great force of the foregoing arguments, there are weighty administrative, economic and military considerations. The whole of the transportation and postal and telegraph systems of India have been established on the basis of a united India. To disintegrate them would gravely injure both parts of India. The case for a united defence is even stronger. The Indian armed forces have been built up as a whole for the defence of India as a whole, and to break them in two would inflict a deadly blow on the long traditions and high degree of efficiency of the Indian Army and would entail the gravest dangers. The Indian Navy and Indian Air Force would become much less effective. The two sections of the suggested Pakistan contain the two most vulnerable frontiers in India and for a successful defence in depth, the area of Pakistan would be insufficient.

A further consideration of importance is the greater difficulty which the Indian States would find in associating themselves with a divided British India.

Finally, there is the geographical fact that the two halves of the proposed Pakistan State are separated by some seven hundred miles and the communications between them both in war and peace would be dependent on the goodwill of Hindustan.

We are, therefore, unable to advise the British Government that the power which at present resides in British hands should be handed over to two entirely separate sovereign States.

56

Sardar Patel to C.R. Reddy

Collected Works of Sardar Patel

PATEL PAPERS, NAVAJIVAN TRUST
16 August, 1946

(Extract)

...There have been considerable changes. The Congress President has been invited to form the Interim Government and, for the first time, the British Government have (shown) the Muslim League its proper place. They have thus given proof of their *bona fides* and it is now for us to make or mar the future of India.

You do not agree with my defence of Pandit Nehru. But you will please appreciate the fact that in defending him, I am defending the organisation of which I am a loyal and humble soldier. You must have seen the resolution which the Working Committee has passed at Wardha and I think you will agree that our President has shown great statesmanship and risen to the occasion in drafting this resolution. If he had erred on a previous occasion on this subject, he had made ample amends. To err is human, but to accept one's error is something much greater.

......

The non-co-operation of the Muslim League has commenced and they are observing this day as their "Direct Action Day". The Congress, claiming to represent the vast majority of the people of India, cannot afford to be weak or to fail to shoulder the responsibility of taking charge of the Government of the country, in spite of all difficulties that may have to be faced. If the British Government and the Congress play the game well, I have no doubt that we shall see India free sooner than many people imagine and neither the League nor any other group of people or interests, however strong or powerful, will be able to stop it.

57

Constituent Assembly To Be Final Authority Regarding Union Army etc.

Collected Works of Sardar Patel

SARDAR'S LETTER—
MOSTLY UNKNOWN-IV
1 June, 1946

DEAR FRIEND,

I have received your letter of 28th May along with its enclosures.[1] The question of formation of Union Republican Army can be considered only by free Indian Government; and, therefore, it is not to be discussed at present. The Constituent Assembly will draft the Constitution for free India and that Constitution will have to be accepted by the British Government by passing necessary legislation in the Parliament.

The defects[2] pointed out by you in the resolution regarding the Cabinet Mission's scheme are known to us all and they can properly be considered at the time of drafting the Constitution by the Constituent Assembly.

The Congress is not against keeping National Army for the country's defence or keeping police for preserving internal peace and order. A few people in the Congress believe in the absolute Ahimsa of Gandhiji and if the Congress were to consist of only people believing in the absolute Ahimsa of Gandhi, it would reduce itself to a body consisting of very few individuals. It is, therefore, high time for you to reconsider your position and make up your mind to join the Congress.

Yours Sincerely,
VALLABHABHAI PATEL

Shri G.V. Subba Rao,
President, Andhra Swarajya Party,
Bezwada.

1 Containing resolutions passed by the Andhra Swarjist Party pleading for the formation of United States of Hindustan and Indian Republican Army.

2 The defects, in the Cabinet Mission Plan, as pointed out in this resolution, among others, were that no definite date for complete action on the main proposals of the Mission was fixed and that it had suggested a group system for provinces which should go, etc.

58

Sardar Patel to Nihchaldas Vazirani

Collected Works of Sardar Patel

PATEL PAPERS, NAVAJIVAN TRUST

2 June 1946

(Extract)

Regarding the clause of grouping, I feel certain that the Muslims of Sind as a whole will not like to be ruled by Punjab and have a capital in Delhi for the Union and one at Lahore for the Group. In my opinion, no province will be willing to sacrifice provincial autonomy. It is against human nature and this grouping is not going to help the Muslim League at all. But our objection to it is on principle. The Cabinet Delegation cannot and should not coerce any province to go into a group against its own will, although it has freedom to opt out later.

I have seen the Syed group's resolution. I dislike entirely their demand for equal representation in the Centre. The Muslim League asked for parity but I opposed it stoutly. Parity in any shape or form is against the very principles of democracy and no amount of quibbling can justify it. Indeed Syed has got a very good opportunity to strike at Jinnah because Jinnah and the League have secured nothing for the Muslims after a struggle of five years against the Congress and after the spreading of so much communal bitterness. His main demand of Pakistan is buried forever. His demand for parity is not accepted. The Muslims in the Hindu majority provinces have lost weightage in the Constituent Assembly. They will be in a hopeless minority. The principle of representation on a population basis is accepted. The only thing that he got, as a face-saving device, is grouping which will be seriously opposed by his own people.

The Muslim Leaguers in their convention at Delhi took oath under which they are bound not to enter the Interim Government till the principle of Pakistan is accepted. All of them are now anxious to go in spite of the pledge... .

59

Setalwad to Patel on Need for A Strong Centre

Collected Works of Sardar Patel

SARDAR'S LETTERS—MOSTLY UNKNOWN-IV

BOMBAY

3 May, 1946

DEAR VALLABHBHAI,

The trend of the negotiations, as appearing in the proposals of the Cabinet Mission so far published, is, I am afraid, disquieting. To have a weak and emasculated Centre with only Defence, Customs and Communications and vest the residuary powers in the provinces is extremely undesirable. What is necessary in a country like India is to have a strong Central Government and Legislature. Even if you vest residuary powers in the provinces, the Central Government should have overriding powers to step in on any emergency arising of which the Central Government must be the sole judge. I imagine a crisis like the present one of food shortage and what would happen if the Central Government had no authority to regulate the food supplies in the whole country. Then how can the whole of Punjab and the whole of Bengal, as they exist now, be made Pakistan provinces when the Muslim population is 52 per cent in the one and 58 per cent in the other? How can Assam with Muslims in a minority be made Pakistan province? How can N.W.F. Province be a Pakistan province when the majority of Muslims there have voted for Congress.

I do hope that merely to secure the immediate elimination of British Power from India, a constitution would not be accepted which we may have to regret afterwards.

Yours Sincerely,
CHIMANLAL N. SETALWAD

Sardar Vallabhbhai Patel,
Camp: Simla.

60

Sardar Patel to Setalwad Affirming A Strong Centre

Collected Works of Sardar Patel

SARDAR'S LETTERS—MOSTLY UNKNOWN-IV
CAMP: SIMLA
9 May, 1946

DEAR SIR CHIMANLAL,

I have received your letter of the 3rd inst. Allow me to inform you that my views are entirely in accord with yours and you may rest assured that nothing will be accepted merely to secure the immediate elimination of British Power from India which would endanger the future security and well-being of the country. As far as the Congress is concerned, it will not be a consenting party to the creation of a weak or loose Centre or to any such arrangement of dividing India into religious groups and handing over the present provinces of Bengal and Punjab, much less Assam, to the so-called Pakistan area.

I fully appreciate your anxiety about the negotiations and I am thankful to you for conveying your views to me.

Yours Sincerely,
VALLABHBHAI PATEL

Sir Chimanlal Setalwad,
Bombay

61

Sardar Patel Against Any Division of Country

Collected Works of Sardar Patel

SARDAR'S LETTERS—MOSTLY UNKNOWN-IV

13 May, 1946

DEAR FRIEND,

I have received your letter of the 6th inst.[1] You need have no apprehension about the matter as there is going to be no agreement between the League and the Congress on the basis of the proposals of the League. The Congress stands for a strong Central Government; and, therefore, there is no question of division of India. The President of the Assam Provincial Congress Committee will certainly be invited if the Congress will consider any change in its declared policy. So long as it stands by its declared policy, no Congressman need have any fear.

Yours Sincerely,
VALLABHBHAI PATEL

Shri Siddhinath Sarma,
General Secretary, Assam P.C.C.,
Gauhati.

1 Shri Siddhinath Sarma had conveyed to the Sardar that regional federation would be disastrous for Assam and it should be an autonomous unit in the Indian Federation.

Sardar Patel in a pensive mood

Sardar Patel in a light moment

Sardar Patel as President of Karachi Congress, declared, "There is no receding from Lahore Resolution of complete Independence."

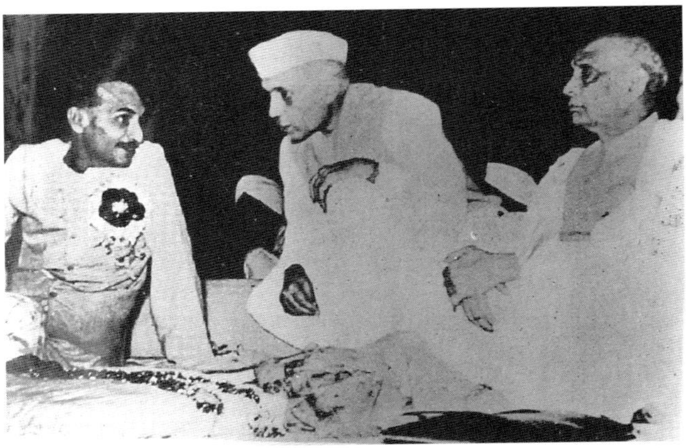

Sardar Patel, Kripalani and Jawaharlal Nehru on the "Quit India" session of AICC, August 1942.

With Gandhiji during Simla Conference, July 1945.

With Gandhiji during Simla
Conference, July 1945.

Sardar Patel going in a Rickshaw to
attend the Leaders Conference in Simla, 1945.

Members of Interim
Government.

Interim Government
with Lord Wavell.

Mountbatten meets Indian Leaders at the Viceroy's House, 2 June, 1947.

Mountbatten addressing Press Conference at New Delhi on 4 June, 1947 to announce the historic "Mountbatten Plan".

First Cabinet with
Mountbatten.

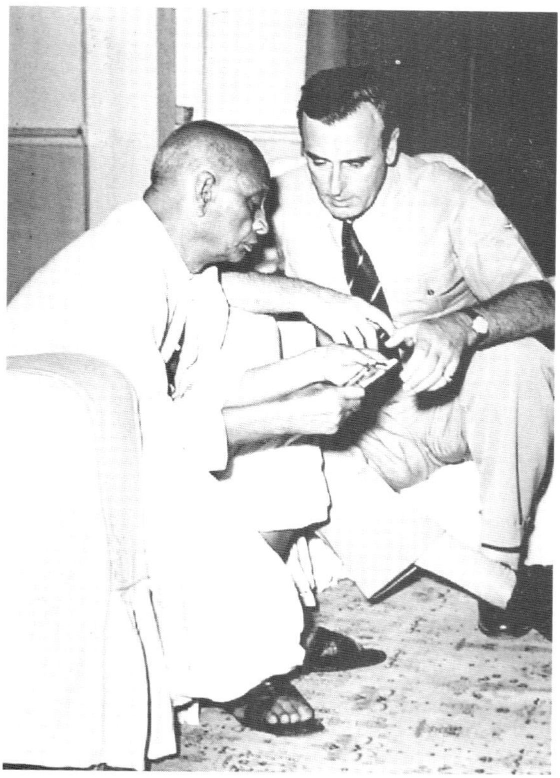

Sardar Patel in intimate discussion with Mountbatten, the Governor General of India.

Sardar Patel
with Jawaharlal Nehru.

62

Maulana Azad Delays Finalisation of List of Muslim Members for Interim Government

Collected Works of Sardar Patel

SARDAR'S LETTERS—MOSTLY UNKNOWN-IV

NEW DELHI

20 August, 1946

REVERED BAPU,

After conveying our opinion to the Viceroy yesterday, we had an immediate reply from him informing us that on seeing Jinnah's interview[1] in today's papers, there was no point in inviting him for having a talk with him. Thus this chapter has ended anyhow. But on our part, we have yet to complete the list of five Muslim Members. We have thought over the matter again and have decided for Asaf Ali, Shafaat Ahmed,[2] Ali Zaheer[3] and Fazlul Haq.[4] Now only one name remains to be settled. In case of Asaf, too, it is subject to approval by him when he reaches here today. This way, Maulana's work is hanging on in his usual fashion. The matter has come up so far though it will be no surprise if there will be changes again today or tomorrow.

There is another development, too, Maulana too is in two minds whether to join as a Member or not. But he says: "I will not join as one of the five Muslim Members. Ought not I be accommodated from the Congress quota?" I did not agree to it as it would have given rise to fresh problems. I have pleaded with him to think over the matter again. But he argued on: "Then I would rather take up the responsibility as Congress President than join the Government". I said: "You are having indifferent health". Yet he harped on the same theme. The matter may come up like a poser before us.

VALLABHBHAI'S PRANAM

Mahatma Gandhi
Sevagram.

1 This was Jinnah's statement to the Press (18.8.46): "Pandit Jawaharlal Nehru would have been nearer the truth if instead of saying that there was lack of co-operation from the League, he had said the Muslim League was not prepared to surrender, and it would have been still more true if instead of saying that the Congress door of co-operation was set open, he had said that Congress door was open to the Muslim League for abject surrender".

2 Sir Shafaat Ahmed Khan; historian and author, Delegate to R.T.C. (Round Table Conference), High Commissioner of India in South Africa (1941-44), Member in Viceroy's Executive Council, for short duration, Member, Interim Government.

3 Syed Ali Zaheer; for short duration Member, Interim Government, India's Ambassador to Iran, Minister in Uttar Pradesh Cabinet.

4 Fazlul Haq; Originally Krishak Praja leader; was also prominent Muslim Leaguer; was Chief Minister, Bengal.

63

Viceroy for Inviting Jinnah Again to Join Interim Government, Muslim Names Delaying Finalising List Due to Azad: Patel to Gandhiji

Collected Works of Sardar Patel

SARDAR'S LETTERS—MOSTLY UNKNOWN-IV

NEW DELHI

19 August, 1946

REVERED BAPU,

I reached here on the 17th at 12 noon by plane. Rajendrababu had reached here on the night a day earlier. He looks improved in health.

Jawahar too had accompanied me from Bombay. He met the Viceroy today at 3 p.m. They had a full and friendly talk.[1] But the Viceroy looked very much perplexed and worried due to recrudescence of violent disturbances in Calcutta since a day or two. So he suggested rather hesitantly: "League is not joining the Government So, in such situation, would you not approve if the Defence Portfolio is entrusted to the Commander-in-Chief?" On Jawaharlal's answering in the negative, he dropped the matter at once.

Maulana was to come a day late. He had wired to us

informing that the list of Members should be handed over to the Viceroy only after his return to Delhi. Hence, on that day, Jawaharlal could only mention the list of members provisionally to the Viceroy and before he took his leave he spoke to the Viceroy that on Maulana's arrival the final list would be prepared by them.

We sat together with Maulana yesterday morning at 9 a.m. He too had returned to Delhi on the night of the 17th. But Maulana, in his usual way, started dwelling on the names again. Hence, nothing so far could be settled. We again met in the evening and yet we could not give a final touch to the list. The names of five Muslim Members to be submitted to the Viceroy are still undecided. At last, we decided to write to all those six or seven persons whose names are under consideration and after receiving their consent, the final list, in this respect, would be drawn. Following this, it was decided to telegraphically communicate to them to come to Delhi. When this was going on, a message came from the Viceroy and Jawaharlal went to see him at 7 p.m.

After meeting the Viceroy, Jawaharlal came to see me. In this interview, the Viceroy raised a new matter. He seems to have been unnerved by the terrible happenings in Calcutta. So he said: "Would you mind if I invite Jinnah once more and persuade him?" Jawahar did not agree to it. So he went on: "If what is happening in Calcutta would have its repercussions elsewhere, it will mean a great burden upon you. So if I would call him once and warn him and persuade him too, your task will be very much easier". On his own, Jawahar conveyed his "No" to the Viceroy; but, at the same time, he told him that he would send a final reply after consulting his colleagues. So all of us met today in the morning and have also sent a reply to the Viceroy to the effect that we were unable to accept his suggestion as it was fraught with the difficulties ahead. Not only that, it would change the entire context to things and that the Viceroy had better keep himself out of it as it was a matter for us to invite him or otherwise. We expect to hear from him till evening and we shall then meet again. But the names have not yet been finalised mainly for the fact that not all of them who were invited to come to Delhi have reached here. Thus our work which ought to have been over till now is proceeding slowly.

Till now, we do not anticipate any trouble. This new suggestion seems to have been mooted here. They did not even care to consult their higher authority. As we have rejected it, they seem to have no courage to do anything against our wishes and there is no likelihood of the changes being made in the list of names that would be submitted by us.

From the Parsees, Bhabha's[2] name has been selected. Matthai's[3] too has been finalised. From the Sikhs, Baldev Singh's name has already been included. Then there will be six out of us including Jagjivan Ram.[4] That includes Rajendra Babu's name also. Only names of five Muslim members have yet to be finalised. Asaf Ali's name is there except that he will have to be consulted when he reaches here tomorrow. From the Sind, Maulana Bux[5] has been invited and he will reach here today evening. One each from the Shias and the Momins will be taken. Still one name remains to be fixed up. The matter has reached so far.

VALLABHBHAI'S PRANAM

Mahatma Gandhi,
Sevagram.
(Original: Gujarati)

1 For the formation of Interim Government.
2 C.H. Bhabha was Commerce Member in the Interim Cabinet.
3 John Matthai.
4 Bihar's prominent Congress leader with an uninterrupted ministerial record of service since 1946; was Defence Minister in the Central Government.
5 Was Member of the Coalition Party in the Sind Assembly.

64

Sardar Patel to D.P. Mishra on Nehru's Unrestrained Observations

Collected Works of Sardar Patel

PATEL PAPERS, NAVAJIVAN TRUST

29 July, 1946

(Extract)

DEAR SHRI MISHRA,

I received your letter of the 11th on the 17th, ...

Though the President (Nehru) has been elected for the fourth time, he often acts with childlike innocence, which puts us all in great difficulties quite unexpectedly. You have good reasons to be angry but we must not allow our anger to get the better of ourselves. We are passing through a critical period and our life's work may either yield successful results or our hopes may all be dashed to pieces by sheer foolishness on our part and the cup which is full of nectar and which is very near our lips may drop down from our hands before we can taste even a drop of it. The situation is full of perplexities and difficulties, but on such occasion seasoned soldiers have to hold their feet firmly and tightly on the ground and brave the tumult and storm through which the country is passing.

You may perhaps be thinking that I must have been consulted. Many Congressmen also think so. But you will be surprised that when I was informed of the new personnel, I pressed for being relieved of the burden. I cannot write to you all in a letter, because it would be unwise, but I feel as much that our cause has been injured at a critical juncture. I cannot afford to get out of it because it would be injuring our cause.

He had done many things recently which have caused us great embarrassment. His action in Kashmir, his interference in the Sikh election to the Constituent Assembly, his Press Conference immediately after the AICC are all acts of emotional insanity and it puts tremendous strain on us to set matters right. But in spite of all his innocent indiscretions, he had unparalleled enthusiasm and a burning passion for freedom which make him restless and drive him to a pitch of impatience where he forgets himself. All his actions are governed by a supreme consideration of reaching the cherished goal with electric speed. His mind has been exhausted by overwork and strain. He feels lonely and he acts emotionally and we have to bear with him in the circumstances. Opposition sometimes drives him mad, as he is impatient. His present action is also the result of a burning desire to take the younger elements with him and although in doing so he has committed a grave mistake. He will not hesitate to rectify it when he realises the grave injustice he has done to others and to the organisation.

You may, however, rest assured that so long as one of us is inside the group that governs the policy of the Congress, the straight and steady march of the ship will not be interrupted.

......

I have written to you at length in order that you may derive some consolation by getting an inkling of my own mind and also with a hope that this passing phase of our political life will not upset you so much as to deviate from our chosen path.

Yours Sincerely
VALLABHBHAI PATEL

Shri D.P. Mishra.

65

Sardar Patel to Sarat Chandra Bose

Collected Works of Sardar Patel

PATEL PAPERS, NAVAJIVAN TRUST
24 August 1946

(Extract)

...Calcutta has gone through an unparalleled ordeal and our

hearts are there with you. In its suffering, we have not been able to do anything. But we have all our sympathies for all those who have lost their lives and who have suffered during these riots. Those who were responsible for these black and inexcusable crimes and who have brought discredit to the city and the country will have to be punished. There will, I hope, be a fair, impartial and independent enquiry. It will take long for Calcutta to recover from the shock. I do not know what will happen to that Government during whose regime such disgraceful events have happened. In no civilised country such a Government should have a day's existence. But we are living in strange circumstances and we have to go through the ordeal. Let us hope that from evil cometh good, and Providence in His wisdom may have inflicted these sufferings for some ulterior purpose.

66

Sardar Patel Urges People to End Fratricidal Fight to Gain Political Objectives

Collected Works of Sardar Patel

BOMBAY CHRONICLE
2 December, 1946

(Extract)

"Whatever happens the Constituent Assembly will meet in Delhi on December 9, as scheduled," declared Sardar Vallabhbhai Patel, Home Member in the Interim Government, responding to the rousing reception given to him by the people of Bombay this evening at Chowpatty.

Speaking on the eve of London talks Sardar Patel said that he himself did not go to London because he believed the solution to India's political troubles must be found in India.

......

Addressing the gathering, Sardar Patel reviewed at length

the political situation in the country since the British Cabinet Mission's visit in April last. The Muslim League and its leader Mr. Jinnah, said the Sardar had threatened all the while that they would not rest content till Pakistan was achieved. The Congress had tried repeatedly to settle with the League but to no avail. Instead Mr. Jinnah has embarked upon the policy of direct action which ultimately culminated in country-wide bloodshed and anarchy. What had happened in Calcutta, Bombay, East Bengal and Bihar were the direct result of the policy pursued by the Muslim League. Under such circumstances, when the League finally decided to join the Interim Government, the Congress was sceptical about its intentions.

The Viceroy made it clear to the League that if it joined the Interim Government it could do so only with the intention of co-operating with the Congress, and also join the forthcoming Constituent Assembly. To this Mr. Jinnah agreed and for a time it was thought that the League's co-operation was certain. The Congress fears were, however, justified for it became evident in no time that the League had come with a determination to obstruct the hitherto smooth working of the Interim Government.

The League again went back on its word when Mr. Jinnah declared the League would not participate in the Constituent Assembly. And now they had come to the final stage when they were invited by the British Premier. Whatever might transpire in London, said the Sardar, he was sure that the League would join the Constituent Assembly at the last moment.

The Sardar further declared: "The Constituent Assembly shall meet on 9th December under any circumstances. It will be an insult to the members and those who elected them if it does not meet."

He added that the Congress was determined to stay in office for all time to come.

Referring to the riots, Sardar Patel said that they were political in nature and not engineered by a few 'goondas' here and there. The moment there was a settlement between the two major political parties the riots together with the 'goondas' would disappear from the map of the country. It was wrong to blame the Home Minister for the continuation of the riots in the city and suggest that Mr. K.M. Munshi would have handled the situation more efficiently. The Sardar remarked: "Times have changed and 1946 is not 1939".

Proceeding the Sardar characterised the work of the 'goondas' as cowardly and appealed to the people to develop the spirit of self-defence instead of relying on the police and the military for help. He said: "You should not allow the fair name of your city to be tarnished by the cowardly acts of a handful of 'goondas'. If you cannot follow in the footsteps of Gandhiji in offering non-violent resistance, you must at least give a brave man's fight in your own way. Instead of blaming the police for their sins of commission and omission, you must learn to do the police work yourself.

Replying to Mr. Jinnah on the issue of Pakistan Patel observed that by running to London Mr. Jinnah could not hope to bring Pakistan nearer. Neither would threats of violence help him in any way. Only by coming to a settlement with the Congress could the Muslims expect to obtain a satisfactory solution of their legitimate demands. The Sardar deprecated the idea of the transfer of population as fantastic and unpractical.

The Associated Press of America report says:

> Tracing the growth of communal rioting in the country, he said that Calcutta marked the real start. He alleged that the Bengal Ministry actively connived with the "direct action" propagators of the Muslim League. It had its repercussions, he said. He mentioned Noakhali where "things dearer than life were ravaged and polluted" and, "we saw what happened in Bihar".

The Sardar appealed for the stopping of riots which "paid nobody." "After all we—Hindus and Muslims—have to live in this country and raise her prestige high," he pointed out.

Apparently answering critics who wanted the Centre to

intervene where the Provincial Governments were unable to maintain law and order, the Sardar said the Centre could not interfere because law and order was a provincial subject.

"People write to me saying that in 1942, when the Congress started a direct action movement, the Centre with all its resources and power came down upon the Congress organisation throughout the country in a sweeping manner. They wanted the Interim Government to interfere in a similar manner.

"But they forget 1946 is not 1942. The wartime powers enjoyed by the then Government are no longer in vogue. Even if they are in vogue a People's Government cannot act in an autocratic manner".

Proceeding Sardar Patel said:

> "If riots continue on a wide basis, it will be difficult for the Government to provide police protection everywhere. People must know how to protect themselves from the goondas' knife and they must organise defence".
>
> "If you believe that the police can protect you at a time of tension like this, then you will continue to get blows. Till you become freedom's soldiers and try to protect yourself effectively, there can be no way out of such a situation".

He told his audience to prepare for self-defence in the event of any attack.

"If you can't do it in the Gandhian way—non-violently—do it violently, but protect yourself," he asserted.

> "If anybody comes to hit you, you have got every right to hit back". He added that he hated people asking for police assistance unnecessarily in the event of trouble.
>
> The conception of Swaraj is one in which the police force will be the minimum required for continuance of the Administration, Sardar Patel said. "This is a great opportunity for India, and we have all to contribute towards it. The opportunity must be seized despite the difficulties that face us and the obstacles that are visible. Only then can we reach our goal—*Purna Swaraj*."

67

Sardar Patel to Stafford Cripps Criticising Governor of Bengal for His Inactivity During Communal Riots

Collected Works of Sardar Patal

SARDAR'S LETTERS—MOSTLY UNKNOWN-IV

NEW DELHI
19 October, 1946

MY DEAR SIR STAFFORD CRIPPS,

I thank you for your letter of the 23rd September which was sent through Sudhir.[1] I am glad to hear that he has been helpful in the formation of public opinion on Indian matters. Your suggestion of sending him back in a more official capacity is under consideration. But here we are, at present, working under great difficulties, of which perhaps you have hardly any idea.

You will, I am sure, remember that when you were here we had a long conversation on the likelihood of communal trouble in India in case there was no settlement with the Muslim League. I told you that there was no possibility of any trouble except in Bengal and Sind and you told me: "You need not be afraid of Bengal as we have a Governor who would immediately put Section 93 into operation in case of any serious trouble". You have heard, I believe, of the "Great Calcutta Killing.[2] Those who have seen the thing can alone realise what it was; but now what is happening in Eastern Bengal[3] is much worse and the Calcutta incident pales into insignificance before Noakhali. In Calcutta, Hindus had the best of it. But that is no comfort. Was Noakhali by way of revenge? My point just now is that the Governor did nothing to prevent the mischief if he had to avoid it. At least, that is the general impression. I will not bother you with the details.

Would you believe that the Governor of Bengal has, all throughout these terrible happenings, been enjoying the bracing climate of a hill-station known as Darjeeling? I myself received many letters and telegrams from the terror-stricken people of this unfortunate area. Similar warnings were addressed to the Viceroy and the Governor but the Provincial Autonomy served as a screen to prevent governmental action. You would realise how difficult it is for an Indian Home to sit in his office quietly day after day when innumerable piteous appeals and complaints are received for some kind of help which would give these unfortunate and helpless victims some protection.

You must have seen that the League has decided to come in the Interim Government at last.[4] But you will see the correspondence that has passed between Mr. Jinnah and Pandit Nehru which has been published and which will give you an idea of the object with which they come in. This is something uncanny in the way things are done.[5] Whilst we fully realise your difficulties, all three[6] of you must at least give some thought to the terrible strain that has been put upon us.

You may share this with your two colleagues. My best wishes to you and them.

I hope you have benefited by the change and rest you had for a month.

Yours Sincerely
VALLABHBHAI PATEL

Hon'ble Sir Stafford Cripps,
Board of Trade,
Millbank, S.W.I.

1 Shri Sudhir Ghose was inmate of Gandhiji's Ashram, figured prominently as a contact man between Members of Cabinet Mission and Congress Leaders especially Sardar Vallabhbhai Patel; for some time attached to Indian High Commission in England as Information Officer; the author of Mahatma's Emissary.

2 Of August 1946 as an aftermath of Muslim League's "Direct Action day". These riots lasting for four days, according to official figures, had taken a toll of 5,000 lives apart from 15,000 wounded.

3 In Noakhali and Tipperah districts of East Bengal a series of communal outbursts had engulfed the countryside resulting in barbaric scenes of massacres, plunders, abduction of women and conversions at the point of bayonet. As Hudson, the author of *The Great Divide*, observes: "There was

evidence that this was an organised operation and not a spontaneous combustion of individual communal hatred".

4 From 15th October 1946.

5 This exchange of correspondence between Jawaharlal and Mohammed Ali Jinnah prior to League's entering into Interim Government did not bring any tangible result; and, in fact, it ended in League's announcement that it was coming into the Government without any agreement with the Congressmen on how to proceed after the new Government was formed.

6 Reference to three Members of the Cabinet Mission: Pethic Lawrence, Alexander and Cripps.

68

Stafford Cripps to Sardar Patel

Collected Works of Sardar Patel

PATEL PAPERS, NOVAJIVAN TRUST
24 October, 1946

DEAR SARDAR PATEL,

Thank you very much for your letter of the 19th. I am so glad that you sent it to me and I shall actually see that my colleagues and the Prime Minister have copies of it.

I realise very fully what a difficult situation you are all in and how terrible are the happenings in Bengal. It is of course quite impossible for us to judge from here exactly what is happening and why it is happening. It seems to us that firm measures are being taken to quell the riots and I hope they will be successful.

I know how exasperating it must be for you especially, but that is always one of the difficulties with a Central Government where there is a large measure of provincial autonomy. The system has many advantages, but it also has its difficulties and drawbacks. We are all very impressed by the way in which your team is tackling its most difficult job and I send you my very best wishes and may your patience not give out.

Yours Sincerely,
STAFFORD CRIPPS

Sardar Vallabhbhai Patel

69

Sardar Patel to Lord Wavell to Use His Special Power to Quell Communal Disturbances in Noakhali

Collected Works of Sardar Patel

SARDAR'S LETTERS—MOSTLY UNKNOWN-IV

28th October, 1946

I desire to bring up the question of Bengal before the full Interim Government for immediate discussion and decision. I have been told by the Hon'ble Vice-President[1] that Your Excellency's view is that the problem of restoring peace and tranquillity in Bengal is your special responsibility and that the Government of India as such, i.e., the Governor-General-in-Council, cannot do anything to give relief to the people of that unfortunate province. It would, indeed, be a tragic paradox if we have undertaken the responsibility of the Government to do anything to terminate the reign of terror which prevails in East Bengal even according to the obviously minimised accounts of those responsible for allowing such to come into being under their eyes. The whole country is deeply agitated about the events as well as about our share of responsibility in the matter. And the question will have to be dealt with in the Legislative Assembly when Members will raise the question in some form or another. It will not be possible for us to deal with it as former governments did.

I have examined the Government of India Act and in particular the 9th Schedule to see whether the Constitution under which we have undertaken this grave responsibility of the governance of India is indeed such as Your Excellency has stated. After an examination of the 9th Schedule of the Act and particular Section 41 thereof, I find that I, as Member-in-Charge of Home Affairs, and each one of my colleagues is competent to propose measures to restore tranquillity in the large and spreading area involved in the present disturbed conditions of Bengal. Though, under the letter of that Section, Your Excellency has power in your discretion to overrule our proposals, our understanding is that Your Excellency will act in accordance with the collective advice of the Cabinet.

I and my colleagues whom I have consulted before writing this are emphatically of opinion:

(i) that the Government of India should at once authorise, if necessary by Ordinance, special officers assisted by adequate staff and military support to proceed to and function in the areas affected and arrest and detain offenders and take all other steps necessary to restore order and tranquillity.

(ii) that we should recommend to Your Excellency that you would immediately exercise the power attaching to your special responsibility as Governor-General and take all steps necessary to take over the duties of law and order in the affected areas, if not in the whole of Bengal, from the hands of the present government of Bengal who have totally failed in their duties in that respect.

I request, therefore, that this matter may be discussed at the Cabinet meeting tomorrow when we shall have to decide our attitude in regard to adjournment motions coming up before the Assembly.

1 Pandit Jawaharlal Nehru.

REPRESSIONS STILL GOING ON
(TELEGRAM)

CALCUTTA
5 November, 1946

SARDAR VALLABHBHAI PATEL
Camp: Calcutta

Noakhali situation still horrible. Free movement for Hindus hazardous. Forced marriages, beef-eating threatened yet. Security impossible without posting military. Stray military patrolling quite insufficient for restoring peace. Oppression repeated no sooner military leaves area. Hindus dare not speak for want of security. Relief rescue impossible without armed *en masse*. Request neighbouring Provincial Governments arrange accommodation refugees Administration opposing rescue on plea rehabilitation which impossible without security. Negligible arrests of miscreants though named. Refugees and villagers starving. New Muslim tactics to set fire to mosques to entangle Hindus and prevent military action. Seasoned paddy fields evacuated. Homesteads and huts require immediate protection against destruction and looting. Renovation of top police administration essential.[1]

PRESIDENT
Noakhali Rescue Relief Committee

1 This telegram was repeated to Mahatma Gandhi, Jawaharlal and a few leading members of the Interim Government.

70

Sardar Patel Invites Muslim League for a Joint Discussion on Cabinet Mission Proposals

Collected Works of Sardar Patel

BOMBAY CHRONICLE
2 August, 1946

(Extract)

"Give up this approach. Much can be done by love; but nothing by holding a pistol to our heads. You cannot get your object by threats. The Congress is not afraid".

This was the categorical answer to the resolution recently adopted by the Council of the Muslim League and the speeches made by Mr. M.A. Jinnah, given by Sardar Vallabhbhai Patel, in the course of a speech at the Jinnah Hall on Thursday evening.

"If you are still keen on freedom," the Sardar appealed to the League, "come, let us sit together like two brothers and arrive at a settlement or let us refer our differences to arbitration and abide by the verdict; and let us jointly break this document (the Cabinet recommendations). Sit with us and let us talk freedom".

The occasion was a public meeting held ander the auspices of the Bombay Provincial Congress Committee at the Jinnah Hall to climax the Tilak Day celebrations. The meeting which was intended to be held at Chowpatty had to be held indoors due to inclement weather and the hall was jammed with people.

Besides the Muslim League resolution Sardar Patel dealt with a number of other subjects agitating the public mind.

With reference to the strike wave, he agreed on the need to cut from above and raise from below, but deplored that all these strikes had degenerated into struggles for leadership. Restlessness was a healthy sign, but people should not rush to hasty and irresponsible action.

......

Turning to the political situation in India, Sardar Patel announced that our struggle with the British was virtually over. They had declared their intention to quit. All his life he had been a disbeliever in British intentions. But he was now convinced that they were prepared to leave.

Whether they were doing so of their own accord or they were being forced to do so was not quite relevant. The fact was that they were quitting. And, therefore, if anybody told him that they were preparing to fight the British, he could not believe it. The preparation could only be for a fight among themselves.

This was the only interpretation he could give to the recent resolution of the Council of the All-India Muslim League. He could smell no fight in it. It was just a manoeuvre to put pressure on the British. If there was any fight it could only be against the Congress.

......

Falling into a serious vein Sardar Patel said that Mr. Jinnah had been abusing him and the Congress. What was their fault. Mr. Jinnah claimed that the Viceroy had given him certain secret assurances and had gone back on them. The Viceroy said he had given no such assurance. Whoever was right, where did Congress come into the picture? The letter from the Viceroy announcing that he had given no assurance of the kind implied by Mr. Jinnah had been published long ago. Why then, did he wait all these days?

The reason Mr. Jinnah cited was that Pandit Nehru, the Congress President, had said something at a Press Conference. This, Mr. Jinnah claimed, had given rise to a new situation. But Congress policy was no secret at any time. It was clearly stated in the resolution of the Working Committee which had been ratified, without the change of a comma or a syllable by the All-India Congress Committee (A.I.C.C.), Congress accepted the full responsibility for its declarations. The Working Committee's resolution said clearly that it accepted the declaration of May 16. It still stood by it. Certainly it had the right to interpret the document. But it made no secret of its interpretations, whatever the new situation had arisen now.

On that analogy, it could be argued that Mr. Jinnah's speeches also gave rise to new situations. While, for instance, the State Paper, expressly repudiated Pakistan, Mr. Jinnah in his speech to the League Council at Delhi had triumphantly announced that it had only concealed Pakistan, He had triumphantly claimed that the Congress had swallowed the sugar-coated pill of Pakistan.

The fact of the matter was, said Sardar Patel, Mr. Jinnah had tried to induce the Viceroy to instal the League in power without the Congress. He had failed and he was venting his chagrin on the Congress. As far as the Congress was concerned, it did not care very much how many seats it got. Let all the seats go to Mr. Jinnah. Only Mr. Jinnah should change his approach. He should cease to be a communalist and become a nationalist. His whole attempt had been to dub the Congress a Hindu body. That Congress had not been for 50 years. It would not be to-day. The Muslims of India were as much a part of the Congress responsibility as any other section of the population.

The speaker referred to the statement of Mr. Jinnah that the initiative was with the Congress or the Government and said that the Congress had gone to his door hundreds of times. He had never once deigned to come to it. How could he expect the Congress to go to him, after the kind of speech he had made? He had abused and insulted the Congress. The Congress was not so helpless that it should go to him.

On that footing no coalition was possible. There could be no coalition between two parties, one of which wanted to go north and the other to go south. The British were going anyhow could not afford to stay any longer. Indians would have to India free and run the administration of a Free India. If there was agreement on that common ground, other things would come easy.

But the fact of the matter appeared to be that Mr. Jinnah wanted the British to give him Pakistan. Comparing Pakistan to a deflated cycle tube, Sardar Patel said that for two months it had been entirely forgotten. It was new being revived and the latest slogan was "Back to Pakistan". Meanwhile all kinds of threats were being held out against the Congress. The Congress, however, could not be subdued by such means.

......

71

Nehru,Patel and Even Viceroy Against Inclusion of Fazlul Haq in Interim Cabinet to which Maulana had to Agree: Patel to Gandhiji

Collected Works of Sardar Patel

SARDAR'S LETTERS—MOSTLY UNKNOWN-IV

NEW DELHI

22 August, 1946

REVERED BAPU,

I could not write to you yesterday. On the 20th, we prepared our final list and sent it to the Viceroy. It included four Muslim Members—one of them being Fazlul Haq. Both myself and Jawaharlal were not in favour of including him. But on Maulana's suggestion, we agreed to accept his name. Yesterday evening, there was a message for Jawaharlal from the Viceroy inviting him to meet him at 9 a.m. to finalise the matter once for all. So Jawaharlal met him. We came to know yesterday that the Viceroy is unwilling to accept Fazlul Haq's name. So we discussed this matter again with the Maulana telling him that neither we nor the Viceroy approve of his name. What for should he then press for him? He came round and let go his insistence for him. So if the Viceroy would again show his disinclination in his case, his name will finally be dropped. If Fazlul is dropped, only three Muslim names remain as finally settled. The remaining two names will be submitted later on. But the list of names finalised already must go to the Press today or at the latest tomorrow.

Asaf Ali is still in Kashmir. He has communicated his consent today on the phone.

The Working Committee meeting has been fixed on the 27th inst. Jawahar wants this matter to be placed before it. Whether he would like you to attend the meeting or not, I cannot as yet say. Possibly, he will not like to trouble you for the sake of this business only.

VALLABHBHAI'S PRANAM

Mahatma Gandhi,
Sevagram.
(Original: Gujarati).

72

Sardar Patel to Wavell Not to Include Ghaznafar Ali in Interim Cabinet Till He Withdrew His Provocative Speech

Collected Works of Sardar Patel

SARDAR'S LETTERS—MOSTLY UNKNOWN-IV

DELHI
20 October, 1946

MY DEAR LORD WAVELL,

Raja Ghaznafar Ali Khan's speech is disconcerting and bodes ill for the future. It should be noted that the speech was made before the impressionable students on the 19th instant, i.e., after his name was sent by Mr. Jinnah as a Member of the Interim Government on behalf of the Muslim League.

Should he not withdraw the speech before he takes the oath of office?

Is the Interim Government to be the arena of party politics and intrigues and for driving in the very partition wedge which the long-term arrangement has withdrawn once for all and replaced it by grouping which in itself seems to be voluntary? What it is and what is its scope is for the Federal Court to decide unless the parties agree among themselves?

In any event the forum for every discussion on the subject is not the Interim Government but the Constituent Assembly.

The Interim Government is to run the Government machinery smoothly during the interim period on purely nationalist and democratic lines. Removal of corruption, communications, scarcity of food and clothing, health of the millions, their education, removal of chronic poverty and crying social reforms including removal of untouchability are the immediate needs of the country. If a wrangle over partition and fomenting of trouble are to take place of the immediate work of administration, it would be a question for the Congress to revise its attitude about shouldering the burden that it has taken over in response to your invitation.

And probably the Raja is not the only League Member to think as he has spoken. Who can say that he does not voice the mind of the League?

It seems to be quite clear that before the Coalition comes into being and portfolios are redistributed, besides the withdrawal of the speech in question, there should be a clear announcement by the Council of the League accepting the long-term arrangement and the text of the resolution of the League Working Committee should be supplied to the present Members of the Cabinet. The date fixed for the meeting of the Council of the Muslim League for the cancellation of the resolution rejecting the long-term scheme by its Bombay meeting should also be announced by the Muslim League.

I am sure you will yourself recognize the necessity of the foregoing requirements if the Interim Government is to run well and the present trouble is to subside.

Yours Sincerely,
VALLABHBHAI PATEL

His Excellency Field-Marshal
Viscount Wavell,
Viceroy's House, New Delhi.

1 From Mr. Ghaznafar Ali Khan's speech before a gathering of students at Lahore: "We are going into the Interim Government to get a foothold to fight for cur cherished goal or Pakistan.... The Interim Government is one of the fronts of the Direct Action Campaign and we shall most scrupulously carry out the orders of Mr. Jinnah on any front he orders us".—See Enclosure:

Enclosure
Ghaznafar Ali Khan's Speech

Ghaznafar Ali Khan, Member-designate of the Interim Government, addressing Islamia College students in Lahore today said: "We are going in the Interim Government to get a foothold to fight for our cherished goal of Pakistan and I assure you that we shall achieve Pakistan. The disturbances which have occurred in many parts of the country after the installation of purely Congress Government at the Centre have established the fact beyond the shadow of a doubt that the 10 crores of Indian Muslims will not submit to any government which does not include their true representatives. The earlier the Congress realise this the better—that no power can suppress the freedom upsurge among the Muslim Nation. We irrevocably stand for Pakistan as our ultimate goal, and I assure you that under the leadership of Quaid-i-Azam Jinnah we shall achieve our goal. In the Interim Government, all our activities should be guided by two considerations, that is to convince the Congress that no government in India can function smoothly without the co-operation of the Muslim League and the League is the sole representative organisation of the Indian Muslims. The Interim Government is one of the fronts of the direct action campaign and we shall most scrupulously carry out the orders of Mr. Jinnah on any front he orders us".

73

Sardar Patel Reiterates Conditions for League Joining Interim Government

Collected Works of Sardar Patel

BOMBAY CHRONICLE
25 November, 1946

In a speech rivalling that to Pt. Nehru's performance on Thursday in its outspokenness, Sardar Vallabhbhai Patel delivered a broadside against the Muslim League at the open session of the Congress here to-day. In the clearest possible terms he said that if the League did not enter the Constituent Assembly there was no alternative for them except to get out of the Interim Government.

Referring to the correspondence which has passed between Pt. Nehru and the Viceroy released today. Sardar Vallabhbhai Patel pointed out how Pt. Nehru had made two points clear.

One was that it the League came into the Interim Government it was to work as a team and not as a separate group.

Secondly, he had said that the League could not enter the Interim Government unless they accepted the Cabinet Mission's Proposals of May 16.

The Viceroy agreed with this position and said that the League too had accepted it. Mr. Jinnah has often accused the British Government of bad faith and of double-crossing. It is now upto the Viceroy to settle accounts with Mr. Jinnah. We have nothing to do with this quarrel, Sardar Patel said.

At the same time he made it clear that as far as the Congress was concerned they were going to stick to their seats. "We will stay there; we will work effectively and we will function as a Cabinet", Sardar Patel emphasised.

They would, however, resign the moment they felt convinced that the British Government was going back upon their promises. Their resignations were always in their pockets, but these would not be sumbitted unless Britain perjured herself and had her name blackened among the nations of the world.

Meanwhile they would not surrender to the war of nerves and resign. They would have to be dismissed.

If Pt. Nehru thrilled the people, the Sardar roused them to anger by his caustic sallies.

Referring to the widespread disturbances which in his view were the result of the political policy of the Muslim League, Sardar Patel said that the time had come for the people to defend themselves. "They can ask for Pakistan? They can ask for all India", he said. But this method would not pay, Poison would produce poison and the sword would ultimately have to be met by the sword. Therefore, he made on behalf of the entire Congress one last appeal to the League to desist from its present course and arrive at a peaceful agreement with the Congress.

74

Sardar Patel Criticises Muslim League's Dilatory Tactics, Constituent Assembly to Meet Regardless of Fate of London Talks

Collected Works of Sardar Patel

BOMBAY CHRONICLE
6 December, 1946

"Whatever happens to the ultimate solution of the communal problem, I trust both Hindus and Muslims have realised that violence and bloodshed will never bring them nearer to the achievement of their goals—either Swaraj or Pakistan; and the best interest of both the communities will be served by deciding to live in peace with one another," said Sardar Vallabhbhai Patel, Home Member, Interim

Government, at a public meeting this evening at the Palan Sojpal Chawl, Dadar, under the auspices of the Bombay Provincial Congress Committee, the Dadar Congress Committee and the Nagarik Samrakshak Dal, Dadar.

......

Tracing the course of events that took place in the country from the time of the failure of the first Simla Conference in 1945, Sardar Patel said that while the Congress had always followed the policy of being as accommodating to the League as was humanly possible, the League was bent upon having its pound of flesh, the impossible Pakistan demand was voiced time and again and the most solemn promises and assurances given by them were thrown to the winds. The latest example of this was the refusal of Mr. Jinnah to join the Constituent Assembly despite the fact that the League President gave definite assurance to the Viceroy that the League would enter the Constituent Assembly.

But the League was not content with stifling the progress of the country towards Swaraj like this. In Provinces where there were Muslim League Ministries they decided to launch "Direct Action" against the minority community. Never in the history of any country, said Sardar Patel, did a Government sponsor "Direct Action" against their own subjects, as they did in Bengal.

The course of events that followed in Calcutta in the latter days and in Bihar and elsewhere, however, said Sardar Patel showed the Leaguers that it was very costly to play such games and their actions recoiled on themselves. He hoped that they would learn the lesson and give up the talk of winning Pakistan by force and by sword.

"Whatever happens and whatever the outcome of the London talks," Sardar Patel observed, "the communal problem would have to be settled in India and by Indians themselves. The British have no place in this sphere and the sooner they quit the scene the better it would be for all concerned. "It was for this reason that I was convinced that no good would be served by my going to London and therefore I declined to go".

Reverting to the intentions of the British in respect of the Indian question, Sardar Patel stated that when the Cabinet Delegation started its negotiations last April, they assured the Congress leaders again and again that they were absolutely sincere about their intention to quit India and about the fact that unlike in the past, they would not make the solution of India dependent upon the achievement of unity between the two communities of India. He was led to believe then that the British were honest and genuine in this assurance, the Home Member said, and he still hoped that he was correct. It remained to see how this was realised in practice.

The Muslim League, led by Mr. Jinnah, was out to obstruct the Congress at every point, by force if necessary, and the country had to meet the challenge.

In this setting, the Sardar continued, it was most imperative that people should not allow themselves to be taken in, due to their cowardice or weakness. "Those who had mastered the ideology of Mahatma Gandhi and were able to practise it effectively should do so. But for the ordinary man who could not practise Gandhiji's non-violence, the best way would be to defend himself and his neighbour with all his strength. Cawardice helps nobody. It only results in more innocent persons being killed", asserted Sardar Patel.

In this connection he recounted the warning he gave to the Bengal leaders who saw him just after the Calcutta Killing, when he suggested to them to prepare themselves and their people to meet the offensive of unsocial elements in East Bengal. "But the Bengal leaders apparently did not realise the seriousness of the situation".

He advised the public to suspend all activities against the community which was not their own at least for fortnight. "This does not, however, mean that you should allow yourselves to be killed. By all means defend yourself and your neighbours with whatever means you can. But do not yourselves go out to kill. I want that perfect calm is restored in Bombay once more and that is why I have come here. I hope you will follow my advice".

Reverting to the London talks he said that this morning he had a telephonic talk with Pandit Nehru who assured the Sardar that he was definitely returning to India by Sunday at the latest in time to attend the first session of the Constituent Assembly. As he had previously announced, Sardar Patel said, the Constituent Assembly would meet, come what may.

Concluding, Sardar Patel said: "We are on the verge of attaining complete freedom. It is for us to take it or throw it. What should we do? I am sure that all sane Indians would not let the great chance that is coming to us go by and that we shall solve our own problems with our brethren of the other community which will make us worthy of the great place we are about to occupy in the world, especially in Asia in virtue of our geographical position".

Earlier Mr. S.K. Patil, President of the B.P.C.C., welcomed the Sardar on behalf of the citizens and assured him that the Bombay people were solidly behind the Congress.

75

"Defend Yourself with Violence or Non-Violence But Don't Run Away" Sardar Patel's Advice to Gujaratis

Collected Works of Sardar Patel

BOMBAY CHRONICLE
2 December, 1946

"Don't run away, don't weep, Don't die in vain, but defend yourselves by all means whether violent or non-violent. Don't look to the police or military for help. Become sepoys of the country and form National Militia", said Sardar Patel addressing a huge concourse of Gujaratis at Variety Theatre this morning before leaving for Bombay.

An address in a beautiful silver casket was presented to him on behalf of the community by Shamjibhai Kheta, Chairman of the Reception Committee. Seth Madhavlal Parakh garlanded Sardar Patel, Swami Vidyanandji blessed the Sardar.

Sardar Patel referred to the Ahmedabad riots, during 1942-43, when the people of Ahmedabad refused to contribute men and money towards the execution of the war. He felt pride at Gujarat's achievement but when he heard of Gujaratis running hither and thither to save their lives, he felt ashamed. Man, he said, was mortal and must, therefore, learn to die. If he died for a noble cause it would make him immortal.

He advised the Gujarati community to mix with the people of the province as "milk mixes with water", Gujaratis were successful businessmen and had accumulated fortune but they should know how to utilise it for a good cause.

76

Sardar Patel to Stafford Cripps

Collected Works of Sardar Patel

PAPERS, NAVAJIVAN TRUST
15 December, 1946

DEAR SIR STAFFORD CRIPPS,

In my last letter I gave you some idea of the amount of strain that was being put on us at this end. Since then events have happened one after another leading up to our being invited to London for discussion. The climax was reached when Jawaharlal returned almost heart-broken... .

When the invitation came (for London) our first instinct was to decline to accept it. But the Prime Minister's appeal and his assurance in reply to our cable created a feeling in Pandit Nehru's mind that refusal to accept the invitation may be regarded as an act of discourtesy; and he left India full of hopes for a message of goodwill and sympathy, but he returned sadly disappointed. He now realises his mistake and the amount of harm that has been done to India by his having accepted the invitation.

We have full appreciation of your difficulties over there. But I must frankly confess that there is very little understanding over there of our difficulties here. You called the League delegation there at a time when there was some realisation that violence is a game at which both parties can play and the mild Hindu also, when driven to desperation, can retaliate as brutally as a fanatic Muslim. Just when the time for settlement was reached Jinnah got the invitation and he was able to convince the Muslims once again that he had been able to get more concessions by creating trouble and violence.

Sudhir (Ghosh) has, I believe, after his return to (London), given you some idea of what has happened here and I need not bother you with details. But I will only say that if strong action had been taken, or had been allowed to be taken here, when "Direct Action Day" was fixed by the Muslim League and when 16 August was fixed as a day of demonstration in Calcutta, all this colossal loss of life and property and bloodcurdling events would not have happened. The Viceroy here took the contrary view, and every action of his since the "Great Calcutta Killing" has been in the direction of encouraging the Muslim League and putting pressure on us towards appeasement.

In London the stage was set against us, and I do not know whether there is any realisation of the amount of mischief that has been done by the statement and by the subsequent debate. With great difficulty, we were able to build a bridge between England and India by our joint efforts—and you know my own contribution. I regret to say that the sense of faith and confidence about the sincerity of Britain that was created by our settlement is being dissipated fast and the bridge is about to crack or collapse.

Your interpretation means that Bengal Muslims can draft the constitution of Assam. It is amazing. Do you think that such a monstrous proposition can be accepted by the Hindus of Assam, particularly after the sad experience of wholesale forcible conversions, arson, looting, rape and forcible marriages? You can have no idea of the resentment and anger caused by your emphasis on this interpretation. If you think that Assam can be coerced to accept the domination of Bengal, the sooner you rid of the disillusion the better. What can we do to satisfy the Sikhs who have admittedly been unjustly treated? If they frame the constitution of Assam in such a way as to make Assam's opting out impossible, what is the remedy in your statement?

You know that Gandhiji at the age of 77 is spending all his energy in the devasted Hindu homes in Eastern Bengal and trying to recover the lost girls and bring back those forcibly converted to their old faith. But he is working against heavy odds, and I have great apprehension that he will end his life there in this fruitless mission. He is surrounded by a very hostile atmosphere. In the event of his death there in these circumstances, what will happen no one can say. I shudder to think of the consequences. But the anger and resentment of the whole of India will be not only against the Muslims, but also against the British to a large extent.

You must have seen what Jinnah has said in London immediately after the debate. He swears by Pakistan, and everything conceded to him is to be used as a lever to work to that end. You wish that we should agree to help him in his mad dream. I am sorry to write to you in this strain, but I feel sad over the whole affair. *You know when Gandhiji was strongly against our settlement, I threw my weight in favour of it*. You have created a very unpleasant situation for me. All of us here feel that there has been a betrayal.

The solution has now been made more difficult, nay, almost impossible. The settlement can only be made if there is no outside interference and the parties left alone. The Viceroy would not give us peace and he and his advisers are all pro-League. We have to work through them. It is an impossible situation, but I do not know whether you will be able to do anything in the matter.

Hope you are doing well.

Yours Sincerely,
VALLABHBHAI PATEL

Sir Stafford Cripps.

77

Sardar Patel Disagrees with Viceroy's Views that Muslim League's Entry into Interim Government Would Ensure Peace

Collected Works of Sardar Patel

BOMBAY CHRONICLE
5 December, 1946

Sardar Vallabhbhai Patel, Member for Home and Information and Broadcasting, Government of India, declared at the Taj this evening that the Government in its programme of nationalisation would only touch the key industries and would perforce embark on a wider programme of nationalisation, if employers in other industries failed to look after the welfare of the workers properly.

Sardar Patel was speaking at a reception given to him by Mr. Ratilal M. Gandhi, M.L.C., and Vice-President of the Indian Merchants' Chamber. A large gathering of distinguished citizens and leading merchants of Bombay was present. It included Mr. B.G. Kher, Prime Minister of Bombay, and his team of ministers Messrs G.D. Birla, Pranlal Devkaran Nanjee, K.R.P. Shroff, Walchand Hirachand, J.C. Setalvad, Hooseinbhoy Lalljee, A.A. Jasdanwala, Sheriff of Bombay, S.K. Patil, S.L. Salim, Sir Cowasji Jehangir, Sir Manilal Mangvati, Sir Byramji Jeejibhoy, Sir Chunilal B. Mehta, Sir R.P. Masani, Sir P. Thakurdas, Sir B. Karanjia, Sir P.I. Rahimtulla and Sir Fancis Low.

Sardar Patel observed that a wave of strikes had swept the country and was proving very detrimental to trade. Loyalty of the working classes was divided. If the industrialists failed to fulfil their obligations to them the Communists would completely capture the Labour stronghold.

He warned the mercantile community against black-marketing and said that if they continued it in defiance of these warnings the Government would have to resort to strict measures.

Sardar Patel expressed the view that the holding of the present conference in London was futile. It would serve no purpose. "I know what the British Government will say. Oh; you are ruling in nine provinces out of eleven. Why can't you be a little magnanimous and concede the demands of the League? This attitude of the British Government is of that category which they adopted towards Hitler".

The London Conference, he said, was a farce. The British Government wanted to enlist world opinion on their side. That was their main object. The world would pass a verdict of fairness on them for calling the Indian leaders to London and regard the Congress unreasonable for declining the invitation.

He replied to the criticism made by the *London Times* on the present situation in the country that if the Hindus and the Muslims continued fighting each other the British would have to stay in India. It was an illusion under which the British were suffering, the Sardar said. They would have to quit the country even if the Hindus and Muslims kept on fighting and hitting each other.

Referring to the entry of the League into the Interim Government, Sardar Patel said that it was believed by the Viceroy that after the League came in tranquillity would be restored in the country. "But I told him that his attempt was like Chamberlain's at Munich".

The Muslim League did not believe in non-violence. They ought to have thought deeply before they observed the "Direct Action Day". It was intended against the British Government, but got directed against the minority community by the majority community.

Sardar Patel described Mr. Jinnah's suggestion of transfer of Muslims to the North as impracticable.

He reiterated his conviction that the Muslim League would come into the Constituent Assembly as it had come into the Interim Government and again declared that the Constituent Assembly shall meet on December 9.

He indicated the Viceroy and the British officials of partisanship towards the League and said that the members of the Civil Service should serve the country loyally otherwise leave it.

Replying to the oft-made criticism that Ministries in certain provinces failed to control the situation, Sardar Patel said that it should also be remembered that the Ministries in tackling the situation had to seek the co-operation of police and officials who were their former enemies. If, for example, in a certain province the police was forced by the Ministry to curb the Muslims they would be dubbed as pro-Hindus and vice-versa. "I can remove the Bombay Ministry from office but I can assure you that the substitute will be less efficient".

A popular Government, he said, must govern the least. Police and military were the weapons of the British Government and not theirs.

He further said that the art of Government was very difficult. "We have yet to learn it. So far we have only struggled."

In the end Sardar Patel said that by internecine warfare neither the Hindus would benefit nor the Muslims. Bombay had a tradition of being a cosmopolitan city and it should maintain that tradition. He exhorted the mercantile community to co-operate with the Provincial Governments in quelling the riots and never to think of looking forward to the Central Government for help, "This is my message to you to-day, let us all resolve that we will restore peace at once".

Earlier, Mr. Ratilal M. Gandhi, welcoming Sardar Patel, paid a glowing tribute to his services to the country.

78

Sardar Patel on Four Edifices for Swaraj Erected by Gandhiji[1]

Collected Works of Sardar Patel

SARDAR PATEL KE BHASHNON
5 January, 1947

(Extract)

......

He laid foundation of four walls and we have not been able to erect even a single wall. This and other universities were founded to impart national education. Many educational institutions were founded in India... . It was the time of Khilafat Movement. Hindus, Muslims and all communities had united... .

Second wall is Hindu-Muslim Unity. If we want real Swaraj, Hindus and Muslims have to be united. On 6the April of 1919 processions were taken out throughout the country in which Hindus, Muslims, Parsis, Christians, Sikhs and Jews had joined, not a single community had been left out, men, women, young and old, rich and poor all were there in the procession, but today distance between the two communities had increased.

Third wall of Swaraj edifice was Swadeshi i.e. Khadi... .

The fourth wall of the edifices is removal of untouchability

......

Gandhiji asked Englishmen to quit India. Today he is prepared to quit if Swaraj means simply to driving out the foreigners, then Swaraj is near. Englishmen shall have to go. We have to make our own arrangements. Englishmen will say we are going, so we shall have to fight with our own weaknesses. If we want Swaraj we cannot fight among ourselves. We must see what Gandhiji is doing, why he is doing, and how he is doing... .

...Only if we manage our affairs properly, we will achieve independence. There is no doubt that Englishmen are leaving. perhaps persons like Churchill yet dream of ruling India. He does not want to abandon a hen laying golden eggs and therefore is instigating Harijans and Muslims. But this game is not going to last long, whether they like it or not they shall have to go... .

India is on the verge of being independent and we shall require lot of efficient persons. At present we don't have competent persons in enough numbers.

If we want real Swaraj, we shall have to mend our ways... .

79

Sardar Patel Foresees Reunion of Partitioned India

Collected Works of Sardar Patel

BOMBAY CHRONICLE
12 August, 1947

(Extract)

"Our first task is to stabilise, consolidate and strengthen ourselves and the rest can have only a secondary priority", declared Sardar Vallabhbhai Patel addressing a mass meeting here to-day held in connection with the Liberty Week celebrations.

Sardar Patel emphatically denied that he and his colleagues agreed to the partition of the country either because of fear or out of a sense of defeat. Under the prevailing conditions in the country partition on the pattern was the best thing possible and he had no qualms about it. In a matter of weeks they had decided the country, the Army, the Services, etc., and this indeed was a colossal task performed. He, however, strongly believed that those who had seceded today would be disillusioned soon and their union with the rest of India was assured.

The Sardar made an earnest appeal to the people to rub out from their minds the memories of the past two years, deem it as a terrible nightmare and forget it, and to look forward with single-minded purpose to make India strong, prosperous and happy. This could only be done by hard toil. A Socialist Government in Britain was calling upon the workers to sweat an hour more a day and the strange contrast here was our Socialists and others preached strikes and encouraged wage-boosts. This could only result, he said, in printing more notes at Nasik and end up in serious trouble.

He welcomed Mr. Liaquat Ali Khan's statement published today and was happy that the minorities in Pakistan would be protected and their rights safeguarded. Such a generous move by the League could not but evoke reciprocity here in India.

The Sardar was sure that all the Indian States would join the Indian Union and none could afford to keep out and live in isolation. He reiterated that first things should be done first and the first job was to get the States to accede and consolidate the Union. The demand of the people in the States for a democratic regime raised an entirely different issue. He could not see how an Indian ruler could exist with his subjects in hostility and clamouring for popular Government.

Sardar Patel said that he would make no efforts to explain away the responsibility of the Congress to divide the country. "We took these extreme steps," he said, "after great deliberation. In spite of my previous strong opposition to partition, I agreed to it because I felt it was convinced that in order to keep India united it must be divided now".

His experience in office during the past year showed that it was impossible to do anything constructive with the Muslim League in. The League representatives during their continuance in office did nothing but to create deadlocks and their role was entirely an obstructionist one. Besides, as he had already once said, he found that all the Muslims, save for a few exceptions, engaged in all capacities in the Government were with the Muslim League. Thus the rot had set in and it could not be permitted to prolong any longer except at the risk of a disaster for the whole country. Indeed at one stage, and it obtained even now to some degree, things had become so bad that with the killing at Calcutta, riots spread all over and it became a perilous adventure for Hindus and Muslims to visit one another's localities. The economic life of the country was paralysed and there was little security of life or property.

The only way out of the sickening situation, Congress realised, lay in the elimination of the third party, the British power. The British, on their part, had declared that they would quit in June 1948. But the period was long. Also their statement promising to hand over power to the authorities in the Provinces gave rise to a vigorous effort to dislodge the Ministries in Assam, the Punjab and in the Frontier. The League succeeded in the Punjab. Even though they failed in the Frontier and Assam, the League movement caused great misery and bloodshed. In order to settle the issue immediately and prevent the slaughter of innocent people, the Congress decided to agree to the division of the country and demanded the partition of the Punjab and Bengal. This was no surrender to the League threats or a policy of appeasement.

Today the partition of India was a settled fact and yet it was an unreal fact. The partition, he hoped, however, removed the poison from the body politic of India. This, he was sure, would result in the seceding areas desiring to reunite with the rest of India. India was one and indivisible. One could not divide the sea or split the running waters of a river. The Muslims had their root in India. Their sacred places and their cultural centres were located here in India. He did not know what they could do in Pakistan and it would not be long before they began to return... .

80

Transfer of Power to Existing Central Government Only Solution for Political Impasse : Sardar Patel

Collected Works of Sardar Patel

BOMBAY CHRONICLE
10 May, 1947

Sardar Vallabhbhai Patel declared today that the current British policy of "remaining neutral but holding power is a way of propagating civil war" and asserted India's political impasse would be broken at once if power were transferred to the Central Government "as it now stands".

The Home, Information and Broadcasting Member said in an interview that functioning of India's Interim Government as a Dominion Government "with the Viceroy standing out" would have two immediate results:

1. "There would be peace in the country within a week. Those who commit acts of violence do so because they feel there is no strong Central power to check them. With Dominion Status, the Central Government would form a strong Centre and would have the necessary power to put down disorder;"
2. "Lacking interference by a third party to whom either side could appeal, the Congress and the Muslim League would settle their differences at once. If there are conflicts in the Cabinet over a question, the majority would rule".

Particular significance was attached to Sardar Patel's statement in the light of a reliable report the Viceroy had sent word to His Majesty's Government that some action must be taken quickly in India to avoid a situation "no one could control" and in view of Mahatma Gandhi's recently reiterated opposition to division of India.

Sardar Patel did not predict what type of settlement might

by expected between the League and Congress over the issue of Pakistan if such a step were taken by the British Government. However, he said the Congress would not coerce any unwilling group or area.

He did say that Section 93 "would vanish in the Punjab" and the Congress and League would agree "possibly to a coalition government".

In the North West Frontier Province, where the League has carried on an agitation against the Congress Ministry for more than two months, Sardar Patel said, "the Ministry would remain. The election was fought only last year on the issue of Pakistan and Congress won".

Sardar Patel characterised the present situation in India as serious and said one of the grave problems was that of private armies now being raised and equipped.

As an alternative in the event the British decided India must be divided, Sardar Patel suggested that power be transferred to the Constituent Assemblies, saying the Muslim League already has a plan for a separate Constituent Assembly.

"The other way is much easier", he added "transfer power to the Central Government. Let the Viceroy stand out and not interfere. Then you have a strong Centre which would be capable of dealing with the problems facing the country, particularly in such places as the Punjab and the North West Frontier Province. Immediately there would be peace in the country"

Sardar Patel reiterated the Congress stands for the May 16 statement "*in toto*" and "in spite of its weakness Congress would like to have a strong Centre. It is absolutely essential that there be a strong army for defence and a strong Central Government.

"The Congress position always has been that it will not coerce any group or area which does not want to remain. At the same time it will not be coerced by any group or community. Congress has accepted that principle since the Cripps Talks in 1942.

"Therefore, if the Muslim League insists that it wants

separation then Congress will not compel them to remain on the Union by force. But it will result in dividing Bengal and the Punjab. If Bengal and Punjab provinces, as they stand today, were put into Pakistan, coercion would come in. Non-Muslims would be forced into Pakistan and there would be a civil war.

"Therefore, if the League insists on partition of India, the same grounds on which it insists on partition apply in the Pakistan areas".

Sardar Patel remarked that "it is a dangerous game that Mr. Jinnah is playing" pointing out that the separation of Burma from India required two years. "And we had nothing in India", he added.

He predicted it would take a long time, perhaps years to divide the Indian army, let alone separate communications, rail, roads and similar interlocking services which span India.

Of the Muslim League President Sardar Patel said that except for the League's temporary acceptance of the Cabinet Mission Plan, Mr. Jinnah's position has remained the same.

"We asked him to refer the question to the United Nations Organisation", Sardar Patel said. "He said 'no'. We asked him to arbitrate. He said 'no'."

81

Sardar Patel Appeals to Sikhs Not to Attack Muslims

Collected Works of Sardar Patel

IN TUNE WITH THE MILLIONS
22 October, 1947

Under a shadow of a unique collection of chandeliers watched by a long row of Sikh Gurus[1] *and the ancestors of the House of Patiala there held in Darbar Hall a Panthic Conference on 22 October 1947 under the gloom of great misfortunes that ever befell the Sikhs in the bloodbath of partition. Lest the Sikh community may arouse to anger and retaliation under this incalculable load of sorrow and distress, Sardar with Baldev Singh, flew to Patiala and assuaged their bleeding hearts and wounded feelings with the balm of this most touching invocation which in piety and spirit has a glow and grandeur of a unique sermon.*

On hearing of the Panthic Conference, I and the Defence Minister, took in mind to meet the Sikh leaders at a very critical moment in their history. I wish to place before you a few words of friendly advice as from one who throughout has admired your virtues of courage and patriotism; and who has nothing but the warmest friendly feelings for the community.

I may recall how with the strong support of H.H. the Maharaja of Patiala, I appealed to your leaders and the vast gathering at Amritsar, for your help and co-operation in securing safe passage for the Muslim convoys through Amritsar. I was gratified at the response to that appeal and I regarded that response as a token of regard which you had been kind enough to show me.

I must, however, warn you against hasty decisions on vital matters in a most difficult situation. I fully appreciate the tempers as have been disturbed under the blows which destiny has visited upon you and the anger that rules your hearts.

But you are a brave people and you must face the situation like brave men. It does not behave the brave to besmirch the honour of your swords and the fair name of your community and the country by spilling innocent blood. The time is for calm and dispassionate thinking over your future course of action and for wisely shaping your conduct to bring glory to your community and the country, and not for bemoaning your fate or counting your losses and vainly hoping to make up for them by retaliation.

The Sikh community has been misrepresented and vilified abroad by certain interested propagandists. You have to rehabilitate your reputation which you have built during the two World Wars. For that, it is not enough to wield the sword but to know how to use it. There is another set of propagandists who are bent on isolating the Sikhs and creating divisions among Hindus and Sikhs. This set is more hostile than the first. We must guard ourselves against this vilest propaganda and give it a lie.

When we accepted partition, it was like our agreeing to have a diseased limb shorn off so that the remaining part may live in a sound condition. But before we could start the process of healing, events have overtaken us.

Evil cannot be met by evil, but by good. Although, we cannot act in entire accord with the creed of non-violence in our imperfect state of mental and moral equipment, we cannot act in such a manner as to degrade the sword which we wield. When the right time and the right cause come, you can use your sword to your heart's content. Now you have to sheathe your sword so that you can raise the moral tone of the people which is now at such a low ebb that lawlessness, contempt of law, attacks on innocent train passengers and brutalities on helpless persons are being perpetuated. It is up to all of us to check that tendency and you can give the right lead in the matter.

We must create the right atmosphere in which we can achieve our cherished objectives of raising the status, our moral sense which seem to have been dulled by the prejudices and anger which cloud our minds. Unless we rise above such prejudices and anger, we can never achieve all that tor which we fought our struggle for freedom.

I appeal to those present here to take decisions consistent with their responsibilities. You must support your Government which is valiantly struggling against heavy odds. It is your own Government which is entitled to your fullest support.

1 A religious teacher, a preceptor, a mentor, elderly adviser.

82

Sardar Patel on Punjab Refugees

Collected works of Sardar Patel

IN TUNE WITH THE MILLIONS
3 September, 1947

Just on his return from the Inter-Dominions conference at Lahore, Sardar Patel, on 3 September 1947 issued this earnest appeal to Government servants to realize the gravity of the unprecedented situation that imperilled the lives of the millions of their countrymen on other side of the Punjab and invoked them to instant call of duty for facilitating swiftest evacuation of the very forlorn and grief-stricken refugees from the place of veritable hell to the abode of safety. How Sardar's heart bled and what solace he was to this uprooted humanity of the Motherland seems echoed in this melancholic note of a Refugee Judge of the Punjab High Court on the passing away of the Sardar: "By his death it is not you (Maniben) alone that has lost a father. The whole Nation has; and those of us who had been thrown out of Pakistan felt his loss all the more as he took us to his bosom and gave us shelter and succour".

I have just returned from a visit to Lahore where I had gone to participate in an Inter-Governmental Conference[1] convened to devise ways and means to restore peaceful conditions in the Punjab with the least possible delay and for expediting evacuation of refugees assembled in hundreds and thousands at various places in both the East and West Punjab. *I should like to say at once that the measures planned and the decisions reached are sound, but they can yield results only if they would be implemented in the right spirit and with singlemindedness of purpose, determination and the full force of the administrative machinery of both sides.*

The immediate objective of these decisions is the swift

movement of millions of men, women and children from their precarious abodes to a haven of safety and peaceful existence.

The gigantic dimensions of the task require honest and efficient working of the administrative machinery in full blast. The Prime Minister is exerting every ounce of his energy at the cost of his health. May I appeal to all Government servants not to spare themselves in the discharge of this sacred obligation to their unfortunate brothers and sisters of the Punjab in their utter distress and desolation. Public co-operation in this stupendous undertaking is a *sine qua non* of success. On workers engaged on Railway and on road transports, and on persons engaged in food supplies, fall a special burden of responsibility which I am sure they will discharge with vigour, courage and devotion.

But on the public in general and on the refugees, who are already fortunately with us, in particular, rests a tremendous duty. *I fully realise that many of them have gone through tragedies of indescribable horror and atrocities of unspeakable bestiality. They and many of their relations and friends have passed through a veritable hell during which human beings have sunk down to levels lower than even the most savage animals*. But they have to remember that any attempt at retaliation or revenge would only divert our energies from the all-embracing task of relief and succour to our friends across the border, and from the obligation of maintaining peaceful conditions without which any efficient organisation of relief is impossible.

I would, therefore, appeal to these friends to exercise all possible restraint and to utilise the bitter experiences through which they have passed, not for accentuating the misery and danger of those who are still let behind, but for creating conditions in which the gigantic task of relief and evacuation can be pursued with the utmost vigour and determination. Let us first engage ourselves wholeheartedly in that pressing task.

If this immediate duty is not discharged with the single-minded determination of all concerned, there is a danger of the breaking out of epidemics as disease taking greater lives

than the senseless slaughter has done. Once it is over then alone can we turn ourselves to the healing of wounds which have been inflicted and redressing the wrongs which have been perpetrated.

1 Sardar attended Inter-Dominions conference at Lahore on 3 September '47 at the pressing call from Nehru on 31 August '47 from his tour in the riot-affected Punjab. Nehru wrote: "I suggest to you, with all earnestness, to come to Lahore for a day. You can come by plane in the morning and return the same evening. Probably I shall return with you. This invitation is also made on behalf of Liaquat Ali Khan".

83

Sardar Patel on Exchange of Population in Punjab

Collected Works of Sardar Patel

IN TUNE WITH THE MILLIONS
11 October, 1947

(*Extract*)

How Pakistan was playing a hide-and-seek game on even the agreed decisions of the Inter-Dominions Conference is eloquently brought to light in this spirited rejoin by the Sardar on 11 October 1947 which he felt constrained to issue in reply to the criticism of the Pakistan Prime Minister on that portion of the Sardar's speech at Amritsar which related to the exchange of population in Punjab:

......

He (Mr. Liaqat Ali Khan) has evidently forgotten that the question of sending out Muslims from East Punjab and non-Muslims from west Punjab is no longer a matter of policy of any one Government, but an agreed arrangement between the Dominions of India and of Pakistan. He, as a participant in the Inter-Dominions Conference in which this agreement was reached and in which the means of its enforcement are being settled should have known better... .

Politicians' memory is proverbially short, but that of the

Prime Minister of Pakistan seems to be shorter. *If, therefore, he deliberately ignores these facts or side-tracks the issues involved the conclusion is irresistible that he is not prepared to own or face the consequences of decisions to which he has been a willing party.*

He (Mr. Liaqat Ali Khan) has also repeated the oft-heard assurances to the minority communities of Pakistan. The proof of pudding lies in the eating thereof. The value of these assurances is written large on thousands of murders, abductions, forced marriages, burnt houses and maimed children, and the treatment of non-Muslim men, women and children leaving Pakistan in utter distress when they are being subjected to most harassing and humiliating experiences... . ...Those who see daily streams of refugees from all over the western Pakistan escaping with just the clothes they stand in can hardly be taken in by it. Those who are left behind are in daily terror of their lives and know not what tomorrow has in store for them.

On the other hand, in India, over three-fourths of the country, Muslims are following their normal avocation and showing no signs of leaving. They are living peacefully in their ancestral homes or on lands in complete protection of their lives and property vouchsafed to them by their Government.

84

Sardar Patel Defends Partition of India as an Evil Necessity[1]

Collected Works of Sardar Patel

SARDAR PATEL KE BHASHNON
11 August, 1947

Today is martyrs' day. It is in memory of those who have been martyrs for achieving independence of our country. It is our bounden duty to remember them. We have been victorious because of their sacrifice. If we do not remember them then we will be disloyal to our country.

After four days alien government will quit India. Now Congress has achieved its goal and our life work is also completed. When Lokmanya died, we had taken a pledge in the Chowpatty ground that *Swaraj is our birthright*. Thereafter in Lahore Congress on the bank of river Ravi under this Congress flag we had taken a pledge to sacrifice our lives for the achievement of independence and decided that Hindus, Muslims, Sikhs, Christians, Parsees all will live unitedly. That is not fully implemented. Therefore, today our hearts are not filled with as much joy as should have been. You must understand that now foreigners will not be able to create impediments in our way. This is a very big achievement.

People say that Congress partitioned India. It is true. We have taken this responsibility after proper thinking and not because of any fear or pressure. I was strong opponent of partition of India. But when I sat in the Central Government I saw that from a peon to high officers are infested with communal hatred. In such conditions instead of fighting and tolerating the interference of the third party, it is better to separate.

After some weeks we will complete one year in Central Government. We entered the government after the genocide in Calcutta. There is much enmity between the two communities. In Calcutta, Lahore and Bombay wherever you go you will see that mini-Pakistans have been formed. No Hindu can enter Muslim locality. No Hindu is able to stay in Rawalpindi. We saw that this problem will not be solved till alien government is here. When British government decided to abdicate power after one and a half years in Assam, Punjab, Bengal, North West Frontier Province—everywhere riots broke out and there were murders on a large scale. We asked the Britishers to leave early. Then they said, "we will go if you mutually agree". So we decided to agree to the formation of Pakistan, but we demanded partition of Bengal and Punjab. We painfully took that decision. As a result the government which was to transfer power in 1948 June decided to transfer it on 15th August, 1947. Army officers, etc, were also divided between the two countries.

Even after partition seventy-five per cent of the total population is on this side. We have to uplift them. Today India is in difficulty. There is financial crisis. India was a debtor country. Now though it has become creditor it is not certain when Britain will return our money. Then what is the gain of being a creditor?

Here words won't solve the problems. There are many scholars. Our Socialist friends talk of Socialist government. I tell them take one province and govern it in a socialistic way. In England there is Socialist government, but there they talk of increase in the working hours while here there is talk of strikes, and increase in wages and salaries. But from where will the money come? By printing promissory notes in Nasik press the wealth of the nation is not going to increase. Where is money in the country? You calculate how many paise as per capita income.

I tell small and big Kings that when the time comes they have to join the Indian Union by fifteenth. After that they will be dealt in a different manner. The concessions which are offered today will not be offered after that date. So if they want to rule they have to sign the Instrument of Accession. In the world today it is difficult to stay alone. When there is hailstorm lonely tree falls to the ground, but the trees which are in the row are saved. They are also the descendants of Ramachandra and Ashoka, yet today you salute even a most junior English servant. They are yet not prepared to accept that Britishers will quit on 15th of August, but when they go and you will feel the breeze of freedom, the gates of your hearts will open.

There should be peace in the country. To fight like wild animals, to stab a woman or a child passing on the road do not enhance the prestige of any community. Only peace will save us. We do not give in to satisfy anybody. We are talking sense. Yet if you want to continue fighting, fight the army way. Cutting each other's throats makes us a laughing stock in the world. The poison which was there in Englishmen's heart has evaporated. Howsoever we fight with each other, one nation is not going to form two nations. Though the country is partitioned, people are not partitioned. Who can partition mountains and rivers? The roots of Muslims are also here. Here there is Jumma mosque, Taj Mahal, Aligarh University, etc. So they have no other go except being one with us.

Since my release from jail I have been saying that it is difficult for Europeans to rule Asia. In Indonesia Dutch people are creating trouble. Last war has not yet dried and there new small battles have started. Again if a big war breaks out, fighters will find their graveyard.

In the government which is being formed today we have to be cautious. The Muslims who were in the army have crossed over to that side and Hindus have crossed over to this side. How can there be nationalist spirit in such an army? Hindu peons, clerks have come on this side and Muslims have gone that side, but when there will be difficulty they are going to come back on this side. Our rule is not theocratic rule. Even after partition our country is very big . Our population is also very large. Forget the past as a bad dream. Forget Pakistan. But when they make efforts to fight we should also be strong enough to repulse them. There should be co-ordination amongst us.

Some today talk of protection of cows. But when we are not able to protect children, women and old men, what is the use of talking about the protection of cows? The countries where there is no ban on cow slaughter the cows are very stout and healthy which we do not find here. If you really want to protect cows then cows should be looked after nicely.

Today we have an opportunity to unite India. Barring some part of Lahore and East Bengal we have now a golden opportunity to integrate India after one thousand years.

We have gained freedom. If we want to work properly there should be peace in the land. If there is no peace, and no food to eat people will say that slavery of British was good.

Forget the history of last one and a half years. Frame the

programme of Congress which would be implemented after 15th of August. Uptill now we have wasted too much time in quarrelling.

Here we are not sitting in such a position that by pushing we will fall. Day before yesterday Jawaharlalji has properly said that those who can show better results than us can come forward, we are ready to handover to them.

1 From the lecture given on Ramlila ground in Delhi on 11 August, 1947.

85

Partition of India Became Inevitable Due to Muslim League's Attitude in Interim Government and Pro-Muslim League Behaviour of Muslim Government Officers: Sardar Patel

Collected Works of Sardar Patel

IN TUNE WITH MILLIONS
11 August, 1947

(When the golden threshold of the ushering and triumphant dawn of freedom was rousing Indian humanity to joys and hopes inexplicable, the Sardar, who knew his work and mission for the resurging India, with a view to channelise this boundless enthusiasm, spoke to Delhi citizens during Liberty celebrations on 11 August 1947 that consolidation, unity and hard work were the imperative needs of the time to make freedom worth having.)

I make earnest appeal to people to wipe out from their minds the memories of the past—treating it as a terrible nightmare and look forward with single-minded purpose to make India strong, prosperous and happy. This can only be done by hard work. A Socialist Government in Britain is calling upon workers to sweat an hour more and a strange contrast here is that our Socialists and others are preaching strikes and encouraging wage-boots. This will only end up in a serious trouble.

I wish Pakistan all success and prosperity. I wish her to be strong because then alone could there be friendly relations and amity between the two States. India harbours no ill-will against Pakistan: and, indeed, it will do all in her power to help the new State.

I am sure all the Indian States will join Indian Union as none can afford to keep out and live in isolation. *First thing should be done first, and the first job is to get the States accede to the Union and consolidate it.* The demand of people in the States for a democratic regime raises an entirely different issue. I cannot see how an Indian ruler exists with his subjects in hostility and clamouring for popular government;

The Congress had pledged to rid the country of foreign domination and, after making considerable sacrifices and bearing prolonged sufferings, it has now succeeded. But the Congress has also strived for United India and a Union of all communities. Unfortunately, it could not lay claim to success on that count. This was due to factors beyond its control. *Their joy on August 15 would have been fuller and greater had not India been divided.*

I would make no efforts to explain away the responsibility of the Congress to divide the country. We took these extreme steps after great deliberation. *In spite of my previous strong opposition to partition, I agreed to it because I was convinced that in order to keep India united it must be divided now.*

My experience in office during the past year[1] showed that it was impossible to do anything constructive with the Muslim League in. *The League Representatives during their continuance in office did nothing but to create deadlocks and their role was entirely an obstructionist one.* Besides, I found that the Muslims, save for a few exceptions, engaged in all capacities in the Government, were with the Muslim League. Thus the riot that had set in could not be permitted to prolong any longer except at the risk of a disaster for the whole country. Indeed, at one stage, things had become so bad that with the killings at Calcutta[2] riots spread all over and it became a perilous adventure for Hindus and Muslims to visit one another's localities. The economic life of the country was paralysed and there was little security of life or property.

The only way out of the sickening situation, the Congress realised, lay in the elimination of the third party—the British Power. The British, on their part, declared that they would quit by June 1948. But the period was long. Also their Statement promising to hand over power to the authorities in the Provinces gave rise to a vigorous effort to dislodge the Ministries in Assam, the Punjab and the Frontier Province. The League succeeded[3] in the Punjab. Even though they failed in the Frontier Province and Assam, the League movement caused great misery and bloodshed.

In order to settle the issue immediately and prevent the slaughter of innocent people, the Congress decided to agree to the division of the country and demanded the partition of the Punjab and Bengal. This was no surrender to the League threats or the policy of appeasement.

Today the partition of India is a settled fact and yet it is an unreal fact; I hope, however, that partition would remove the poison from the body politic of India.

India is one and indivisible. One cannot divide a sea or split the running waters of a river. The Muslims have their roots in India. Their sacred places and their cultural centres are located in India. I do not know what would they do and it would not be long when they would like to return.

Despite the division, it must be remembered, we have 80 per cent of the country with us which is a compact unit with great potentialities.

The main task before India today is to consolidate herself into a well-knit and united power. The obstacle of foreign domination has gone but there are serious problems that confront us. economically, India is in a sad plight. The War has resulted in making India a creditor Nation[4] but that does not mean much. The United Kingdom is our debtor and owe us a huge amount. But they do not appear to have anything to pay us now. In fact, the Big Powers have so arranged their economies that smaller and poorer countries remain at a disadvantage.

The need of the hour is to increase the wealth of the country and this can only be done by putting in more and more work and thus increasing production. This necessitates preservation of peace in the country. For one year now, there has been disorder in the country. Now that Pakistan has been established, there should be no more fights between Hindus and Muslims. *If, unfortunately, there would be a recurrence of strife, it would not be the cowardly killings of innocent people, but it would be between two armies of the two States.*

I appeal to people not to indulge in mutual strifes but create a calm atmosphere and engage themselves in constructive activities essential for the building up of a new India.

With the exit of foreign power, the princes will have to adjust themselves to the democratic order. The days of those rulers who do not command the confidence of their subjects are numbered. The majority of the States have acceded[5] to the Union and I appeal to the rest to join the Union before August 15. The States which will not come in now, but might decide to join at a later date, would have to accede on different terms. These days no State can afford to live in isolation.

I should also warn the people to exercise reserve in judging the role of princes at the present juncture. The rulers were not free uptill now and many of them do not even now believe that Paramountcy is lapsing on August 15. Many of them are descendants of great and benevolent rulers of the past ages, and I have no doubt that they will have no hesitation in pursuing a correct policy and become popular rulers.

Essentially, our main problems are domestic. Ever since my release from prison,[6] I was saying that Imperialism was on its last legs not only in India but in all Asia. The British are quitting India and I hope that Dutch imperialism will also meet its end in Indonesia.

In future, there would not be any more separate electorates or weightages and special treatment. Every community must get what is its due.

India has nothing but goodwill towards all. But if her safety is endangered she must have strength to defend herself; and, for that, people must work hard.

1 When the Sardar was Home Member in the Interim Government from 2 September 1946 till the dawn of Independence.

2 This was an aftermath of Muslim League's "Direct Action Day" observance on 16 August 1946. It had resulted in unprecedented holocaust in Calcutta where on 16 August and four to five days onwards riot, murder, arson and pillage were the order of the day involving very heavy damage to life and property. According to a rough official estimate, nearly 5,000 lives were lost, over 15,000 persons were injured and about one hundred thousand were rendered homeless.

3 In Punjab after the fateful 1945-46 elections. Coalition Ministry consisting of Congress, the Unionist Muslims and the Akali Sikhs was formed under Khizr Hyat Khan's premiership. But due to Muslim League's disturbances during early part of 1947 Khizr Hyat Khan yielded and resigned thereby practically making a room for the Muslim League Ministry to come to power and sealing the fate of Punjab towards division. How horrible the situation then and afterwards in Punjab can be gauged from Sardar's Mussoorie Statement during May 1947: "In the present adverse circumstances, the minorities in Punjab must organise and adopt all possible means to defend themselves against organised acts of vandalism, arson and murder, etc."

4 On the eve of World War II, according to British calculations, India was a debtor country. During War, subject India having been made one of the major feeders to British war-effort, as per ex parte British accounting. India tilted the balance in her favour by £ 1,250 million showing indirectly how incalculably was India bled white to save England from ruin and devastation.

5 Except the States of Hyderabad, Junagadh and Kashmir.

6 On 15 June 1945 from Ahmednagar Fort where with other members of the Congress Working Committee the Sardar was detained since early August 1942.

86

Sardar Patel and Nehru Explain Issue of AICC Delegates Before Country Faced Partition or Balkanisation

Collected Works of Sardar Patel

BOMBAY CHRONICLE
16 June, 1947

(*Extract*)

The All India Congress Committee (A.I.C.C.) passed the

resolution accepting His Majesty's Government (H.M.G's) June 3 statement by 157 votes to 29.

Two hundred and eighteen members were present and 23 members did not vote.

Pandit Jawaharlal Nehru and Sardar Vallabhbhai Patel wound up the debate on the resolution which lasted nearly eight and a half hours. Both Pandit Nehru and Sardar Patel bluntly told the Committee that the alternative before the Committee was either to accept Partition or to be faced with complete Balkanisation and anarchy.

Both leaders declared that today there was no responsible authority in India to maintain order. Their first concern should be the establishment of a stable Government in India which could ensure peace and progress... .

Swami Sahajanand, the Bihar Kisan Leader, opposing the resolution, said that the Congress had always said that it would be no party to a division of the country and it would not use force to keep within the Indian Union any unwilling part. The present resolution, however, put a premium on division. The British could do what they liked, but the Congress could not "cut up a living body", for India was not yet dead. "There would not be just two parts of India but many more. Since Mr. Churchill had agreed to this Plan, and he was no friend of India, there was bound to be something sinister about the Plan".

Mr. Sudhir Chandra Roy, supporting the resolution, said that undoubtedly a United India would have been the best solution. But was that possible when a section of their country-men was bent upon secession? Speaking as a Bengalee, he preferred the present Plan to the May 16 statement under which the whole of Bengal would have come under group "B". The situation in Bengal was such that a solution of the problem could not brook any delay. He, therefore, accepted the June 3 statement.

Mr. Ansar Harwani opposed the resolution. It was

surrender to Mr. Jinnah's obstinacy. The situation, he said, was identical with the situation of Britain in 1939, when Mr. Chamberlain had adopted a policy of appeasement.

Mrs. Aruna Asaf Ali, President of the Delhi Provincial Congress Committee, said that some of those who were vigorously opposing the resolution today had on all previous occasions accepted the decision of the Working Committee. They forgot, however, that the resolution that was before them was the logical consequence of those earlier resolutions to which they had associated. The Socialists, she said, did not oppose the Working Committee decisions just for the sake of opposition but because they had known that the British were planning to shake the revolutionary urge in India.

The present situation was created as a result of joint conspiracy between Mr. Jinnah, Mr. Churchill and Mr. Amrey.

The Congress had expressed its readiness to accept Dominion Status, but this was a far cry from the Congress' demand of complete independence for the whole of India. India had been caught in the British trap. She said that she would have agreed to Pakistan if it could solve the present problem; but unfortunately it did not put an end to communal strife in the country, and at the same time divided the country into two. Concluding, Mrs. Asaf Ali said that she would ask them to vote one way or another. They must exercise their own judgement.

Pandit Jawaharlal Nehru and Sardar Vallabhbhai Patel then addressed the Committee.

Pandit Govind Ballabh Pant then wound up the debate and the A.I.C.C. carried the resolution of the Working Committee by 157 votes to 29. On the first count the votes were 153 for and 29 against, but after a recount the President Acharya Kripalani announced that the resolution had been carried by 157 votes to 29... .

87

Sardar Patel to Gandhiji on Difficulties Created by League, Communists and Socialists

Collected Works of Sardar Patel

Sardar Shrino Patro

NEW DELHI
1 February, 1947

(Extract)

REVERED BAPPU,

Received your letter dated 24th.

League is now on warpath.[1] Let us see what happens. It appears that kings are not going to behave well. Here many a time your advice is needed, but what can be done? We are doing what we thing proper, but difficulties are mounting... .

May God save us.

Your health might be good.

VALLABHBHAI'S PRANAM

Mahatma Gandhi

1 Members of Muslim League had joined Interim Government, but they were not taking part in the deliberations of constituent assembly.

88

Pandit Nehru Defends Acceptance of Partition

Collected Works of Sardar Patel

BOMBAY CHRONICLE
16 June, 1947

The Congress, Pandit Nehru declared, could not afford to act in an irresponsible manner by passing high-sounding resolutions. A responsible body must not think in terms of today only, but there was a tomorrow and a day after that. It would be ridiculous to suggest that the British do everything before they quitted. The June 3 statement, he said, could not have come about had there been no agreement. It was not like one of those old decisions of the British Government which they could accept or reject. The acceptance for which he was wholly responsible, did not mean that he agreed to every word in the statement, but he agreed with the fundamental principles therein.

The riots in Rawalpindi, Multan, Amritsar, Calcutta, Noakhali, Bihar and elsewhere, Pandit Nehru said, presented the situation in a different light. To suggest that the Congress Working Committee took fright and therefore "surrendered" was wrong. But it was correct to say that they were very much disturbed at the prevailing madness. Homesteads burnt, women and children murdered and why, he asked, were all these tragic and brutal things happening? They could have checked them by resorting to the sword and the lathi, but would that solve the problem? Some people from the Punjab had said that the Congress had let them down. What he to do? Should he send an army? He was bitter and India's heart was broken. The victims in Rawalpindi said that they were being killed in order that the League might rule. The wound, he said, must be healed. With whatever they were able to salvage, they must plan out a programme on the basis of partition.

It was sufficient for the House to compare what happened in Noakhali and Calcutta and again what happened in Bihar. By supreme efforts the Congress was able to control the situation in Bihar but they could do nothing in the Punjab. Why did such things happen in the Punjab and why was the Khizr Ministry broken and how was it that no one seemed to be capable of controlling the Punjab disturbances? The answer was patent.

The Congress Working Committee passed a resolution in favour of the partition of the Punjab into two administrative provinces. *Partition was better than murder of innocent citizens*. After the resolution was passed, the Committee received numerous complaints from Bengal that Bengal also should be divided. The underlying principle in the case of the Punjab and Bengal was one and the same.

Pandit Nehru repudiated the allegation that he and two others decided the fate of millions. The Bengal Provincial Congress Committee and other responsible organisations in the province strongly supported the partition proposal.

The next question that arose was, having divided the Punjab and Bengal, had the Congress abandoned the Sikhs and the Hindus? An answer should be found. By high-sounding resolutions the Congress would not be able to help them. Even when the Punjab was one they were not able to help the people. An answer to this problem would no doubt be found. However, there was no reason why the minorities there should be tyrannised and persecuted. There might be individual cases of rioting, but there was not much room in future for organised attacks on the minorities. He had nothing much to say about Sind and so far as Sylhet was concerned, there was to be a referendum and he could not forecast the result. He was much worried about the N.W.F.P. If Bengal and the Punjab went out, the Frontier would be isolated. The question was now the subject of consultation between the Committee and the Frontier leaders.

Deploring the disturbances in the country, Pandit Nehru reiterated that Governmental authority had almost collapsed. The British were no longer interested because they were leaving. This probably explained why some officers asked the victims who came to them for help to go to him (Nehru) or Sardar Patel for help. They were not desirous of shouldering any further responsibility and many had become callous.

Stating that any controversy over the question of Dominion Status versus Independence was meaningless, Pandit Nehru said that what the Congress demanded was that the Government should function as a Dominion Government and Conventions must be established. The acceptance of

Dominion Status was without prejudice to the Republic Resolution adopted by the Constituent Assembly. But the composition of the present Government was such that no agreement could work and no Convention could be established and the Viceroy, therefore, suggested the June 3 statement and the Congress accepted it.

Pandit Nehru said that all talk of Pakistan and Hindustan was due to misunderstanding. Both from practical and legal points of view India as an entity continued to exist except that certain provinces and parts of certain provinces now sought to secede. The seceding areas were free to have any relations they liked with Foreign Powers. The Government of India was intact and there should be no further confusion of Hindustan and Pakistan and people should not allow such ideas to grow.

The present, perhaps, Pandit Nehru said, is the most difficult period full of trials and tribulations. Today, we have to shoulder responsibility. The first thing we have to do is to establish the independence of India firmly and set up a strong Central Government. Having established a strong and stable Government all other programmes will not create much difficulty. The Congress has a heavy responsibility. You must bend all your energies to strengthen the Congress organisation. We have to face dangers, both external and internal, and if we are not strong we will go down.

Concluding, Pandit Nehru made a passing reference to the Indian States. He said he would have something to say on the subject when the next resolution came up for discussion. However, he was confident that the Congress would be able to deal with and solve the problem of the States. And if they proceeded on the right lines the seceding provinces would also rejoin the Union.

He asked the A.I.C.C. not to vote for the resolution out of any sympathy for the Working Committee but they must do so out of conviction.

89

Sardar Patel Pleads with AICC Delegates to Accept June 3 Plan

Collected Works of Sardar Patel

BOMBAY CHRONICLE
16 June, 1947

Following Pandit Nehru, Sardar Vallabhbhai Patel, in a vigorous speech, at the All India Congress Committee this afternoon, extended his full support to H.M.G's Statement of June 3. Looking at the Cabinet Mission's proposals, today, in the light of his experience in the Interim Government during the last nine months, he was not at all sorry that the State Paper had gone. Had they accepted the State Paper, the whole of India would have gone the Pakistan way. To-day, they had 75 to 80 per cent of India, which they could develop according to their genius and make it strong. The League could develop the rest of the country.

The League Council, which met in camera, evidently nursed the ambition to capture the whole of India after August 15. It was the duty of every Congressman to work unitedly to make India strong, to build up an efficient army and strengthen her economic position.

The House had listened to their leader Pandit Nehru. Never in the history of the Congress before the All-India Congress Committee had to take a decision on such an important issue. He fully appreciated the apprehensions of his brothers from Sind and Punjab. Nobody liked the division of India, and his heart was heavy. But there were stark realities of which they should take notice of. The choice was whether there should be just one division or many divisions. The fight to-day was not against the British. The British have no desire to stay on in India, and if they wished to stay, they desired to do so only with India's consent. And definitely they had no desire to govern this country.

The May 16 Plan, Sardar Patel said, no doubt gave to them united India. The Congress agreed to it in spite of its shortcomings. But there was a snag in it. The Plan could not be executed if one or the other party withheld co-operation. Thus the State Paper was in the nature of an imposed award. But the position to-day was different. The Congress must face facts. It could not give way to emotionalism and sentimentality. They must coolly assess the pros and cons and arrive at a deliberate decision.

Sardar Patel denied that the Working Committee accepted the Plan out of fear. We had never known fear. He deeply regretted the many massacres. In one family of 33, there were two survivors. Many were maimed and disabled for life. They had gone through all that. But he was afraid of one thing, and that was that all their toils and hard work these many years should not go waste or prove unfruitful. They worked for independence, and they should see as large a part of this country as possible become free and strong. Otherwise there would be neither "Akhand Hindustan" nor Pakistan. Further by taking any course other than the one which the Working Committee had suggested, would not only be injurious, but would also make the Congress the laughing stock of the world. Here was a chance for India to attain her independence. Was she going to throw it away? It would be incorrect to say—first let the British go away, then all questions could be solved. How were they to be solved and what would happen afterwards?

His nine months in office, Sardar Patel said, had completely disillusioned him of the supposed merits of the State Paper. He had noticed that Muslim officials, right from the top down to the Chaprasis, except for a few honourable exceptions, were all for the Muslim League. There should be no mistake about it. Mutual recriminations and allegations were the order of the day. He had watched it for nine months. The police had fired and people told him that the 'Meos' did it. What could he do or what could he say, under the circumstances?

The May 16 Plan was gone and he was glad. That Plan left much room for conflict and bickerings. The Congress was opposed to Pakistan, but yet the resolution before the House accented partition. Whether the All India Congress Committee liked it or not there was already Pakistan in action, both in the Punjab and in Bengal. Under the circumstances he would prefer real Pakistan because then they would have some sense of responsibility.

Under the State Paper the whole of India would have been subjected to an intolerable situation. The communal veto, which was given to the League, would have arrested our progress at every state. The majority would have to stand and look on and they would have been able to do nothing in the administration. But now they had a chance. They could eradicate the plague of communalism, weightage, etc. which existed in no other Constitution in the world. Now no more weightages. They (League) said that they required corridor, and there was an outcry elsewhere. By shouting back, no problem could be solved. What was required was silence and hard work.

Sardar Patel sympathised with the minority in Sind. But mere sympathy without power was no good. They must build up strength.

He would appeal to Congressmen in general to be prepared to shoulder responsibilities. Internal wranglings would weaken the country.

At first the British said that they would withdraw by June 1948. It was felt that the intervening period was too long. Now they were going away on August 15 and even this intervening period was too long. The continuance of the present situation each day injured the country.

There should be complete unity, and there was no room for groups in the Congress. He would invite the opposing groups to join them and share the responsibility for the good governance and progress of their country. Always sitting in the opposition and disagreeing led to dangerous habits.

Sardar Patel said that they had now a great opportunity to develop over the three-fourths of India. They had not much time to waste. There was food shortage. There was labour unrest. In Multan food and cloth had been burnt. He had been told that for another four years we could not expect any import of textiles and if so even the small ration of 12 yards per head could not be kept up. Conditions were such that everyone should apply himself to his work energetically. He had heard many complaints against the Congress. The criticism should be met.

Freedom was coming. Congressmen should work hard to make that freedom a living thing and to make India strong. They might have a five-year plan and work to schedule. They must build up industries. They must build up the army, make it strong and efficient. It would serve no purpose indulging in vague criticism of the Congress. Nor would it do as was the case with the Communists, who alternately backed the British and then the League, to denounce the Congress. The Working Committee had not placed the resolution before the All India Congress Committee in a light-hearted manner but did so with a clear conscience (cheers).

On the question of Indian States, Sardar Patel referred to Travancore and said he would like to know how that State could become a Sovereign State. Probably the statesmen who made declarations of independence and sovereignty did not understand the implications of those terms. So long as the Congress continued to have a foothold in Travancore there was no question of "independence and sovereignty".

90

Sardar Patel's Reports on Minorities and Fundamental Rights Highly Applauded by All Sections of Constituent Assembly

Collected Works of Sardar Patel

BOMBAY CHRONICLE
28 August, 1947

(*Extract*)

Sardar Vallabhbhai Patel, Chairman of the Advisory Committee on Minorities, Fundamental Rights, etc., submitting the reports of the committees to the Constituent Assembly, today congratulated the various minorities who had taken a correct perspective of the problems and helped in arriving at unanimous conclusions on many items... .

...The Committee had taken into consideration the points of view, sentiments and feelings of the minorities, big and small, and as far as possible tried to meet their wishes... .

On the question of weightage they had agreed that there should be no weightage and the various communities should be represented according to the proportion of their population. They had thought it fit to agree to reservation of seats, in proportion to the population of minorities. Some of the minorities had gladly surrendered their rights. They desired neither separate electorates nor reservation and wanted to merge into the Nation and stand on their own legs. He congratulated those who had taken that stand and sympathised with those who wanted to be statutorily helped. The question of representation in public services had also been amicably settled.

It was proposed, the Sardar went on to say, to provide some sort of an administrative machinery to see that whatever safeguards provided were given effect to and continuous vigilance was kept to see the safeguards were given proper effect... .

...Sardar referred to the position of the Anglo-Indians. That community at present enjoyed certain privileges and concessions... . These grants would be continued to be given, but progressively decreased till such time they were able to stand on their own legs. In view of the numerical smallness of the community no provision could be made to reserve seats for them in the Legislatures... .

...In regard to the Parsis they had voluntarily abandoned any claims for concessions. Though small, the Parsis were a very powerful community and perhaps most wise... . Sardar Patel congratulated the Parsi community for the stand they had taken.

The Christian community had agreed to have reservation according to their population and abandoned the claim to separate electorates or other concessions... .

There remained, however, Sardar Patel said, one matter of controversy and that was on behalf of the Muslim League and the Scheduled Castes. A point was raised that members of those communities should poll certain percentage of votes of their community to be declared successful in the elections. The matter was discussed and the Advisory Committee rejected the suggestion by a large majority.

Sardar Patel then presented the reports.

Mr. Panjabrao Deshmukh congratulated the framers of the reports on doing away with separate electorates and weightage for minorities. They had, in the past, barred all progress. The term minorities itself was a British creation which has succeeded in dividing the country... .

Separate electorates were the creation of the British to divide Hindus and Muslims who fought shoulder to shoulder in 1857 to gain their independence.

Mr. Ayyangar made a fervent plea to Muslims to join with the other communities in creating a secular state. The result of granting separate electorates would be the creation of small

Pakistan in each village. On the other hand, if they had joint electorates with reservation of seats, the different communities would have to come together... .

Despite the creation of Pakistan, there were still Hindus and Muslims living in both States. There had been too much talk in the past of treating the Muslims in India as aliens and Hindus "in Pakistan as aliens." Would separate electorates further encourage those separatist tendencies or would they discourage them?... .

Replying to the debates, Sardar Patel said he was surprised that there should have been such a debate on the motion.....

His mind went back to those days when the question of separate electorates was first discussed. Many eminent Muslims had recorded their view that communal electorates were a serious flaw in the body politics. Many Englishmen had also admitted that the country had to be partitioned today because of separate electorates.

Sardar Patel said: "When Pakistan was conceded, at least it was assumed there will be one Nation in the rest of India and that there will be no attempt to thrust the Two-Nation Theory here. It is no use saying, we shall ask for separate electorates but will abide by your decision. We have heard this for many years and the result of this agitation was, they said, separate electorates or anything else were not sufficient for their protection. Therefore, they demanded a separate State. We said, "Alright, take it, but for the rest 80 per cent India you agree there shall be One Nation".

"Do you still want there should be Two Nations? Will you show one free nation which has a religious basis? If this unfortunate country is to be again oppressed by this, even after its division then woe betide it. It is not worth living for.

91

Sardar Patel to Bozman Hoping Pakistan Might Return to India

Collected Works of Sardar Patel

SARDAR'S LETTERS MOSTLY UNKNOWN
NEW DELHI
11 July, 1947

(Extract)

MY DEAR BOZMAN,

Thank you for your letter of 1st July, 1947... .

......

I fully appreciate your reasons for disliking the decision to divide India. Frankly speaking, we all hate it but at the same time see no way out of it. We nurse the hope that one day Pakistan will come back to us... .

Yours Sincerely,
VALLABHBHAI PATEL

G.S. Bozman, Esq., C.S.I., C.I.E., I.C.S., Ridgway Road, Kettering, England.

92

Sardar Patel's Call to the Youth to Serve the Nation—At the Special Convocation of Banaras Hindu University on 25 November, 1948

Collected Works of Sardar

(*Extract*)

(Nothing was of so much importance to Sardar as the realisation by the youth and the people of the paramount needs of the resurging India. It was his very earnest call to the youth of his time that they should so build themselves, in character and vision, as to be mighty instruments of service to nation.

This call of the departing father reverberates again and again in this unique address to students of Benaras Hindu University at its special Convocation on 25 November, 1948)... .

I agree with your Vice-Chancellor that here came[1] one and the sole leader of our Independence Movement, viz. Gandhiji. It was his austerity and his *tapasya* (Penance) that brought us this gift of freedom. I claim to be nothing more than an obedient soldier of him like the millions who obeyed his call. *There was a time when everyone used to call me his blind follower, but both I and he knew that I followed him because our convictions tallied.* I am not one given to debates and verbal disputes. I hate prolonged discussions. *For several years, Gandhiji and I were in perfect agreement. Mostly, we agreed instinctively; but when the time for a big decision on the question of India's Independence came we differed.* I felt that we had to take Independence there and then. We had, therefore, to agree to partition. I came to this conclusion after a great deal of heart-searching and with great deal of sorrow. But I felt that if we did not accept partition, India would be split into many bits and completely ruined. My experience of office of one year[2] had convinced me that the way we were proceeding we were heading for disaster. *Gandhiji felt that he could not agree with this conclusion. But he told me that if my heart bore testimony to the rightness of my convictions, I could go ahead.* Our leader whom he nominated as his heir and successor[3] was with me. Gandhiji did not oppose us nor did he consent to what we thought was right and proper. Even today I do not repent for having come to that decision, though it was with a great wrench of the heart that we did so.

We undoubtedly made some mistakes. Its responsibility attaches to some people; but I do not wish to enter into those details. I am convinced that the decision we took was to the nation's benefit. People do not know what would have happened if we had not accepted partition. At the same time, we were convinced that partition was worth accepting only if the foreign power quitted as quickly as possible. We, therefore, made it condition that we would accept the partition of the country if the British left in six or eight weeks' time. The pace at which the legislation[4] was passed and the unanimity behind it in the British Parliament were probably a record in British history... .

India today is one and united. There is no question now of any foreign pockets... .

But unity and integration are not enough... .

India's freedom is only a year old. We have to nurse and nourish it. We have to devote proper care and attention for its growth When India attains proper place in the comity of nations and has peace, tranquillity and contentment, you may have some leisure for your fancies... .

If Pakistan goes its own way and becomes a theocratic State, ours is not that way. *While protecting our religion, we have to follow the path whereby we can protect all creeds and religions.* Let us not get involved in communal wrangles. But, at the same time, we should guard ourselves against any danger to our national existence... .

1 Sardar here refers to Gandhiji's visit to Benaras Hindu University on 4 February 1916 at its opening ceremony when Gandhiji had delivered a speech that had irked Dr. Annie Besant and many among the Princely Order for his pungent remarks on India's crushing poverty amidst that pomp and glory.
2 In the Interim Government
3 Shri Jawaharlal Nehru.
4 Indian Independence Legislation, 1947.

93

Sardar Patel on Economic Situation in India

Collected Works of Sardar Patel

IN TUNE WITH THE MILLIONS

5 January, 1948

(Extract)

(Sardar's was a very pragmatic approach to economic affairs

of the country. But it was imbued with humanism and urgency of the time. More production and equitable distribution were the sheet-anchor of his economic policy and with a fair deal to all instruments of production, Sardar with his robust enthusiasm and prodigious zeal was applying himself wholeheartedly to the work of economic reconstruction of the land with the same doggedness and spirit as he had applied himself in solving the problem of States. This speech which the Sardar gave at the luncheon party at Calcutta on 5 January 1948, may be termed as one of his major speeches on the subject. True, it is that the Government of India's economic policy was then in evolution but as far as the Sardar was concerned he was wielding his mighty influence in welding Labour, Capital and Government to ensure plentiful production in the shortest time possible to give relief and succour to the common man and make him feel the glow of Swaraj:)... .

You have asked: Why did we accept partition? It is a long story, but you should be able to appreciate matters better because Calcutta had tasted the bitter experience of the League Ministry. Businessmen thought of leaving the city, but I advised them to stay on because I was certain that no power on earth could take away Calcutta from India. Although, therefore, we all have to suffer the blow and shock of partition, if we are able to extract good out of evil, I have no doubt that we shall eventually gain and not lose in the transaction.

We have now to settle down to the task of reconstruction. *In the last few months we have had to shoulder a burden that would have broken the back of any government; but we have been able to acquit ourselves creditably in dealing with this critical time... .*

94

Not an Inch of Kashmir Will Be Yielded: Sardar Patel Assures People of Bengal

Collected Works of Sardar Patel

THE HINDUSTAN TIMES
5 January, 1948

(*Extract*)

Addressing a mammoth gathering on the Calcutta maidan, India's Deputy Prime Minister, Sardar Patel, made an impassioned appeal to the people for patience and forbearance... .

He added: "We adhere to the principle of referendum, but if a decision is sought to be made by force, we have no alternative then to reply to the same with force. Anyway, even an inch of Kashmir will not be yielded. India wanted to be liberal in settling affairs with Pakistan and wanted to live and let live. But if Pakistan wanted to shell India with the money received from India, it could not be allowed."

......

Expressing his deep-felt sympathy with the people of Bengal in the affliction which the separation of East and West Bengal had brought about, he said: "We have all been deeply affected by it, but it is profitless now to go into the question as to why we accepted it. Our main task is and should be to extract good out of evil".

There was no reason why despite partition there should be a wall of hostility between East and West Bengal... .

Sardar Patel continued that even though they were overwhelmed by the disturbances after the Independence Day, they had accomplished a great deal. They had carried out successfully and effectively separation of armed services, stores—both civil and military, and of many other large undertakings incidental to partition.

They had settled all this out of court and in addition they had carried out an exchange of 40 to 50 lakhs of people on each side. Any Government in the world would have been overwhelmed by such tremendous responsibilities, but they had weathered the storm and turned the corner.

If they reflected on the condition of India today, Sardar Patel said, they would realise how critical the position was. India was short of food and had to pay a heavy price for imports to make up the deficiency. If they had to digest freedom they had to have a strong army which involved considerable equipment for the three services—Army, Navy and Air Force.

......

Describing the critical situation which faced India today, Sardar Patel said that the country was saved from fragmentation by the accession of States... .

Criticising those who unnecessarily brought in the controversy of a secular versus Hindu State, Sardar Patel emphasised that there could be no serious talk of a Hindu State. But one fact was indisputable. There were 4.5 crores of Muslims in India, many of whom had helped the creation of Pakistan. How could one believe that they would change overnight?

The Muslims said that they were loyal citizens and, therefore, why should anybody doubt their bona fides? To them we would say: "Why do you ask us, search your own conscience".

Emphasising that India only wished to be left alone, Sardar Patel said: I would tell Pakistan, you have now got Pakistan. I wish you enjoy it. It is only when your teeth are soured that you need come back to us. You make Pakistan a heaven on earth. We ourselves welcome it, after all we shall also benefit from it".

......

"I can tell you this, if we had not accepted partition, India would have fallen into bits. Now that we have been able to salvage a major part of India and have been able to build it

up into an extensive single unit, let us make it powerful. If we become prosperous and powerful, I have no doubt that small bits of territory round India would themselves seek our shelter.

"If young men behave with discipline and if we unite our ranks we shall certainly achieve that destiny. The world is looking to us to see how we avail ourselves of our hard-won freedom. Let us not do anything which will make us hang our heads in shame. Instead, let us act in a manner which will not only rehabilitate the prestige and reputation which we have lost by the recent unfortunate events, but also enhance it and carve out for India a glorious place in the comity of nations".

95

Sardar Patel Appeals to Muslims to Give Their Loyalty to India

Collected Works of Sardar Patel

IN TUNE WITH THE MILLIONS
6 January, 1948

(Nowhere did the Sardar speak so candidly to the Muslim Community as in his famous speech at Lucknow before a vast assemblage of men and women on 6 January 1948. To Muslims, he then earnestly appealed that they must give practical proof of their loyalty to Mother India and not keep themselves unconcerned and away from issues concerning the vital interests of the soil of their birth. In no case should they seek to ride on two horses was his friendly warning and the truest of advice to them. Alas? such a candid telling had proven a bitter pill for some of the so-called nationalist Muslim Leaders of the day; and, principally, it was they who had sought to malign the Sardar in Press and even mislead the Mahatma on this fundamental aspect of Sardar's approach to communal harmony and peace:)

I am a true friend of Muslims although I am dubbed as their greatest enemy. I believe in plain-speaking. I do not know how to mince matters. I want to tell them frankly that mere declarations of loyalty to the Indian Union will not help them at this critical juncture. They must give practicable proofs of their declarations.

The ever-vacillating, indecisive and non-committal attitude of Pakistan must change in her own interests. The Junagadh and Kashmir incidents have brought their evil intentions to the fore. If they seek to split the rest of India too, let them say it boldly and let us decide the issue in open field.

The carvation of Pakistan is being hailed as a heaven for Muslims. We should be glad if they indeed make a heaven of it. But they must realise that the enemies of Pakistan are within Pakistan itself and not outside. If Pakistan collapsed, she would collapse by her own sins and follies.

Today my mind turns back to those days when, in this city of Lucknow, the foundation of the "two-nation theory" was laid. It was said that the Muslim culture and traditions were not akin to those of Hindus. They were a separate nation. Muslims of this city played an important role in fanning this theory. A few nationalist Muslims protested against it. They made common cause with the Hindus because both of them were perturbed at the advocacy of such a theory and raised their voice against it. But my Muslim League friends made a strong plea for separation. They said that they were not satisfied with separate electorate and with the safeguard of the minority rights. They only wanted separation and establishment of a separate State. Throughout the breadth and length of India the Muslim Leaguers spread this doctrine of separation. To a major part, the Muslim youth also came under their influence. They accepted it as the whole truth.

In Calcutta, on August 15, they launched a "Direct Action" movement to give a direct blow to those who still did not believe in the "two-nation-theory". We then thought if there was to be a division of the country, let it be divided. Let them manage their own affairs and we will manage our own. We were then facing the problem of getting rid of the alien rule. So we accepted the division of the country.

I will be happy if Pakistan becomes strong, happy and prosperous. But I wonder if even after separation we shall have a breathing time. It is said that plans for sabotaging Pakistan are being hatched in Hindustan. But I would assure you that plans for nullifying Pakistan are being hatched in Pakistan itself. It is the ugly situation in Pakistan that ultimately will ruin it. Sometimes, they lay blame on the Hindus, sometimes, on the Sikhs and, sometimes, on the Central Government for creating troubles. But I must tell you that if Pakistan falls, it will not fall on our score but due to her enemies within.

The Muslim Leaguers call me as their greatest enemy. Formerly, they used to call Mahatma Gandhi as their enemy number one. Now they think of Gandhiji as their friend and have substituted me in his place for I speak the truth. They believed that if they had Pakistan they would ensure full protection to Muslims. But have they ever thought of Muslims living in India? Have they ever sympathised with them?

No sooner did we attain freedom than came the massacre in Punjab and that lowered our prestige abroad. Then came the Junagadh issue quickly followed by the issue of Kashmir. We took up this issue with Pakistan. But they replied: "We are not concerned? It is the Azad Government in Kashmir and the Kashmiri Muslims who were responsible for the aggression". But it is no secret that the Frontier tribesmen were having their rations, war material, motor-trucks and the petrol, etc. from Pakistan itself.

Only as a last resort Indian Government referred the issue to UNO. But Mr. Zafrullah Khan[1] says: "Why did we take to washing the dirty linen outside"? But are they not satisfied with washing their dirt in the Punjab during the last four months? It was a deliberate lie.

To Indian Muslims, I want to ask only one question. In the recent All India Muslim Conference,[2] why did they not open their mouths on the Kashmir issue? Why did you not condemn the action of Pakistan? These things create doubts in the minds of people. So, *as a friend of Muslims, I want to say a word and it is the duty of a good friend to speak frankly. It is your duty now to sail in the same boat and sink or swim together. I want to tell you very frankly that you cannot ride on two horses. Select one horse whichever you like best.* Those who want to go to Pakistan can go there and live in peace; let us live here in peace to work for ourselves.

The Muslim League Government in Pakistan professed that they would make suitable arrangements for the minorities there. But ask the Sindh refugees today? They say it is impossible to remain there. Pakistan is drifting towards lawlessness. If they want to fight with us we have men, material and resources too. Pakistan is a baby of yesterday.

I see there is an urge among the youth for military training. Military training is a good thing and there is a need for it. I appeal to young men to unify India from all sides. Let them not forget that India came to ruin because of her own stupidity. Let us not repeat that folly in future.

If the problem of States had not been handled properly, there would have been *Rajasthans* in the body politic of India. As soon as Paramountcy lapsed, I came in touch with the *rajas*. I explained to them the present political situation. I also carried home to them that it was only due to our internal squabbles that India lost her freedom. I am happy that they have understood me.

To critics, I would like to say that since August 15 when we took over charge of the Government we have been able to do an enormous amount of work. What about the work relating to partition setting at naught the steelframe of bureaucracy, the division of assests and liabilities and the stupendous refugee problem? I am sure that if such a burden would have fallen all of a sudden on any government, it would have cracked under its weight. But we proved equal to the task. As a matter of fact, the manner in which we have discharged our duties has raised our prestige in the world.

For the reconstruction of India, only two things are the needs of the time. A strong Central Government and a formidable army. By army I mean all its branches—Naval, Air and Land forces. For a strong army, industries for the production of necessary material are absolutely necessary. So if there is labour unrest, strong and formidable army cannot be built up. Unless we produce more how can we share the profits; India is not an industrial country. She has to be industrialised first.

1 Pakistan's Foreign Minister, then representing Pakistan's case about Kashmir in the UNO.
2 At Lucknow, which was held only a couple of. days prior to Sardar's delivering this famous speech.

96

Consolidation of India Our Primary Interest After Partition: Sardar Patel

Collected Works of Sardar Patel

THE HINDUSTAN TIMES
22 January, 1948

(*Extract*)

Sardar Vallabhbhai Patel, India's Deputy Prime Minister, addressing a mammoth meeting at Ahmedabad, emphasised that the two bare essentials for preserving the hard-won freedom of India... .

...The division of the country, which was agreed upon as a condition precedent to the attainment of freedom, brought with it many serious problems, especially in the Punjab and Bengal.

The position of communalism grew in intensity and thousands of innocent men, women and children were either killed or thrown out of their homes. That besmirched the fair name of India and the reputation which free India should have earned was lost.

Peace had been established, Sardar Patel said, only with the help of police and military. There was, however, lurking suspicion and distrust in the minds of the people. That was why Mahatma Gandhi went on a fast. Gandhiji felt that there was no real peace in the hearts and the so-called peace was only through the police. Gandhiji's fasts had always produced good results.

Sardar Patel said that they accepted Pakistan—division of the country—deliberately in the belief that it was a lesser evil. Now that it had become an established fact, they should not act in a way which would worsen the relations between the two Dominions. He was charged by the Premier of Pakistan with attempting to sabotage Pakistan. He wanted to assure the authorities of Pakistan that the Government of India desired peace and prosperity for Pakistan and would do everything to make that Dominion strong and happy, because that was to the advantage of both. The Government of India had shown generosity on every issue arising out of the division of the country. It had been appreciated by all impartial observers.

Sardar Patel emphasised that the Muslims of India should have no cause for mistrust or suspicion. Peace was necessary for the rehabilitation and all-round progress of the country. If the fruits of Swaraj were to be enjoyed to the full there should be no recourse to police and military.

97

India's Tribute to Sardar Patel on His 74th Birthday

Collected Works of Sardar Patel

IN TUNE WITH THE MILLIONS
30 October, 1948

(*Extract*)

(This candid and invigorating speech of the Sardar on 30 October 1948 at Bombay, when he, as a man of Destiny, was being felicitated with unusual warmth and feelings by the Bombay citizens on the eve of his 74th birthday, indeed surveys the Indian political and economic scene of 1947-48 with an eye of a juror keeping ever before him the larger goals of the country with a rare determination to reach them within his little left lifetime itself, fills us with amazement about the unfathomable and versatile capacity of the Sardar to fill in the leeway of the ages.)

......

You know what India had to put up with in the course of one year. We had to pass through many difficult and critical times. Sometimes, day and night, we were anxious and apprehensive lest we make a slip which might spell disaster to India. Many were there who did not expect or believe that we could survive. When I accepted partition, in a sense, I was unwilling and was full of sorrow. *It went against the grain of all my innermost feelings, against all we had to live for, and against all we had aspired*, but in another sense, we accepted partition willingly and after a full weighment of its consequences. We felt that if we could not remain united we must part. We could not have secured India's freedom by any other means. If we had not partitioned India, the consequences of what would have followed would have been much worse than what actually took place as a result of partition. At that time, we were quarrelling and fighting bitterly amongst ourselves. The third party[1] was reaping the full benefits out of the dilemma in which we were placed and out of the situation in which we had landed ourselves. We had to pay the price for our liberty. It was then we decided that, if the foreign government undertook to leave as soon as possible, the price of partition was worth paying for. *We suffered grievously as a result of partition. A limb was torn as under and we bled profusely*. But it was nothing as compared to the troubles that would have been in store for us and with which we would have had to put up. I have, therefore, no regrets for accepting partition. My experience of Government had convinced me that if we went on like the way we were carrying on, we would lose everything that we held precious.

The leaders of Pakistan who called it "moth-eaten Pakistan" accepted partition with mental reservations. *We know that their motives were bad and that they were prepared to practise bad faith on us. We realised that if it was so and they were minded to invade India at a suitable opportunity, we should be fully prepared to meet the contingency.* We know that just as in securing Pakistan outside elements were with them, they were with them also in the nefarious designs they harboured. *Integration and unity, therefore, became our first essential.*

At the time India was partitioned, it was part of the settlement that paramountcy would lapse and that the rulers would be free to enter into new relationship or to keep aloof. But nobody could have been so innocent or ignorant to presume that overnight small rulers could be converted into "Their Majesties." That position would have been so full of dangerous possibilities and potentialities that we would not have been a willing party to it. It was at this time that several rulers, led by patriotic and good intentions, decided to cast their lot with us. Even those who had striven to remain outside were finally converted, some of them even at the last moment. Three States alone remained outside—Junagadh, Hyderabad and Kashmir, and it was in these States that Pakistan found an opportunity to intervene. We warned them not to intervene in our domestic matters like thieves and dacoits, but they did not heed us.

......

There were forces in England also ranged against us and secretly planning for a reference of the dispute to the UNO.[2] There were negotiations about the sale of Goa. There was constant smuggling of arms to Hyderabad... . *But we shall not put up with any interference in domestic matters, even if it involved the end of India, the end of Pakistan and the end of the world.*

One thing is clear. *We shall do what the interest of the people of Hyderabad demand and what they themselves desire... . This is a domestic matter and we will not tolerate any interference from Churchill or men greater than he.*

They say we should remain in the Commonwealth. We will

decide that question in accordance with the best interests of India. *If Churchill feels he alone can defend us let him remain in that Fool's Paradise.*[3] *Let him first try to defend England. Today truth, love and justice alone can save the world.* The world cannot bear a third war. Churchill's way is the way of ruin... .

......

We have made India one, but it has to be strong and united. We have to lay strong foundations of peace, tranquillity and good government... .

1 The alien rule.

2 It was practically from June 1948, after his last-ditch unsuccessful efforts to seek a solution to Hyderabad issue through Lord Mountbatten that Nizam with his friends in England was preparing his case for UNO and Churchill's indictments against India during June and July on the floor of the House of Commons were in fact a preparatory move to bolster Nizam's case against India in the UN Forum. But in spite of Nizam's references to Security Council during July-August 1947 the matter, in real sense, came to be discussed on 15th September 1947 when Indian Army troops were already converging on Secunderabad from West and East. But this cooked up complaint had lost its edge through the instrumentality of the Nizam himself as, after his surrender to Indian Government on 17 September, 1948, he wrote to UNO that he now decided to withdraw his case.

3 During June and July 1948, Sir Winston Churchill, as Leader of Opposition in British Parliament had raised the issue of Hyderabad with venom and vigour and he made several insinuations against India for its approach to Hyderabad issue. Churchill was trying to prove an imperialist case that Britain still held its obligations towards Hyderabad and that Hyderabad has the choice to choose between India or Pakistan or remain Independent.

98

Sardar Patel's Appeal to People of Saurashtra to Make It A Garden City

Collected Works of Sardar Patel

THE HINDUSTAN TIMES
25 January, 1949

(*Extract*)

Addressing a public meeting at Rajkot, Sardar Patel made

an impassioned appeal to the people to co-operate with the Government in making Saurashtra self-sufficient in food and cloth.... .

"We had agreed to the partition of India", the Deputy Prime Minister went on, "for without that India would have been balkanised. Today we have consolidated the country. But if we had not succeeded in winning over the Princes and induced them to play their part the situation would have been difficult for them as well as the people".... .

99

Sardar Patel Warns Pakistan Not to Drive Out Hindus from East Bengal, Otherwise They Would Have to Face Dire Consequences

Collected Works of Sardar Patel

IN TUNE WITH THE MILLIONS
4 November, 1948

(Extract)

(*Nothing was dearer to the Sardar than the fullest protection of his Motherland? And when Pakistan was at the height of its bellicose attitude towards the minorities in East Bengal and the beautiful valley of Kashmir already locked in war, the Sardar, in his historic speech at Nagpur on 4 November 1948, while calling upon people to realise true duty to nation amidst dangers to her security spoke like a thunder: "We are India's guardians and as long as we live, we are not going to tolerate all these dangers to our national existence." Here again, among the top leaders of the day, the Sardar was the first man to issue a resounding threat to Pakistan that if Pakistan was bent on its precipitous course to drive out Hindus from their homes in East Bengal it would have to compensate by parcelling out a portion of its territory to resettle the lakhs of those unsettled.*)

These are days when slogans and cries can be of no use to us. *Instead, we have to concentrate on how to make ourselves stronger. If we do not do this, we shall never realise the sweetness of our freedom.* We shall not know whether we are free or still slaves. Just as a blind man cannot appreciate that value of a jewel placed in his hand or a monkey who is given a jewel merely breaks it, similarly we shall either not appreciate the gift of freedom that has been given to us, or we shall destroy the very freedom which we have secured through so much sacrifice. If we do not realise the true worth of freedom, we shall be doomed.

The world is now disturbed; The World War has affected the morale and atmosphere of every country. We have also grievously suffered. We have also fallen from our high moral pedestal. *During our struggle for freedom, the path which we had selected was one of sacrifice, abnegation, truth, unity, love and justice. When we became free, we strayed away from that path.* If you heed the advice which I am giving you, the country stands to gain. Otherwise, I would be like what happened with Gandhiji, whose advice we did not heed although through his austerities we won freedom and whom we had to lose? We are repenting over it terribly today? We cannot merely be satisfied with replacing the White Sahibs with the black ones. *He must get the state of real Swaraj.*

Every soldier of the Congress should understand this plain and simple fact. Formerly, they used to be rivals in offering sacrifices and self-denials and in undergoing sorrows and miseries? They are now scrambling for places of power and authority. They are absorbed in provincialism.

We do not feel we are all Indians, as we did before when we had to rid the country of foreigners. Instead of unifying our country we are out for splitting[1] it up. If we persist on that road, we are going to lose everything that God has given us.

......

A true citizen must realise his duties and obligations: otherwise Swaraj is an empty name. We have to achieve stability. *India's position today is such that if only it knew how to grasp the opportunities that lie in its way, it would secure its rightful place in the comity of nations.*

This is not the time for provincialism, but for promoting feelings of brotherhood, neighbourliness and oneness... .

Do you think that having secured all this, we are going to fritter away our hard won freedom? We shall not tolerate any danger or damage to the country's interests. We have not spent our lives and made sacrifices merely to see our achievements destroyed in this manner... .

......

Are we to stage this profitless show of provincial politics and provincialism, while they are engaged in a life and death struggle? *We have become old, but we are India's guardians and as long as we live, we are not going to tolerate all these dangers to our national existence.*

......

You must offer support and co-operation to your Government to the maximum of your capacity. Make the country strong... .

! Here Sardar Patel refers to Congressmen's growing restlessness over linguistic redistribution of the country which to a greater degree brought to surface local rather than national considerations.

100

Sardar Patel Over Gandhiji's Fast

Collected Works of Sardar Patel

IN TUNE WITH THE MILLIONS
16 January, 1948

(*Extract*)

(*In this remarkable speech in reply to Civic address of the Bombay Corporation on 16 January 1948 Sardar Patel unravels the anguish of his heart over the ordeal of fast that Gandhiji at that hour of his life had to go through at the altar of Unity and Peace. The Sardar X-rayed it from the plane of worldly life tracing the genesis of discord and the part that Muslims should play towards that Unity. This is a revealing speech in the sense that though the Master and the Disciple differed in their approaches towards that consummation, yet they were working towards the same end in the light of their revelations and judgements of the time.*)

As a result of our freedom struggle we have succeeded in eliminating foreign domination. But all that we have aspired for has not been achieved. We had hoped to achieve peace by getting rid of foreign domination. Actuated by the same motives, we accepted partition; but subsequent events presented a different shape of things. Our prestige went up when we secured Independence but later events have marred it. *If, in spite of having achieved Independence, Gandhiji has to fast today in order to achieve real Hindu-Muslim unity, it is a standing shame to us.* In brief, our happiness at having won the freedom has received a rude shock.

We have just heard people shouting that Muslims should be from India. Those who do so have gone mad with anger. At the same time, we have to sympathise with such people who have lost their dear ones and their valuables. People in thousands are pouring into Kathiawar deprived of everything that they possessed. Anger rules their hearts and it turns their minds topsy-turvy. But we have to tolerate all this. At the same time, so long as we are in the Government, we have to govern also. *If we cannot act as trustees to the entire population irrespective of caste, creed or religion, we do not deserve to be where we are.* I frankly ask myself: “Are we to admit before the world that we are not fit to rule?”.

......

I am a frank man. I say bitter things to Hindus and Muslims alike. At the same time, I maintain, as I have said a number of times, that I am a friend of Muslims. If Muslims do not accept me as such, they also act like mad men. They do not seem to understand the right or wrong. For their attitude, however, I cannot forsake truth nor can I descend from the pedestal of duty. Some of them went to Gandhiji and complained over my Lucknow speech in which I was critical of them for not deprecating the attitude of Pakistan towards Kashmir. They went and spoke to Gandhiji many things and Gandhiji felt compelled to defend me. That also pained me. For, after all, I am not a weak person who would like to be defended by others.

The real task is still in front of us, namely, the planning of the future shape of things in this country. The opportunities for doing so have come, but we seem to have no realisation of it.

The supreme task of the moment is to live up to the real spirit. It is in that spirit that we have decided to hand over Rs. 55 crores which we had agreed to allocate to Pakistan out of our cash balance. I can assure you that when we settled this sum we acted in a spirit of generosity and goodwill. The financial Advisor[1] to the Pakistan Government admitted that the settlement was generous. *The London Economist* was also of the same view. I had then made it clear that even for a single item I would not like to go to the Tribunal;[2] but, at the same time, I emphasised the fact that the whole agreement would be implemented simultaneously along with settlement on other issues. *I could never have agreed to the proposition that all gains were theirs and losses ours.* They, however, claimed it in isolation. We all decided that this was entirely wrong and it should be resisted. Pakistan papers and spokesmen when they heard of it, emitted poison. *When Gandhiji undertook the fast, we thought we could clear the atmosphere. For, after all, when we were throwing money like water, why should we cavil at the payment of Rs. 55 crores if it meant some relief to Gandhiji's mental agony*? We hope it will evoke some response from Pakistan. But if it does not, the fault is of our fate. It is true we have to take the people with us. But we have also to think of Gandhiji. We take a short-range view while he takes a long-range one.

......

Nevertheless we cannot blind ourselves to the fact that we have achieved something by making India more united today than it was at any time during the past several centuries. We should unite more, but that requires a determined effort. In such united India, Muslims should feel as secure as the rest of the population. *For this, however, Muslims will have to change their outlook. They must forget the lesson of the two-nation theory which has been taught to them...* .

1 Sir Archibald Rowlands.
2 Arbitral Tribunal.

101

Sardar Patel Exhorts Youth of the Country to Make India Strong and United

Collected Works of Sardar Patel

THE HINDUSTAN TIMES
5 November, 1948

(*Extract*)

Sardar Patel, Deputy Prime Minister of India, exhorted university students to realise their responsibilities, to prove themselves worthy of the country's hard-won freedom and to make India strong and united. He was addressing a convocation of Nagpur University specially held to confer on him the honorary degree of Doctor of Laws.

......

"It is for our universities to train young men to understand and shoulder that responsibility. The great university of life is full of experiences but to make full use of those experiences all of us—students, teachers and professors—have to be cautious and on our guard. The essential requisite to enable us to discharge that responsibility is character. If your character is lacking and if you leave the precincts of the university without having fully developed it, you shall have wasted an opportunity of a lifetime".

......

Dealing with the different conditions which prevailed in the universities today Sardar Patel said: "In many universities and even in Government services different ideas are inculcated in our young men. Some teach them that Congress Governments and administrators are inclined towards Muslims and are, therefore, against Hindu culture. I should like to warn them that after partitioning India there is no question of India thinking in terms of one community or another. We are not going to do anything which would be contrary to our principle of justice for all communities—Hindus, Muslims, Christians, Parsees, etc. If we create a contrary atmosphere we inevitably run into danger.

"*All communities have their proper place. Their religion is their concern....*

Deploring the present increasing signs of provincialism Sardar Patel castigated those who were thinking in terms of being Maharashtrians, Gujaraties, etc. "All this is poisonous growth", he said "and you must avoid it". It is only foolish and ignorant people who can think on those lines. They do not seem to realise what dangers face our country.

......

Concluding, Sardar Patel asked the students to resort to self-analysis. "I have placed before you in a few words the essence of my experiences which I have gained over a number of years. You have placed on me great responsibility and I have to prove worthy of it. I also thought I should tell you what is your responsibility which you have to shoulder and of which you have to prove worthy. Work more and speak less. Think over what I have told you and make the country strong. My prayers are with you. May God help you".

102

Sardar Patel for Preservation of All Religions in Democratic India

Collected Works of Sardar Patel

SARDAR SHRINO PATRO-II
NEW DELHI
23 March, 1950

(Extract)

SHRI SWAMI NIJANANDJI,

I have your letter dated 11 March 1950... .

The Government does not interfere in any way in the matter of religion. But there are some who in the name of religion encourage hypocrisy, and the public complain to the government. So for the welfare of the people we have to interfere. In Hindu religion many evil practices like untouchability have crept in. Because of that crores of Hindus have left their religion and have embraced other religions. These days there are many who save their interests in the name of religion... .

Swami Shraddhanandji,
Bharatiya Vidyalaya,
Haridwar.

103

Sardar Patel Advises People to Develop Sense of Unity

Collected Works of Sardar Patel

THE HINDUSTAN TIMES
15 May, 1950

(*Extract*)

......

Pleading for strengthening the Congress, Sardar Patel

observed: "We have one organisation which has got us freedom. That is the Congress. All of you showed considerable sympathy and contribution to the growth of it. Now when you have got freedom, it is for you to strengthen it more and not to think that it is no more useful. You may feel that there may be other parties. If there are other parties which are likely to handle power and do better than what is being done at present, by all means do so. But do it decently and in a civilised manner. Do not start the hoax of communism or communalism. Do not leave the path of tolerance".

"When I heard some of the people of the State saying for the first time 'Hinduism in danger' then I feared whether Hindus have disappeared from here".

"There was one Hindu who made reputation for India all over the world. That was Gandhiji. And yet it was a Hindu who killed him. Is that Hinduism? Do you preserve Hinduism by that method? How many castes, creeds and sub-castes are there in Hindus? Even amongst Christians are they one? Let us follow our own religion and if we follow it properly, then nothing is in danger. Let us live as decent men—either Christians, Hindus, Muslims, Sikhs or Parsees. No religion prospers which is based on intolerance. Those days are gone. No nation prospers unless that nation has character.

"Hinduism can never be in danger in India. We are a vast majority. But even without majority, have we not produced men of religion in the past? In the past we have spread the culture all over India. Shankaracharya was one of them. When he died, how young he was, but he did not raise the cry of Hinduism in danger. Religion is a matter between the man and his Maker"... .

104

Sardar Patel Warns People Against Bloody Revolution and Condemns Resort to Violence

Collected Works of Sardar Patel

THE HINDUSTAN TIMES
16 May, 1950

(*Extract*)

......

"I warn you all against any such false cry being raised. We have paid enough for such things in this land. Do not do anything of the kind any more. Let us Hindus, Christians, Parsees, Jews and Muslims, who are here, live in peace and harmony and let us try to be happy. Let us conserve what is good in society and let us build for the future well-being of society".

......

"I would appeal to you to create an atmosphere of goodwill and harmony and live in peace, learn to live in peace and learn to love your neighbour whether he is a Christian, Muslim or anybody else. Let us follow our own religions according to our own tenets and conscience faithfully".... .

......

"Let us begin on solid foundations of unity and harmony".... .

105

Sardar Patel Warns Delhi Police to Suppress Communal Disturbances Impartially

Collected Works of Sardar Patel

BOMBAY CHRONICLE
8 September, 1947

The following appeal has been issued today by Sardar Vallabhbhai Patel, Home Minister, Government of India:

"Delhi is again in the grip of a very serious menace to law and order. In the past, the officers and men of the Police Force and of the Civil Administration had set a very high standard of efficiency and impartiality in dealing with communal disturbances. I am sure I can rely on them to maintain and if possible to improve upon their standard. I appeal to every member of the Force and the Civil Administration to contribute his level best to a speedy restoration of peace and tranquillity in the capital city.

I would like to emphasise that if the evil is to be nipped in the bud, each one of them must behave in an exemplary manner and serve the general public irrespective of caste or community. Any act showing partisanship in favour of one or other community will be attended with most serious consequences to the perpetrator and no slackness of duty will be tolerated. I am mentioning this not because I expect any such slackness from such a splendid force but because I feel that all of us must rise above the surcharged atmosphere of prejudice and passion and discharge our duties with determination and devotion. It must be remembered that if Delhi is disturbed the Central Government cannot function efficiently and the people whom we are to serve will suffer.

To the people of Delhi I make an earnest appeal not to lose their sense of proportion and be carried away by a false sense of sympathy towards bleeding Punjab and those who try to disturb the peace of Delhi are doing great disservice to the people of the Punjab and discouraging the Government of India. The refugees from the neighbouring provinces coming to Delhi will be abusing the hospitality of the people of Delhi if they do not show self-restraint and behave as good citizens".

106

Sardar Patel's Plea to Delhi Citizens Not to Cut Lifeline for Refugees, Ask for Assistance for Mass Exchange of Population

Collected Works of Sardar Patel

BOMBAY CHRONICLE
13 September, 1947

(*Extract*)

Appealing to the citizens of Delhi to contribute their utmost to the maintenance of law and order and essential services in the capital city, India's Home Minister, Sardar Vallabhbhai Patel, broadcasting tonight said that Delhi was not only the nerve centre of the administration but had become the focus of non-official organisations and, therefore, to disturb the life of Delhi was "to deal a deadly blow to the very life of the community throughout India. It is also cutting the life-line through which alone can the free flow of refugees be maintained".

"Let us not," he added, "concentrate on mutual fault-finding but on mutual assistance so that we can, each one of us, lend our hand to the speedy solution of the vast problems which an evacuation virtually amounting to mass exchange of population entails".

......

Let not any one remain under the impression that we are not fully alive to the dimensions of sufferings and misery that have been inflicted on our unfortunate brethren and sisters on the other side... . They look to us to rise to the occasion. This stupendous task is going to consume every ounce of energy and every bit of our resources. To place any obstacles in the way of its fulfilment or to divert our attention from it involves playing with the lives of millions of men, women and children who are lying in hourly peril and whose patience and resistance are wearing away every moment. I do fully appreciate the feelings of those who have taken refuge with us; the feelings of anger that rule their mind; the amount of bitterness that has affected their outlook; and the depth of sorrow that afflicts their heart.

......

It is, in these circumstances, that I make this appeal to all of you to contribute your utmost to the maintenance of law and order and essential services in this capital city. Delhi is not only the nerve-centre of the administration; it has also become the focus of non-official organisations. To disturb the life of Delhi is, therefore, to deal a deadly blow to the very life of the community throughout India. It is also cutting the life-line through which alone can the free flow of refugees be sustained. Let each one of you, therefore, calmly reflect on the part which you are playing in your respective spheres and outside and whether the consequences of such actions as you might be taking are promoting the object we all have at heart or whether they are hindering the task of saving the lives or relieving the sufferings of lakhs of our people... .

......

Let us not, therefore, concentrate on mutual fault-finding but on mutual assistance so that we can, each one of us, lend our hand to the speedy solution of the vast problems which an evacuation, virtually amounting to mass exchange of population entails... .

107

Sardar Patel Details Government's Achievements, Conditions in Country Most Reassuring, Communists Free to Preach Ideology Peacefully

Collected Works of Sardar Patel

THE HINDUSTAN TIMES
18 March, 1949

(*Extract*)

......

Referring to the Muslims in India, the Deputy Prime Minister said: "Except for sporadic activities of their old organisations such as the Muslim League and the Muslim National Guards which I think they would do well to forget and give up in the light of the present conditions, they have on the whole kept the peace of the country and have settled down somewhat disillusioned but more or less willingly to their new loyalties. I can assure them that as long as they behave as loyal citizens of this country, they shall have every protection to their lives, property and religion which this Government can extend to them".

"No better proof of this could have been given than by the steps we took to guarantee their safety in the city of Delhi itself. We willingly agreed to keep their houses vacant against the return of those who had fled to Pakistan, although a large number of homeless refugees were at our hands. The work of restoration of mosques, which has been virtually completed, and the one-way traffic of the return of refugees from Pakistan are sufficient testimony to the peaceful and amicable relation which prevail in this country. High posts both in the army and civil service as well as in public life continue to be shared by them. Thus the cause for which Gandhiji fasted and for which he had to lay down his life has been fulfilled".

Sardar Patel continued: "In return for all this, the

Government does not expect from the Muslim anything more than what it demands from other communities, namely, a complete and unquestioned loyalty to their State. I feel certain that the more easily and quickly the Muslim community accommodates itself to that new loyalty, the greater would be the impression that they would create on the majority community and more willing and generous would be treatment which they would get from all concerned"... .

108

Sardar Patel for Reservation of Seats to Scheduled Castes Only for 10 Years? No Such Reservation for Other Communities Including Muslims

Collected Works of Sardar Patel

THE HINDUSTAN TIMES
27 May, 1949

After a powerful speech, eminently fitted to the occasion, by Sardar Patel, the Constituent Assembly approved the decision *to end reservation of seats for all minorities except the Scheduled Castes*. The concession for the Scheduled Castes will last only for a period of ten years.

Winding up the two-day debate, Sardar Patel told the House that they were changing the face of history. It was the decision which would alter the very character of India and the members should vote with the full consciousness of the great responsibility they were taking upon themselves. They were laying the foundation of a truly secular democracy in India.

Replying to those Muslims who still demanded separate electorates and reservation of seats, Sardar Patel said that having worked for the partition of the country and for a free homeland they should go there to enjoy the fruits of that freedom, leaving this country in peace. There was no place for them in India.

Warm praise for Sardar Patel and profound satisfaction at the decision were the main features of the speeches. It was in an atmosphere of cordiality that representatives of the Sikhs, Muslims and Anglo-Indians gave their support to the proposal. But the feelings of the whole House were expressed by the Prime Minister, who intervened as he himself said, to associate with "this historic turn of our destiny" and to support the "historic motion".

109

Sardar Patel Asks People for Full Support to Government in Economic Reconstruction

Collected Works of Sardar Patel

THE HINDUSTAN TIMES
7 November, 1948

(*Extract*)

......

No service could be greater at this critical juncture than that of subordination of our ownselves to the country's freedom, security, economic stability and reconstruction, Sardar Patel emphasised.

Sardar Patel said: "In the critical times through which the country was passing, I appeal to every citizen to make his maximum contribution to the solution of our problems. The ultimate sanction of Government is popular support. Our broad requirements are settled and clear. We must have a modern army, economic contentment and stability. A disciplined and responsible citizenship, and a firm administrative fabric are the essential requisites as well as expression of the unity and strength.

"India holds a prominent position in Asian policy. That position must be justified and maintained. These objectives have to be achieved with the same tenacity of purpose, the same determination, the same single-minded devotion and the same unity in our ranks as we brought to bear on our struggle for freedom. Complacency and weakness would be as fatal today as they would have been in the struggle".

"India is a land of varieties of religion, culture, habits and languages. Yet throughout history it has evolved a synthesis of harmony and oneness which has been the admiration of the world and the secret of its preservation. We have to live up to this precious heritage and demonstrate to the world that while religions, habits, thoughts and languages may divide, the country unites us".

......

Let us first consolidate the freedom which we have won after such a prolonged and hard struggle before we think of subsidiary, narrow, parochial or sectional loyalties. No service can be greater at this critical juncture than that of subordination of our own selves to the country's freedom, security, economic stability and reconstruction.

110

India Ready for Peace But Ready for War Too: Sardar Patel's Stern Warning to Pakistan

Collected Works of Sardar Patel

THE HINDUSTAN TIMES
7 January, 1948

(*Extract*)

"We want to live in peace and let Pakistan live in peace; but if Pakistan is itching for conflict and war, it should come out in the open instead of resorting to back-door tactics in Kashmir," declared Sardar Patel, Deputy Prime Minister, addressing one lakh people here at Lucknow.

Sardar Patel said: "Pakistan will perish under the weight of its own lies and falsehoods and not through our force though powerful and resourceful as we are to do the job".

Referring to the Pakistan Foreign Minister, Mr. Zafrullah Khan's recent statement, Sardar Patal said: "We have been washing this dirty linen for four months in the Punjab and if we have to wash any more dirty linen then we shall have to go to Lahore and Sialkot.

"In view of our delicate nature of relations with Pakistan we have to bring out land, air and naval forces to a very high pitch of efficiency".

Referring to the conference of Nationalist Muslims in Lucknow, Sardar Patel said that it was surprising that 70,000 Muslims had collected in Lucknow but they did not say a word about what Pakistan was doing in Kashmir. It should not surprise Muslims if doubts were entertained about their loyalty. They could not ride on two horses. Those who were disloyal could not remain in India for the atmosphere would become too hot for them. He was saying this as a friend of the Muslims. It would be a great tragedy and matter of shame to us if one of the greatest Muslims who had been with us had to leave India... .

111

Sardar Patel Confident of Early Solution of Kashmir Problem

Collected Works of Sardar Patel

THE HINDUSTAN TIMES
6 December, 1948

(*Extract*)

"We have made elaborate arrangements to defend our borders and no foreign power dare attack us," declared Sardar Patel, Deputy Prime Minister, replying to a civic address presented to him last light on behalf of the citizens of Gwalior, Lashkar and Morar.

......

Warning the Hindu Mahasabha and the R.S.S., Sardar Patel said that the Government were determined to prevent any communal organization from entering the political sphere. He appealed to misguided R.S.S. young men to give up their harmful activities and join the Congress... .

Sardar Patel made an earnest plea to members of the R.S.S. to change their outlook. They (R.S.S.) must understand that the Government of India could not tolerate any challenge to peace and tranquillity in the State... .

Sardar Patel said that every loyal Muslim must be treated as our brother and if anyone thought he was at liberty to trouble the Muslims, then the freedom won was not worthwhile.

......

"Those who wish to rule by anger must go the way Ravana went. It is none of the individual's concern to deal with any disloyal Muslim. That must be the duty of the State. But a loyal Muslim must be treated as your own brother. If you think that you can go on constantly troubling loyal Muslims because they happen to be Muslims then our freedom has not been worthwhile".

"I, therefore, say to those Muslims who have left India that their strength and prosperity will be a source of pleasure to us. But those who are here must be treated with love and affection. We should create an atmosphere in which everyone can live in confidence and security. In that task I want your co-operation. You must conduct yourself in a manner which renders a police force unnecessary"... .

112

Lord Mountbatten's Letter of Appreciation to Sardar Patel

Sardar Patel's Correspondence

THE VICEROY'S HOUSE
NEW DELHI
14 August, 1947

DEAR SARDAR PATEL,

I cannot leave my active participation in Cabinet work without writing a line to express my sincere appreciation of the loyal support you have given me as a Member of the Interim Government during my short period of Viceroyalty. No one could pretend that the Coalition Ministry was an easy partnership, particularly with the partition looming so large in the background; but you and your colleagues made my task easy and thus proved yourselves true statesmen of whom your country can well be proud.

It was indeed fortunate that a statesman of your vision and realism should have been associated with all the discussions on the 3 June Plan and with all the subsequent vital and delicate negotiations with the States. After our first "tussle" I always felt we should become friends, and I believe history will prove that friendship played a very vital part in obtaining a peaceful solution and a speedy transfer of power to a Dominion of India which, with the States, will be greater than "British India" was by itself.

Thank you also for your trust and support in the problem of the Indian States—future generations will appreciate the full effect of the wise policy you have followed.

With this letter I am sending you a small informal photograph of myself, in the hope that you will accept it as a souvenir of the historic time when we were colleagues together in the Cabinet.

All best wishes to you and to the Dominion of India.

Yours sincerely,
MOUNTBATTEN OF BURMA

The Hon'ble Sardar Vallabhbhai Patel.

113

Sardar Patel's Reply to Lord Mountbatten

Sardar Patel's Correspondence

NEW DELHI
16 August, 1947

MY DEAR LORD MOUNTBATTEN,

Many thanks for your very kind letter of 14 August. I am overwhelmed by the personal references to me and by the generous terms in which you have referred to such assistance to you as I have been able to render in the very difficult and complicated task which was entrusted to you by His Majesty's Government.

You were good enough to call me a stern realist and it is as such that I make bold to say that, when the history of the six months of your Viceroyalty comes to be written, it cannot but accord to you the major share of the credit for the manner in which the manifold difficult tasks have been accomplished and for the transformation which has been made in Indo-British relationship during these fateful months. India and Indians have always been quick to respond to understanding and sympathy. Both Britain and India must congratulate each other that in you they at last found one so abounding in these virtues, essentially a man of speech and action, frank and painstaking and genuinely sincere and anxious to deliver the goods. The only regret of ours is, and of the future historian will be, that we should have had the benefit of your wise counsel and the privilege of your able guidance at a much earlier date.

I personally have a great deal to thank you for. It is possible I have taxed your patience and consideration severely during the last few months of great mental stress and strain, but I have always found in you a ready response which has often dispelled the clouds of anxiety and concern. In fact, what you have achieved in the way of friendship and goodwill merely emphasises what the long line of your predecessors have missed as a result of studied aloofness and failure to take into confidence leaders of public opinion.

I am also grateful to you for the kind thought which prompted you to send me your photograph as a souvenir of our collaboration during these historic times. I shall always prize it as such.

May I add a word of gratefulness to Her Excellency for the humanitarian service which she has rendered to India at a time when it was sorely needed? Her keen insight into human psychology and vigilant interest in the removal of human suffering and misery have touched the hearts of thousands with whom she has come in contact.

Yours Sincerely,
VALLABHBHAI PATEL

H.E. Viscount Mountbatten of Burma
New Delhi.

114

Sardar Patel's Letter to Stafford Cripps

Sardar Patel's Correspondence

28 February, 1947

MY DEAR SIR STAFFORD,

The last I heard from you was when I received your letter of 21 December, 1946. Since then events have happened in quick succession leading up to the final declaration of HMG fixing a date for complete withdrawal from India.

During this interval, we have passed through a period of suspense, anxiety and terrible difficulties. On your side also you had to face serious troubles.

You have seen Pandit Nehru's statement, which represents our reactions to the declaration. There are some obsecure points of very great importance which require elucidation, but that can be done at the appropriate time. The real problem, however, which requires early solution, is the present arrangement of the Interim Government. It has to be solved soon if the declared policy is to be implemented properly.

I hope that the new Viceroy will come with full instructions so that the process of transference of power may proceed smoothly and rapidly.

I must congratulate you and your colleagues for the bold and courageous step that you have taken, and I have no doubt that, if the policy is implemented in its proper spirit, it will result in establishing permanent friendship between our two countries.

You had once written to me to send Sudhir[1] (Ghosh) there if possible in some official capacity. He is now coming there as Public Relations Officer. He will need help and guidance in the initial stages as he is new to the type of work he has to do.

Kindly give our love to Lady Cripps.

Yours Sincerely,
VALLABHBHAI PATEL

The Rt. Hon'ble Sir Stafford Cripps.

1 Unofficial emissary of Congress in Britain before Independence; later appointed Public Relations Officer at India House for a brief period.

115

Stafford Cripps' Reply to Sardar Patel

Sardar Patel's Correspondence

BOARD OF TRADE
MILL BANK LONDON, S.W.I.
4 March, 1947

MY DEAR VALLABHBHAI,

How nice of you to send a letter by Sudhir, with whom I had a long talk last night. Both Isobel and I were delighted to hear from you and to know that you are getting along well so far as your personal health is concerned. You must take care of yourself because you are terribly precious to India just now in these last final months.

I have felt very much for all your difficulties and anxieties and we have hurried forwards to come to a decision as quickly as other urgent matters allow. With (Herbert) Morrison[1] away ill, Aneurin Bevan[2] with pneumonia, Ellen Wilkinson[3] dead and (Ernest) Bevin[4] off for a long spell at Moscow, we are a depleted team and we have more work than ever.

The bitter cold still persists and it's just started snowing again; I am afraid Sudhir and his wife will feel it very much.

I believe with patience we shall get through this transition without any major trouble, but we must be patient. I am sure you will like Mountbatten enormously as I do and respect him. He is very advanced in his views as you will find and you will like him too.

God bless you and keep you fit and strong for your great job. All our love.

Yours sincerely,
STAFFORD CRIPPS

Sardar Vallabhbhai Patel

1 MP (Lab).) for Hockney South from 1935; Home Secretary and later Foreign Secretary in Attlee Cabinet.

2 British Labour politician; in world war-II was frequently a "one-man opposition" against Churchill; Minister of Health in Labour Government, 1945; Minister of Labour, 1951.
3 Labour politician and active campaigner for women's suffrage in Britain? elected MP, 1924 and 1935; Parliamentary Secretary to Ministry of Home Security, 1940? Minister of Education, 1945.
4 MP (Lab.) for Wandsworth Central? Foreign Secretary in first Attlee Government.

116

Sardar Patel to Ismay

Collected Works of Sardar Patel

PATEL PAPERS, NAVAJIVAN TRUST
19 December, 1947

DEAR LORD ISMAY,

I am most grateful to you for your letter sent from Bombay and much appreciate the kind thought which prompted you to send it.

As you know, our country has been the victim of misrepresentation for years in the past. We thought that after India attained her independence, past controversies would cease and men prominent in public life in England would forget their past opposition to India's freedom and reconcile themselves to an attitude of friendship and goodwill, but I regret to find that our former opponents, including your old chief, still harp upon the same old tune wherever they get an opportunity to fling mud at us. This is all the more regrettable since, I make bold to say, no other people and no other country in the world could have forgotten and forgiven the bitterness of years so easily as we have done. It was as if overnight we buried the past and entered upon an entirely new relationship with your people. You have yourself seen how that friendship and goodwill burst forth when the psychological opportunity came on 15 August. It is now for your statesmen and your country to capitalise that friendship and that goodwill and not to let these be smothered by old controversies in their new form.

You have been singularly fortunate (and I somehow feel in that circumstance India has also been lucky) that you came to India with Lord Mountbatten and thereby were able to see at close quarters how India reacted to the final gesture which your people made to us. You have also seen how we faced perhaps the most difficult task that was ever set to any country's government. You have also witnessed the manner in which the country as a whole and the administration have accustomed themselves to the great and vital change from foreign rule self-government. *It is now for you to convince your Old Chief whether you have had to deal here with men of straw or with men of substance.* I am sure, if you could succeed in doing something to remove such misapprehensions as exist among the conservative party, and particularly its gifted leader, about men and affairs in India, you would be rendering a signal service not only to this country but also to your own; for I genuinely feel that in the continued friendship and goodwill between our two countries lie the interests of both.

I should also like to say how much I have enjoyed the occasions whenever social or official engagements have brought both of us together. Your frank and straightforward manner of presenting views which you sincerely held was always welcome to us and we felt that your advice had the weight of experience of men and things which is a rare asset, particularly in the critical times through which we have passed. I, therefore, send my best wishes to you with all my heart and hope that whenever you feel like having a holiday you would not forget that warm welcome awaits you.

Yours Sincerely,
VALLABHBHAI PATEL

Lord Ismay

ANNEXURE I

Sardar Patel Stresses Need for National Unity

Collected Works of Sardar Patel

SARDAR'S LETTERS—MOSTLY UNKNOWN—IV

8 February, 1946

DEAR FRIEND,

I received your letter of the 18th January[1] but on account of my pressing engagements outside Bombay. I could not give you a reply earlier.

I have no doubt that what I have said in the public meeting about Pakistan is true and I stand by it. That does not mean that I am any the less anxious for Communal Unity than anyone in this country. It is easy to raise communal hatred and to make demands from a foreign power in the hope that the interested power will view the claim with favour because the Congress is fighting for the liquidation of that power, but it is not easy to gain this objective without bloodshed and anarchy. My opinion about Pakistan is not based on any communal grounds and I am quite aware of the fact that millions of Muslims, Christians, Sikhs and others agree with me in my view. If I am mistaken in my expression of opinion, from which any communal bias is noticeable, I would be prepared to correct it. *I believe in the sacred ideal of National Unity and I hope to stand by it till the end of my life.*

Yours Sincerely,
VALLABHBHAI PATEL

S.A. Bhimjee Esq.,
Bombay

1 Extracts from Correspondent's letter: "With due respect and honour, I draw your attention to your speech on 14th inst. in which you said: "If Pakistan is to be achieved Hindus and Muslims will have tc fight. There will be a civil war". There are many other Muslims including the writer who are imbued with the same spirit. Pakistan may be a communal issue with the League but that is not so with us in the Congress... . Do not negotiate with communal leaders as this puts us all in a false position. I hope one day you will be a stronger pillar of Hindu-Muslim Unity".

ANNEXURE II

Sardar Patel to Balvantrai, British Government Cannot Enforce Any Mad Scheme Like Partition on Us

Collected Works of Sardar Patel

SARDAR'S LETTERS—MOSTLY UNKNOWN-IV

9 February, 1946

MY DEAR BALVANTRAI,

I was delighted to have your letter of 15th instt.[1] and I am thankful for the suggestion you have made, we have done our best to impress the Parliamentary Delegation about the disastrous consequences that are involved in the proposed mad scheme of Pakistan based on communal hatred and I think we may not have to organise a petition of the type you propose at the present stage. It is not in the power of the British people or the British Government to impose any such insane scheme on this country against our will.

I am glad to see that you have kept your head cool and clear and are keeping good health at this age.

Yours Sincerely,

VALLABHBHAI PATEL

Shri B.K. Thakore, Bombay.

1 The correspondent had suggested to the Sardar that a mammoth petition containing lacs and lacs of signatures from every province should be collected on a statement stating clearly that to press for Pakistan was only to play for the most devastating and utterly unjustifiable civil war and it should be forwarded to the Viceroy in order that he should verify as many of the signatures as he might deem fit before forwarding it to His Majesty's Government.

ANNEXURE III

Sardar Patel Endorses Banerjee's Views on Partition

Collected Works of Sardar Patel

SARDAR'S LETTERS—MOSTLY UNKNOWN-IV

NEW DELHI
14 April, 1946

DEAR FRIEND,

I have received your letter of the 7th inst. I fully appreciate your feelings on the question of partition of India and I am in full sympathy with your views. I am also aware of the depth of feeling of nationalist Bengal in this respect. Individual expressions of opinion need not disturb you but the Congress, as a whole, stands for the unity of India and it cannot agree to any division of which you have such grave apprehensions. *I shall do my best to see that nothing is done to disturb the unity of India.*

Yours Sincerely,
VALLABHBHAI PATEL

Shri D.N. Banerjee,
Dacca.

Notes: This was in reply to Banerjee's letter dated 7th April 1946 to Sardar Patel "The question of partition is a question of principle and not a question of vote by a blind and ignorant multitude inflamed by communal maniacs and fanatical demagogues.

We have heard that you are deadly against the partition of India in any shape or form. We, therefore, earnestly look forward to you to prevent people, acting in the name of Congress, from being a party to any compromise on this question.

ANNEXURE IV

Sardar Patel Permits Banerjee to Publish His Correspondence on Nehru and Partition

Collected Works of Sardar Patel

SARDAR'S LETTERS—MOSTLY UNKNOWN-IV

NEW DELHI
21 April, 1946

DEAR FRIEND,

I have received your telegram this morning asking permission for publication of our correspondence.

I am prepared to give you my views for publication which will serve the purpose you have in view:[1]

"I fully appreciate your feelings on the question of partition of India and I am in full sympathy with your views on that subjects as expressed in your letter of the 7th inst.[2] I am also aware of the depth of feeling of nationalist Bengal in this respect.

Individual members of our committee while expressing their personal views may have laid emphasis on one of the other part of the Congress resolutions on this subject. But I can assure you that all of us are united on the one question, *viz.*, that the Congress as a whole stands for the Unity of India and it cannot agree to any division of which you have such grave apprehensions. How can the Congress disregard the combined will of a province?

A Curzon can do it but not a democratic organisation like the Congress. But even what Curzon did was undone by Bengal and it would be easier for Bengal to assert its will against any attempt to repeat such folly by any popular organisation. I am, of course, bound to do my best to see that nothing is done to disturb the Unity of India".

You can publish this as an extract of my letter to you. I trust this will satisfy you.

Yours Sincerely,
VALLABHBHAI PATEL

Shri D.N. Banerjee,
Dacca.

1 To allay anxiety in fear-stricken Eastern Bengal due to clamours for partition of the country.
2 Ibid., pp. 213-14.

ANNEXURE V

Sardar Patel to Ruler of Sandur Appreciating His Stand on Unity of Country

Collected Works of Sardar Patel

SARDAR'S LETTERS—MOSTLY UNKNOWN—IV

SIMLA
13 May, 1946

DEAR FRIEND,

I have received your letter of the 5th inst.

I am glad to have an assurance from you that the State will be prepared to make sacrifices towards a united and Free India. Your fears about any expectation of such sacrifices to be made by the princes on the basis of divided India are wholly unfounded. The Congress stands for United India and nothing in the world will be able to move the Congress from that position.

The reports that may have reached you about the Chancellor of the Chamber of Princes are not known to me and so far as I know they may be wholly untrue. Whatever may be the personal opinion of H.H. The Nawab of Bhopal, he cannot go against the wishes of his brother princes whom he represents as Chancellor.

I am sure, as you are there the Chamber of Princes will turn down any scheme favouring the division of India.

We are going down to Delhi tomorrow. The Conference[1] has ended in a failure as was expected from the beginning. There is no meeting ground between the League and the Congress as there is no possibility of agreement on fundamentals between the two organisations.

The Mission tried its best for nearly six weeks but it has failed. The next stage of the Mission now begins and that will probably be taken up at Delhi immediately after our going there. Let us hope that there will be no failure in this important stage for which the Mission has come to India.

Yours Sincerely,
VALLABHBHAI PATEL

H.H. The Ruler of Sandur,
The palace,
Sandur.

1 Convened by the Cabinet Mission.

ANNEXURE VI

Sardar Patel Explains Iftaqaruddin's Plea to Congress to Accept Pakistan Led to His Expulsion

Collected Works of Sardar Patel

SARDAR'S LETTERS—MOSTLY UNKNOWN—IV

4 June, 1946

DEAR FRIEND,

I have received your letter of the 10th May.[1]

You are not right in saying that Mian Iftaqaruddin was ridiculed for advocating unity between the Congress and Muslim League. The Congress stands for Hindu-Muslim unity and that policy has always been advocated by the Congress. What Mian Saheb wanted was that Congress should accept the Muslim League's demand of Pakistan and it was impossible for the Congress to do so. If that was his stand, he was told that his place was in the League and he understood it properly and joined the League. It was no sin on the part of

Mian Saheb to advocate Congress-League unity, but I do not understand what you mean by the Congress Working Committee encouraging the Muslim League to adopt a wholly unreasonable and impossible attitude. The Congress Working Committee has done nothing of the kind.

Yours Sincerely,
VALLABHBHAI PATEL

Shri M.M. Ahmed,
New Delhi Congress Committee,
New Delhi.

1 The Correspondent had complained to the Sardar that "Iftaqaruddin was ridiculed for advocating unity between Congress and the Muslim League. As a result of this ridicule, Mian Saheb left the Congress fold. At that time, I thought that Congress has put an end to the policy of appeasing Muslim League and I welcomed it. But the knocking at the door of Muslim League by the Congress has not ceased as is apparent from the recent statements and efforts of the Members of Congress Working Committee".

References

1. Chopra, P.N.
   a) The Gazetteer of India (History and Culture), Volume-II, Publications Division, Ministry of I&B., Govt. of India, 1973.
   b) India's Struggle for Freedom (Books for Millions), Publications Division, Ministry of I&B., Govt. of India, 1989.
   c) Historic Judgement on Quit India Movement, (Justice Wickenden's Report), Konark Publishers (P) Ltd., 1989.
   d) Quit India Movement (British Secret Report), Thomson Press (India) Ltd., 1976.
   e) The Sardar of India, Allied Publishers Ltd., 1995.
2. Chopra, P.N. and Others
   a) A New Advanced History of India, Prentice-Hall of India (P) Ltd., 1996.
3. Chopra, P.N. and Prabha Chopra
   a) Collected Works of Sardar Patel—Volumes from III to XV, Konark Publishers Pvt. Ltd., from 1993 to 1999.
   b) Inside Story of Sardar Patel (The Diary of Maniben Patel: 1936-1950), Vision Books (P) Ltd., 2001.
4. Das, Durga
   a) Sardar Patel's Correspondence. Volumes III and IV, Navajivan Publishing House, Ahmedabad, 1972.
5. Hodson, H.V.
   a) The Great Divide (Britain-India-Pakistan)—With An Epilogue Covering Events—1947-1985, Oxford University Press, Karachi, 1969, 1985.
6. Moon, Penderel
   a) Wavell (The Viceroy's Journal), Oxford University Press, London, Delhi, Karachi, 1973.
7. Kulkarni, V.B.
   a) The Indian Triumvirate—A Political Biography of Gandhi-Patel-Nehru, Bharatiya Vidya Bhavan, Bombay, 1969.

8. Philips, C.H. & Wainwright, Mary Doreen.
   a) The Partition of India (Policies and Perspectives, 1935-1947), George Allen and Unwin Ltd., 1968.
9. Shankar, V.
   a) Sardar Patel—Selected Correspondence, 1945-1950, Volumes I & II, Navajivan Publishing House, Ahmedabad, 1976.

Index